COMPANY
COMMANDER

COMPANY COMMANDER

MAJOR RUSSELL LEWIS MC

Virgin BOOKS

2 4 6 8 10 9 7 5 3 1

First published in the UK in 2012 by Virgin Books

This edition published in 2013 by Virgin Books,
an imprint of Ebury Publishing

A Random House Group Company

Jacket Photography: The U.S. Army

Extract from *The Afghan Campaign* by Stephen Pressfield,
reproduced by kind permission of the Random House Group Ltd.

www.randomhouse.co.uk

Addresses for companies within The Random House Group Limited can be
found at: www.randomhouse.co.uk/offices.htm

The Random House Group Limited Reg. No. 954009

A CIP catalogue record for this book is available from the British Library

The Random House Group Limited supports the Forest Stewardship Council®
(FSC®), the leading international forest-certification organisation. Our books
carrying the FSC label are printed on FSC®-certified paper. FSC is the only
forest-certification scheme supported by the leading environmental organisations,
including Greenpeace. Our paper procurement policy can be found at:
www.randomhouse.co.uk/environment

MIX
Paper from
responsible sources
FSC® C016897

Printed and bound in the UK by
CPI Group (UK) Ltd, Croydon, CR0 4YY

ISBN: 9780753540312

To buy books by your favourite authors and register for offers, visit:
www.randomhouse.co.uk

This book is dedicated to all those that I have had the honour to command and fight alongside. It is particularly dedicated to those who paid the ultimate price. They remain forever in our hearts.

2 PARA Battle Group Roll of Honour Afghanistan 2008

2nd Battalion, The Parachute Regiment

Private Daniel Gamble

Private Dave Murray

Private Nathan Cuthbertson

Lance Corporal James Bateman

Private Jeff Doherty

Warrant Officer Class 2 Michael Williams

Private Joe Whittaker

Corporal Jason Barnes REME

Private Peter Cowton

Private Jason Rawstron

Corporal Nicky Mason

2 PARA Battle Group

Trooper Robert Pearson QRL (ASG)

Marine Dale Gostick ASC RM

Lance Corporal Kenneth Rowe RAVC and Sasha

Ranger Justin Cupples 1 RIRISH

In 2 PARA Battle Group Area of Operations
Warrant Officer Class 2 Daniel Shirley APTC
(ex 2 PARA)
Corporal Anthony Mihalo USMC
Lance Corporal Juan Lopez Castaneda USMC
Lance Corporal Jacob J. Toves USMC

In Memoriam
Sergeant Phil Train
Corporal Gareth Gwyther

CONTENTS

List of Maps   ix

Maps   x

Author's Note   1

Prologue   3

April – The Journey Begins   11

May   97

June   161

July   227

August   261

September   313

October   355

Epilogue   389

An Appeal   395

Glossary   397

Acknowledgements   401

LIST OF MAPS

1. SANGIN AREA WITHIN HELMAND PROVINCE
2. B COMPANY 2 PARA AREA OF OPERATIONS

CONTACT MAPS

WEDNESDAY 21 MAY
FRIDAY 23 MAY
TUESDAY 24 JUNE
TUESDAY 12 AUGUST
MONDAY 18 AUGUST

SANGIN AREA WITHIN HELMAND PROVINCE

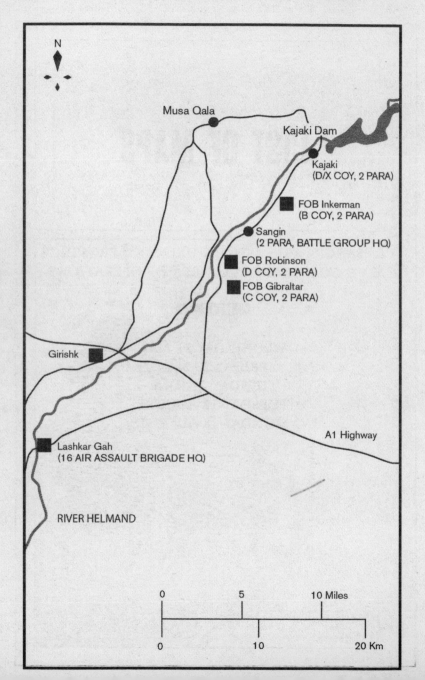

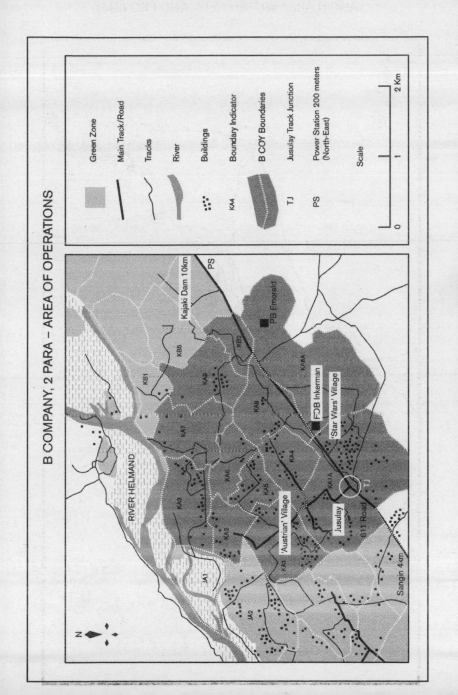

B COMPANY, 2 PARA – AREA OF OPERATIONS

AUTHOR'S NOTE

I had wanted to join the army from a very early age. My grandparents took me to the Royal Tournament when I was four and from that point I was hooked. By the age of 13 I was obsessed and, by headmaster's decree, was allowed to join my school's cadet force a year early. When I was 14 I read an incredible book called *2 PARA Falklands* by John Frost. I remember thinking what incredible men these were. Outnumbered, poorly resourced and in horrendous conditions, these men fought not one, but two battles. I never believed, in my wildest imagination, that I would end up commanding, in battle, men like these.

At the age of 19 my dream came true when I passed the selection board to become a British Army officer. It was while at Sandhurst I decided I wanted to join the Parachute Regiment. They appeared to be the best regiment in the infantry They had be – they are the only ones with their own physical selection.

I commissioned in 1994. The physical selection for the Airborne forces – P Company – was as brutal as I expected it to be. After parachute training I joined 2 PARA in Northern Ireland. I found it incredible to be joining the organisation that I had read about in John Frost's book; what was even more incredible was the fact that there were still Falkland veterans in the battalion. I even had one in my platoon. I learnt a lot.

My career progressed steadily. I trained recruits and while doing this superb job I met my future wife, Andrea, an officer in the Queen Alexandra's Royal Army Nursing Corps, who was training medical recruits at the same time. I became 3 PARA's mortar officer and was a company second-in-command for tours to Kosovo and Northern Ireland. I returned to 2 PARA as the surveillance officer for another Northern Ireland tour and then became the battalion's operations officer before being selected for promotion to major. All I now wanted was to be a company commander in a PARA battalion.

I attended staff training and worked in defence procurement, buying small arms, ammunition and surveillance systems for the army. It was during this period that the regimental boards sat to decide who would go where. As ever, there were more people than available company command places and I sweated for a few months waiting to hear my fate. Late in 2006 I received the news – I was to return to 2 PARA as Rifle Company Commander. My dreams had come true. Not only was I returning to the battalion I had spent the most time with, but I would also be going on 'operations'. 2 PARA was chalked in to deploy to Afghanistan in April 2008.

PROLOGUE

'Sir ... sir ... are you awake?' The voice of one of my signallers drags me from my sleep. 0300 hours is never a nice time to get up. I am amazed at how well I manage to sleep with all that is tumbling around in my mind. I am conscious that within four hours I will probably be in a huge contact.

Private Crisp checks I am awake before heading back to the operations room. The signaller tasked with waking me up invariably brings me a cup of tea, which is always a welcome treat at such a horrendous time in the morning. I roll out of my camp cot, have a slurp of tea and head in to the storage room where I keep all of my kit. By midway through the tour it is too hot to sleep inside; the temperatures are hitting 45C by day and 28C at night, so a lot of us have moved our travel cots outside. You still sweat and ingest a lot of dust but sleeping inside is even worse – it feels like being in a sauna.

Company headquarters all sleep in the briefing area, near the ops room. Next to the briefing area are a couple of mud buildings that formed the original compound out of which morphed the forward operating base (FOB). I share one room with my two sergeant majors and we keep our kit stacked up in there.

As I glance around there is activity in most directions as people prepare themselves and their kit for patrol. To protect our night vision we keep the lights off and work on head torches. This means that each soldier is working in his own little glow, cocooned from reality for a few more minutes.

I have another sip of tea and then start the laborious process of 'getting it on'. Like a time-honoured ritual of the samurai or a Teutonic knight, we all have rituals and sequences that allow us to get our 'armour' on. Trousers and boots first – the boots are always a challenge. As we wade through drainage ditches and streams when on patrol, boots always get wet. They then dry far too quickly, so they shrink. This means that you have to stamp and kick your way in to them and enjoy a couple of minutes of one-size-too-small before they stretch back. Next, my undershirt goes on.

I leave putting on my body armour until the last moment so, once dressed, I go through my kit check. Rifle and pistol – as dust free as possible. Radio and night-vision goggles – fresh batteries and quick check to see that they are actually working. Magazine and grenades all in the correct place and then water bottles, all topped up. Once I am happy with my kit, it is just a matter of waiting. We have to carry a crippling load. The body armour alone weighs more than 13 kilos. Once you add ammunition, water, radio, night-vision goggles and spare batteries it is between 30 and 40kgs; not great to carry around the green zone in 40C heat. Yet my load is probably at the lower end of the spectrum; the lads will be carrying a lot more ammunition than me, so many of their loads will be pushing 45kgs. One thing we are not is agile! This becomes an issue when you are fighting an opponent who is wearing loose clothing, flip-flops and carrying an AK-47.

Invariably, I sit on my own before going on patrol. Some people seek the comfort of others, I like to sit quietly and gather my thoughts. We are all thinking and feeling the same, though. A mixture of pre-game nerves and anticipation. Deep down we don't really want to get hurt but we know there is a distinct possibility. By midway through our tour we have all been in contact and have all seen the horrors of friends and colleagues being injured and killed. As paratroopers, we like to think that we are tough but we have also seen the fragility of the human body when faced with modern high-velocity weapons. As the commander I take my mind off these thoughts and think through today's tactical plan. I try to identify any friction points – an officer's technical term for spotting the parts of the plan that could go wrong.

There is a lot of pressure on the commander. It is my plan, therefore my responsibility. I know that if/when it all starts to go wrong people will turn to me to make the decisions. I have to remain confident and project a belief that my plan will work. If I don't believe in my plan, why should anyone else? I take the time to think it through and try to empty my mind of distractions. Mostly, I think about how painful it's going to be on my shoulders lugging all of this equipment around.

Twenty minutes before departure my group start to gather in the briefing area and get our kit on. Body armour, webbing and daysack all strapped and cinched in place. It feels heavy almost instantly, so we sit around and chat until ten minutes before we are due to leave. I then make my way down to the rear gate with my signallers.

Whilst I am going through my own little routine, those on the patrol will be doing the same. A company patrol comprises of between 60 and 90 people, which as a group is quite an unwieldy beast to coordinate. By the time I arrive at the rear gate to the FOB there is a whole melee of activity going on.

I find a quiet spot and sit down. I rest my load up against the Hesco blast wall and watch the proceedings. Soldiers are clustered in small groups, talking; you can see the odd glow of a last cigarette in a cupped hand. Platoon sergeants are busy checking kit and there is often the odd expletive and raised voice as someone points out that they have forgotten something or a particular piece of technology has now stopped working. 'Well go and f*cking get it then/get it f*cking sorted' is the inevitable, sympathetic response. I watch as a lone soldier jogs off into the darkness to rectify whatever problem he has just pointed out.

I sit, taking this all in. There is radio traffic in the headset attached to my left ear and I can hear various call-signs checking communication. The activity starts to build as we approach the departure time. People start getting in to the correct order of march and equipment is checked again. One minute out a final flurry of radio checks confirms that every-one's communications are still working. One by one, the platoons check in with myself and the ops room to let us know that they are ready to depart. I sit quietly, answering on my radio when necessary and suppressing my anticipation.

As a young officer I had the privilege and good fortune of having a company commander who had served with the SAS. He gave me a phenomenal piece of advice, which has fortunately stuck with me through my whole career. His advice was simply 'cool on the net' (even better when said with a Bob Marley accent – 'coo-ool on da net'). The net is slang for the radio network. He explained that when you, the commander, speak on the radio, everyone can hear you. They are listening not only to your words but also to your emotion. They will read as much in to *how* you are saying something as to what you are saying. If you panic, they will panic. If you are calm and measured, they will stay calm and measured. So before you speak on the radio, take a second, think through what you want to say and then be 'cool on the net'. This advice is some of the best I have ever been given.

So, once all of the call-signs have checked in and told me that they are ready to go, I sit back, take a second and prompt myself – 'cool on the net'. I also have my own little tradition, so I lean over and whisper to my radio operator 'let's get it on'. He grins back and I reach for my radio to let the lead platoon know that they are clear to start the patrol. I let the ops room know that we are departing.

I then watch the scene unfold. It is one that I would see many times and it would become burned into my mind. It has come to epitomise the bravery and dedication of all of the soldiers that it was my honour to command.

Once I have sent the command on the radio I watch the ripple in front of me as the message is passed up and down the line by voice. The waiting is over – it's show time. I focus on the lead cluster of soldiers. The last bright glow of a cigarette is amplified through my night vision. A last draw before it crashes to the ground in a shower of sparks to be extinguished by the grind of a boot. I watch intently as the soldiers help each other up – their loads are too big to get up unaided.

Once on his feet the lead soldier jumps up and down to try and get his load seated and as comfortable as possible. You can't ever get it comfortable, there are just degrees of discomfort. He shrugs his shoulders and clicks his head side to side, working out a few kinks but ultimately going through his own pre-match ritual and getting his game face on. He is the point man. The very first man in this whole snake that will weave its way out into the green zone and actively hunt out the enemy. I can't see his face but I know him. A young nineteen-year-old private. He has probably been out of basic training less than a year, yet already he is in the middle of a war. He joined the Parachute Regiment because he believes they are the best and the hardest regiment in the British Army. Since serving in the battalion he believes this more than ever. The indoctrination and the tribal rituals have worked. He is a paratrooper. He feels fear, but he isn't going to show it. He is scared. He is scared because he is at the very front and, statistically, the most likely to walk in to the enemy. He has seen the horrors of war. He has seen mates injured and some killed. He knows exactly what a bad day looks like. So he is scared, very scared. But he doesn't show it. He doesn't want his mates to see any emotion so he just shrugs his load and clicks his neck. A final nod to his section commander and then he heads off. Confidently, shoulders up, chest forward. Not a backward glance, nor a faltering step. 'Bring it on,' he says to himself.

As I sat there on countless occasions watching this scene unfold I realised I was watching the bravest man I had ever met. He knew the risks; he knew the pressure. Within two hours of departure we would invariably be in a contact. Huge battles initiated by the enemy, where massive volumes of machine-gun fire and rocket propelled grenades (RPGs) would rain down on us. This fire would most often be directed at the lead group and, for a few precious minutes, the whole battle would centre on them.

He is the point man, the very tip of the spear. He has 70 paratroopers behind him with enough weaponry to start a third world war: rifles, machine guns, rocket launchers and hand grenades. Artillery, mortars, Apache helicopters and fighter jets are all a radio call away. But that lone soldier might as well be on his own. It doesn't matter what's behind him. He knows there is only the enemy in front of him.

On all the patrols that I led I never once saw the point man as much as flinch. When told to go, he shouldered his load, tightened a few straps and headed straight out. As I watched him disappear into the darkness, the feeling of humility and honour constantly overwhelmed me. I was humbled by his bravery but, most of all, I realised what an incredible honour it was to command men such as these.

This is our story. B Company, 2 PARA, who for six months in the summer of 2008 battled it out for a small piece of territory in North Helmand. But actually it's his story. That lone paratrooper, heading out into the darkness, without even a backward glance. This story is dedicated to him. It was an honour and a privilege to command soldiers such as these. That lone soldier is the bravest man I have ever met.

APRIL – THE JOURNEY BEGINS

There have been differences in the summer and winter tours since the British Army deployed to Helmand. The winter season is often quieter, as the conditions are too challenging and the enemy want time to rest and recuperate. We are to take over from the Royal Marines, who have had a quieter tour than last summer's, but have still suffered deaths and casualties.

In November 2007 I visited Afghanistan as part of the 'commanders recce'. The command group from 2 PARA spent a week with the Royal Marines, seeing how they did business. We used this visit to shape our training.

Our training has been demanding, both mentally and physically. Months of general and then specialist training to make sure that we are as best prepared as we can be. There has been so much to learn, or refresh. New weapon systems, new vehicles, new procedures and more assets than any of us have seen before. It is a challenge pulling together so many moving parts. Training always grinds you down and in the end all of us just want to get to Afghanistan and get on with it.

Deploying to Afghanistan is both sobering and exhilarating. For nearly all of us this is our first time 'to war' and, while putting brave faces on it, we know that our futures are very uncertain.

FRIDAY 4 APRIL 2008

I steal a furtive glance around the cabin of the aircraft. Once satisfied that the bulk of my fellow travellers are asleep, I reach in to my daysack and pull out a brand-new, hard-bound A4 notebook.

On the first page I write *The Odyssey*, followed by the date and the flight details – *RAF flight, Brize Norton to Kandahar* – and underline everything neatly.

I sit back and start to gather my thoughts. There has been a lot of pressure: the build-up training; the emotion of saying farewell to those that I love. For now though, I need to push all of that to the back of my mind and focus on the job at hand.

I have kept a journal for the past four years. It is a habit I have adopted and it has become a source of therapy for me. A source of light relief and a way of capturing people, events and thoughts. I have found it a useful reference to dip into. Looking at this nice new journal I realise that the following six months could be the most interesting yet. I deliberated over bringing a journal. We were under such tight weight restrictions that at one point I was going to leave it behind. I am glad that I didn't.

The past few months have been demanding and intense. The training has put us through our paces. The commanding officer (CO) is old school – tough and uncompromising. He rightly sets high standards and expects them to be met. Plus he believes in pushing you to your breaking point. This gives an understanding of how best to use your skills – and which aspects of your performance need to be improved. Sound logic but it makes for an uncomfortable ride. We have been through our share of discomfort. I keep thinking about the exercise in January where the temperatures were minus-7C and we swept across a broad, open, expanse of Yorkshire moor, attacking compounds made of logs. I wonder how useful this was going to be for a summer tour where the temperatures average 45C and where the fighting will take place in a green zone that appears to resemble a jungle.

I think the company is in good order and ready for the challenges it might face. The company is the base fighting unit of the British Army. It is commanded by a major who is assisted by a warrant officer, known as the company sergeant major (CSM). My CSM – Martin Thorp, or 'Thorpy' – is a bundle of humorous energy. He is tough, fit and very funny. He is also a qualified paramedic, a skill which I am hoping we won't need. We have a really good relationship that I know will see us through the challenging times.

The company itself comprises three platoons, each of roughly thirty soldiers commanded by a lieutenant and assisted by a sergeant. My platoons are numbered 4, 5 and

6. They are the same on paper but very different in character; 4 Platoon is comfortable with itself – a bit more relaxed and more chatty than the other groups. Our sister battalion 3 PARA has given us 5 Platoon, a driven bunch, very professional and very tight-knit; they are fortunate to include people who were on the 2006 tour. Also driven and incredibly competitive is 6 Platoon – its members want to be the best in the company. I have a fair idea of the strengths and weaknesses of each but I am going to have to wait to see how they perform 'on the day' before I can get a true feel.

This is the interesting thing, though. We are all new to this. Most of us have been on operational deployments before – I have done three tours in Northern Ireland and been to Kosovo and Iraq; but this feels very different. This feels like it will test us more than ever before and allow us to join the ranks of the warriors. We want to be practitioners, rather than just study the theory. I realise that this may sound odd to most people. Why would you want to get into a gunfight? The easiest way I can describe it is to use a sports analogy. Imagine going to every training session but never playing a game. You understand all of the theory, but you aren't really sure how it will work on the day. We want to get on the pitch and play the game.

I know that there will be significant pressure on me. The company commander is the last level of *Fingerspitzen* or fingertip command. The CO is in charge of the battalion and he will give orders but these will be what he wants doing, not how he wants it to be done. This is mission command. As the company commander, I will take this direction and make it in to a plan; a plan that the lads will carry out but one that I will direct. It will be my plan, with all of the implications of ownership that go with it. I feel pretty confident though. I have spent a long time preparing myself. I have studied neurolinguistic programming to help me develop visualisation techniques to ensure that I can produce my 'A' game when it is most required. I have 'modelled excellence', so that I have a series of role models in my mind to help me behave appropriately in a given situation. I realise that in certain situations my confidence and the confidence I project will be crucial. I have studied military history, searching for the pearls of wisdom from leaders past. There is no secret key. I think leadership is about trying to be the right person, doing the right thing, at the right time. If all else fails I intend to fall back on the US Army Infantry Battle School's motto, 'Follow me'.

Saying farewell to Andrea and Rufus – my wife and cocker spaniel – was horrendous. The time off we have had recently was lovely and I have become a bit of a home bird. Good food, nice wine, open fire; it has been wonderful. Then the time came. Andrea dropped me off around the corner in camp so that I could get myself together before seeing the lads. Perception is everything. We said goodbye and I watched as they drove off, Rufus's little face in the back window. It broke my heart. I had to get my 'game face' on and go and join the lads. Once there, the feelings passed. You could tell by the banter that we were all experiencing the same thing – anxiety, excitement, a leap into the unknown. As the Company Commander, it is up to you how much banter you get involved with. Everyone knows that you are the boss. If you want to be aloof that is up to you, but I figure this will be a very lonely experience if you are too stand-offish. I am happy to get stuck in, as I need the release as much as everyone else.

So for now I am sitting back and gathering my thoughts. A good piece of advice when being moved by the RAF is to consider yourself a piece of luggage. No emotions, no feelings – just a lump of baggage.

It is an eight-hour flight and we soon start the procedure for the landing at Kandahar. We are told to put on our helmets and body armour before they dip the lights in the cabin. It is a strange experience. All of us have luminous tabs on the back of our helmets so that we can follow each other at night. With the dimmed cabin and the bumpy ride I am mesmerised by the rocking and swaying of the luminous green blobs. Then, with a bump, we are down. Afghanistan.

TUESDAY 8 APRIL

I am finding Bastion incredible, a really impressive set-up. Once at Kandahar we were moved here quite swiftly by C-130 transport aircraft and now I am just waiting to move forward to Forward Operating Base (FOB) Inkerman, where we will be based for the tour.

A FOB is effectively a launch platform. It is a place of security from which you can administrate and conduct missions. It does not have a fixed template, it is just a piece of real estate that fits the purpose.

We have been through an in-theatre training package which is quite good, although everyone is wrung out from the travel. The package is designed to bring us up to date with the very latest information and techniques and cover some topics that aren't so easy in the UK.

They stack us up in transit accommodation, which has bunk beds four high and houses 200. There is noise all night.

Fortunately, this isn't for too long. After a number of mandatory briefs and some practical exercises, we move into a decent tented camp. This will be our rear base while we are at the FOB. The facilities are good: nice food, toilets that flush, showers, a few shops. I think six months here would be pretty pleasant.

I am waiting and the tension is starting to build, though 40 Commando Royal Marines, who we're relieving, are looking after us well. People keep asking me where I am going. When I reply 'Inkerman' I get a mixed reaction. Most burst out laughing and the others do a sharp intake of breath and mutter 'good luck'. This could become quite off-putting, so I try to ignore it.

Each night there is an update brief. The HQ staff goes through all of the activity throughout the area of operations (AO) for the day. So far my flight has been delayed. Each day I have been ready to go but the FOB has come under attack, so the RAF hasn't been able to fly the helicopters in. I realise that, emotionally, I can't dwell on any of this. I will take the FOB as I find it; saying that, FOB Inkerman has become a bit of an urban myth round here. It really seems to be the badlands. For now though it is all about waiting. I will see what happens.

WEDNESDAY 9 APRIL

Today could be the day! Who knows? It is raining, which I am quite surprised at. I mean really raining. I have got all of my kit ready. Moving it around is a pain. The body armour weighs almost 14kgs, I have a rucksack, grab bag, daysack and all sorts hanging off me. I struggle down the track until

– fortunately – the company quartermaster sergeant (CQMS) picks me up and drives me to the airhead where the CH-47 Chinooks will pick us up. After all the false starts I don't know if this will just be another laborious exercise in moving my kit from one side of Bastion to the other. It looks promising though.

As I stagger on to the back ramp of the Chinook, with 12 of my commanders, I can feel the adrenaline pumping. I always enjoy helicopter rides but this one should be particularly special. It's all looking good and before I know it the whine of the turbine starts up and the rotor blades begin to turn. It looks like we are on our way. The Chinook has so much kit on board it struggles to take off. Slowly, it rises off the pan; you can feel the pilot fighting to do so. Suddenly the nose dips and the pilot throws the weight forward. It builds momentum and we are off, gaining speed and height as quickly as possible so that by the time we clear the outskirts of Bastion we are at 2,000 feet.

Due to the noise from the rotors, communication is impossible. I have ear defences in to protect my hearing from the high-pitched whine. It sounds like the inside of an electric drill. I can't move as I have kit piled on top of me so all I can do is sit back and try to enjoy the flight. Suddenly there is a huge burst of fire as the door gunner lets rip with his machine gun. Immediately I think 'this can't be happening'. I am panicking that we are going to get shot down and I'm not even going to make it to the FOB. I try to run through in my head what I would do if we are shot down but this appears pretty futile. Helicopters are not designed to crash-land. The message is then passed – the gunner was just test-firing his weapon. Brilliant! He could have warned us.

Suddenly the helicopter flares and everything disappears in a huge brown dust cloud; luckily I have my goggles on. The buffeting is intense as we land. I stagger off the back ramp and I am bodily manhandled in the right direction – the Royal Marine reception party is here to meet us.

I continue down the human chain, carrying as much as I can and watching as soldiers dart in and out of the helicopter, appearing with sacks and boxes. Everything is done very quickly and before I know it the pitch of the helicopter increases and it is on its way. The dust settles and all goes quiet. I look up to see a face grinning at me, the Royal Marine company commander – Ade. A relaxed, confident, humorous marine, he is clearly very pleased to see me. We were on a course together three years ago, so we know each other quite well.

After all of the waiting, all of the training and the odd false start, I am finally at my forward operating base, FOB Inkerman.

The overall campaign construct in Afghanistan has evolved over time. The initial campaign in 2006 saw 16 Air Assault Brigade and our sister battalion – 3 PARA – conduct ferocious and wide-reaching operations. 3 PARA was spread thinly and had to fight for territory throughout the summer before the next brigade could consolidate its gains. The next evolution were the 'platoon houses'. These were houses that an entire platoon took over and operated from within, to target a certain area. While the theory is sound and the British Army's counter-insurgency experience supported it, the plan didn't really work in Afghanistan. With only 30 men, a platoon is too small a unit to conduct patrols and also protect and administrate itself. Hence the evolution to the company outpost and the FOB. A company is big enough to protect its firm base and conduct patrol activity.

FOB Inkerman was originally a small patrol location established by the Grenadier Guards in June 2007 and was named after their Inkerman Company. Since then it has expanded to reach its current size. There are currently 220 soldiers in the FOB. That is a lot of people in quite a small place. The FOB sits six kilometres north-east of Sangin town centre.

My initial impressions are good, though my head is swimming with a kaleidoscope of thoughts, feelings and ideas. The mantra I keep repeating to the lads is 'it's a marathon, not a sprint'. We have to pace ourselves. We will be here for six months and we need to be going at the same speed by the end that we are at the beginning. I have to remind myself of my own mantra.

It feels surreal though. I have been personally preparing myself for 'combat' and command for three years. The pre-deployment training has been intense. Once I knew my company was going to FOB Inkerman I spoke to Sergeant Radcliffe, my intelligence sergeant, and he got me as detailed a map as possible of my AO. I pinned it on my office wall and spent most spare moments staring at it, trying to imagine what it would look like and how it would feel. The map was not very detailed. The FOB was just a small square with a number of dots around it denoting compounds. In front of the FOB ran a road called the 611 and then the infamous green zone, a five-kilometre belt of green hatching up to the river Helmand. There wasn't much to be gleaned from the map.

Briefings during our training had not added that much more. There were plenty of pictures of the FOB, showing an almost medieval mud fort with desert on one side and lush fertile fields resembling a jungle on the other. But that was it. It has been impossible to get any real sense of what it would actually look like. Hence the multitude of thoughts and feelings. An overwhelming sense of adventure and relief that I am finally here, but also the realisation that the company will be here for six whole months and there is the likelihood of some dark days.

It is great to be taking over from someone that I know. Takeovers and handovers can be like rutting season, with egos and testosterone flying in all directions. The outgoing party wants to be acknowledged as the alpha male, whilst the incoming party wants to prove that they are actually far harder. This can be quite tedious and means you don't actually achieve much.

So it is good to see Ade. As we aren't throwing our egos around no one else feels the need to either, so the handover period should be pain free.

40 Commando have done an excellent job. Their tour has been challenging – as all the tours seem to be – but they are still in good spirits. Royal Marines are a good bunch and although there is a level of professional rivalry between the marines and the paras, there is also a begrudging respect.

No amount of staring at a map or looking at photographs has prepared me for the FOB. It is far bigger than the picture I have created in my mind. It is the size of six football pitches and it is ringed by Hesco walls. Hesco walling is made up from wire-bound sacks filled with aggregate that, when constructed properly, offer excellent blast protection. The walls are at least ten metres high and two metres thick.

The location of the FOB is logical. It is on an elevated position so it automatically dominates the surrounding area. The FOB naturally creates its own security bubble. It is at least ten metres above the 611 road and the green zone, offering excellent observation in all directions, thus making it easier to defend. Crucially, the original compound has a well, which has been enhanced with a borehole. The FOB is self-sufficient in water, which takes a huge burden off the resupply chain. Water is pumped from the borehole through a purifier so that all water in the FOB is safe to drink. The water is heavily chlorinated so it tastes like it has come from a swimming pool. The FOB also has an emergency supply of 50,000 litres of bottled water in case the pump goes down. That sounds like a lot of bottled water but it isn't when we are talking about 220 people conducting serious manual labour in 45C heat. The beauty of the borehole is that it means that we don't have to ration water. There is plenty for drinking, showering and washing clothing.

Directly in front of the main part of the FOB, down at road level, is a secondary compound. This was originally manned by the Afghan National Army (ANA) but is currently unoccupied.

The 611 is a two-lane track that links Sangin to an area just short of Kajaki. It is a busy road and during daylight hours gets a lot of traffic. The road forms a natural boundary between the green zone and the desert. To the north-east of the 611, and on the side that the FOB sits on, there is nothing but desert. Rolling, rocky, undulating desert that stretches for 40km before it hits stunning snow-capped mountains. The views at dawn and dusk are spectacular. Dotted around the desert are compounds of varying size, ranging from a single small dwelling to football pitch-sized compounds with entire families living in them. The Afghan existence looks hard, but none more so than for those who live out in the desert. The labour involved in getting water makes it look completely impractical.

Our helicopter landing site (HLS) is just outside the FOB in the desert and there is a 'bottom' gate, as it is known, that allows access in and out. The gate is covered by an elevated bunker known as a sangar. All of the sangars around the FOB are manned twenty-four hours a day.

To the west of the FOB is a village which stretches for about a kilometre away from the FOB and is heavily populated. The majority of the occupants are farmers who own compounds and fields out in the green zone. Due to the fighting, a lot of the compounds directly in front of the FOB are not safe to occupy, so the occupants of the village tend the fields to the front and bide their time, hoping that we and the Taliban go away. They just want to farm and be left alone.

The village is referred to as Star Wars village; it looks very much like Luke Skywalker's home planet of Tatooine in the *Star Wars* films. Similar to many North African villages, it is a labyrinth of vaulted compounds and dim passageways. It looks like it has been there for ever. We are told that the occupants are friendly.

To the north-west of the 611 and directly in front of the FOB is the infamous green zone. This is a miracle of Afghan ingenuity and a testament to the Afghans' phenomenal capacity for irrigation projects. It is a five-kilometre belt stretching from the river Helmand to the 611, an agricultural zone literally carved out of the desert.

The FOB's commanding position allows it to overlook the green zone all the way out to the river. On the far bank of the river is a steep incline and then nothing but more rocky desert.

The front sangar of the FOB offers the most commanding views. The sangar is big enough for eight people and has a collection of heavy weapons and observation devices. There is a 40mm belt-fed grenade launcher and a 7.62mm general purpose machine gun (GPMG) giving us quite a reach. To the right of this bunker is a small firing bay for the Javelin anti-tank rocket – a heat-seeking 'fire and forget' missile. This really extends our ability to hit the enemy. Inside this bunker is a huge pair of binoculars; colloquially referred to as 'ship's binos'. These allow you to see comfortably out to at least 5000m.

I find myself drawn to this front sangar and the green zone. Ade has shown me around the inside of the FOB but I am more interested in the outside – that is where the enemy is.

I have spent a long time in the front sangar already, gazing out at the agricultural jungle in front of me. Sweeping the binos from left to right, near to far, trying to take in as much as possible. What hits me is how stunning it is. The alluvial run-off from the river makes the green zone incredibly lush and fertile. It is a mixture of tended fields, tracks and tree-lines. What also strikes me is how much activity there is. As the green zone supports so many peoples' livelihoods, there are always people working the fields, both day and night.

As I gaze through the binos an Afghan male pops into view. He appears through a gap in the trees. He gently sweeps down a track (Afghans do not rush unless they have to) and then disappears from view. I try to focus in and see his face. Who are you? Are you Taliban? Are you my enemy or just a farmer? It is a strange sensation, sweeping the binos and knowing that at this exact moment my enemy is out there. Is he watching the FOB? Watching me? I know he is out there, I just can't see him.

The fertility of the water from the river allows for an incredibly tight and productive agricultural cycle. We have arrived in poppy season. The poppies are a foot high and within weeks they will rise to waist height, ready for harvest. After the poppy there is an initial growth of corn, followed by harvest and then another growth of corn or wheat before the winter. The locals are put under a lot of pressure to grow poppy as opium – produced by the flower's seedhead – is used to fund the Taliban's campaign. Unfortunately the poppy is often grown at the expense of wheat so the locals need supporting through the winter.

For the locals in our area the agricultural cycle is every-thing. I quickly realise that it is for us, too. Our weapons systems are optimised for longer-distance engagements. Between harvests, before crops have had the chance to grow, the conditions are perfect for us. The gaps between the compounds and the open fields mean that engagement distances will often be 200 metres plus – great for our marksmanship training. The enemy, with his AK-47 and poor training, are not good shots at this distance. We are. Once crops start to grow the engagement distances shrink. Really shrink; sometimes down to only one metre. This doesn't really provide much of an advantage to the enemy – we are still incredibly well trained and just as good at close-quarter battle as we are at shooting at distance. It just makes the commanders' job – especially mine – that much harder. Coordinating the movement of 70 people across fields and hedgerows is relatively straightforward, if you can see them. Coordinating the movement of 70 people through corn that is two metres high and so towers above head height, where you can see only the man in front of you and the man behind you, is something completely different. The responsibility I will have, especially when calling in fire, is significant. If I don't know where everyone is, there is the danger that I will bring fire down on my own soldiers. This is my worst nightmare. I realise that when on patrol the ability to create a picture in my mind, based on what is happening on the map, is essential.

At 1505hrs Ade is showing me around the FOB when the Taliban decide to introduce themselves. An SPG-9 – a Soviet rocket – shoots over the FOB and lands just outside, followed by a second rocket that lands just in front of the ANA compound. We sprint for cover and make our way to the ops room. Once we have an update we move to the north sangar to coordinate the response. By the time we get there the marines are returning fire with 81mm mortar, 105mm artillery, 40mm grenade launcher, .50cal and general purpose machine-gun fire. This fire is directed on to the identified rocket firing-point. I have to admit, the firepower is impressive; I just can't stop grinning. There is so much fire going on, including two Javelin anti tank rockets that I have to laugh. The 105mm air-burst looks impressive and the noise is – dare I say it – exactly like footage from the

Falklands, a screaming rush followed by a crump. The fire continues for ten minutes before a Dutch F-16 jet is brought in and conducts two gun runs. After that a US F-16 joins in but all has gone quiet. What a welcome. My first day at the FOB and we are already under fire.

THURSDAY 10 APRIL

In the morning, Ade delivers a set of verbal orders for a patrol into the Star Wars village. He follows the British Army's standard patrol orders format and delivers them to all of the junior commanders who will be on the patrol, from lance corporal up. The set format means that everyone knows what information will come out, and where. It is good to listen to the construct of his orders and I decide that I will always give a full set of verbal orders before one of my patrols and I will follow the orders headings. It sets the context and ensures that a patrol doesn't appear *ad hoc* or not thought-through.

This patrol will be fairly short, which I am grateful for as it is going to take a while to configure the best way to carry my kit and get used to the load.

At 1500 we head off out of the side gate next to the artillery's 105mm light guns. This is referred to as 7 RHA gate. The marines move well tactically, and Ade has a good knowledge of the village and the movement that is required to patrol through it. He moves groups through the village itself and leaves one outside the village to 'satellite' around. Of course we are next to the FOB, so we have that providing overwatch as well.

As it is my first patrol in Afghanistan I have a lot to take in but Ade soon convinces me that the village is fairly benign. There may be an element of Taliban coercion but overall the locals are fairly onside. Throughout the winter the FOB had to provide flour and cooking oil as the locals had grown nothing but poppies last year.

The locals appear to be a mixture of curious and indifferent. There is no real hostility and, as ever, the kids follow us as if we were the Pied Piper. Sergeant Radcliffe does most of the talking to the locals through an interpreter and appears to have some success. He is the perfect man for this job as he is an affable, talkative, happy Scouser. They keep clustering around him and appear mildly amused by his antics.

At one point we stop next to a cluster of older males. Ade quickly explains that the village does not really conform to the Afghan norm. Traditionally, a village would have an elder. As this village is a hotchpotch of farmers thrown together for convenience there isn't really one head of village. This makes our job that much harder – who should we be dealing with? Sergeant Radcliffe just wades in and chats to a cluster of older-looking men. He sits with them and quite quickly they offer him some tea. He accepts, which I am impressed with. He doesn't get much information from them but, more important, he has started some form of dialogue.

We continue round the village and it becomes apparent to me that my current kit configuration is not up to the task. A good friend of mine – Mike Newman – works for a firm called Edgar Brothers, a supplier of top-grade kit, and he ensured that my company was really well looked after before we deployed. I have an excellent array of pouches, but the belt isn't great. Everything keeps sagging and dragging my trousers down. I quickly realise that drop-leg holsters are a waste of time and decide to have a good reorganisation once we get back in. I need to email Mike and ask for a decent belt.

We continue the slow amble around the village and it gives me a good chance to chat to Ade. The patrol continues to be well received, one of the platoons is even asked to play football with some of the young kids. The game gets going but the surly teenagers quickly put a stop to it. They push in and confiscate the ball. They cuff the young kids around the head and glower at us. This doesn't look like open hostility. More to do with teenage ego. Shame, but it is a good indication that there is the potential to expand the 'hearts and minds' strategy.

We head back in and I immediately reconfigure my webbing. Ade gives another set of orders for tomorrow's patrol and then it is early to bed.

FRIDAY 11 APRIL

'Mate, you awake?' Ade asks. It is 0400 and I am already awake. I have been for a while. It is pouring with rain and the sound of it hitting the tin roof above, woke me up hours ago. Plus there is the anticipation. We are heading into the green zone on this patrol. My first time.

The sound of the rain and the darkness reminds me of the jungle. I have been to Brunei and Belize on jungle warfare courses and the routine is to get up before dawn, invariably in the rain, and get on your cold, damp patrol kit.

I dress quickly and head in to the ops room. I make myself a cup of tea and have a custard cream – I'm not in the mood for breakfast.

We head out through the ANA compound, across the 611 and straight into the fields opposite the FOB. It is so dark I can't see anything. The night vision goggles (NVGs) aren't helping that much as the rain is so heavy it is obscuring the lenses. I just concentrate on following the man in front.

The fields in front of the FOB aren't really the green zone and we soon come to a two-metre wide drainage ditch which marks the zone's real start. I am confronted with a single narrow log that straddles the ditch. It is now greasy with rain and mud from people's boots and it is the only way of crossing over the mini torrent that is cascading down the drainage ditch.

'That's all I need,' I think to myself; the marines will love it if the paras' Company Commander falls in. I watch in dismay as the marine in front skips over in two bounds. I get on with it and manage to get over. I push on and hear the sound of someone falling off the log and crashing into the ditch. He is met with sympathetic giggles all round.

We continue with the patrol but I don't really see much until the sun starts to come up. I am watching Ade to see how he is controlling everything and it is impressive. He has a good grasp of the ground and knows where all of his guys are. He keeps updating the ops room so that they can develop their understanding as well. He has a lot going on and this is without the enemy interfering.

Once it is light, I get a better feel for the ground. We are sweeping up the belt of compounds that sit 500 metres in front of the FOB. I have studied them quite intently through the 'ship's binos' in the front sangar, so it seems odd to be now walking amongst them. The compounds are all deserted. They show a lot of battle damage. These compounds were originally cleared by the Royal Anglians over a year ago as part of Operation Pulk and they have remained unoccupied ever since. They are close enough to the FOB for the Taliban to use them to mount attacks. This resulted in constant exchanges of fire, so the locals sensibly decided to move out.

We continue over the next two and a half hours to sweep through these deserted compounds in the pouring rain. There is no hint of enemy activity. I wonder if they are sensibly sitting out the bad weather.

The conditions make me realise how grim the winter tour must have been. We are constantly in and out of drainage ditches, which are quite chilly. This is in April; it can't have been much fun in January.

The patrol passes without incident and before I know it we are heading back in. Once in, there is a quick patrol debrief. All of the commanders gather back at the briefing area and the company second-in-command (2IC) and the intelligence sergeant ask questions to gather as much information as possible from the patrol. This debrief is short as no one has seen anything of interest. After that I clean my kit and try to find somewhere sheltered to dry it out. A useful day that has given me a lot to think about.

SATURDAY 12 APRIL

I wake up early so I decide to go to the gym. It is a habit I want to get in to while I am here. Going to the gym sounds grand but in reality it is a single stack of Hesco wall made into a compound with random bits of real and improvised gym kit, all of which has seen better days. There are two exercise bikes, a stepper, a barbell and a whole host of pots filled with concrete and bags filled with sand. It is nice to be able to do some training though. I go on the step machine and do some pull-ups. It's quite pleasant in the cool of the early morning and lovely to watch the sun climb higher, illuminating the beautiful rugged mountains to the south. The birdsong cheers me up. Due to the water and the food in the FOB, there are always a lot of birds. I have identified finches and swallows but I am not sure about the others. In the evening the bats begin their low swoop over the camp, which is always good to watch.

Today is a no-fly day for the helicopters, so I won't be getting any more of my lads in. I have about half, mainly the support elements. My mortars and fire support group are here. The snipers have arrived, which is good news. I have a chat with Corporal Berenger, my sniper commander, and we start hatching plans. I can see a lot of utility for the snipers out here and I am going to use them as much as possible. The .338 sniper rifle has incredible range but I think the L96 7.62mm sniper rifle will be better for patrolling in the green zone. We will need to experiment and the snipers themselves will have to find out what works best for them.

I spend most of the afternoon moving my kit into one of the back rooms with my two sergeant majors. There are clusters of rooms around the briefing area, which are part of the original compound. It is good to have a bit of space. I just want to get myself sorted. I marvel at my book collection. This was another area I was concerned about before leaving – having enough to read. I am an avid reader and I always have to have a book on the go. I only brought a couple with me, but have managed to accrue quite a few from the outgoing marines. We obviously all have similar tastes. Mainly military history, humorous novels and some science. Bill Bryson's *A Short History of Everything* seems popular. Having this space to spread out in is great and I even have a shelf to stack everything up on neatly. I acquire two large metal boxes that mortar bombs come in. In one I place spare ammunition, hand grenades, spare batteries etc. The other I fill with luxuries: sweets and books. This helps keep everything organised. I know the sergeant majors will be hounding me if I drift in to clichéd officer bad administration.

Once the sun has set I go up on the ramparts and look out to the green zone. There are a lot of noises – crickets and insects – and the odd light from a far-away compound; lots of shadows. It is very odd looking into the green zone. You feel like an observer into another world. You are gazing at this strange, distant land. It almost feels like a stage or film set, created for us to do battle in. It doesn't look anything like I expected and I enjoy just staring out, wondering if the enemy is staring back. He is out there somewhere and I am pretty certain our first meeting is in the not-too distant future.

It is my birthday today, which feels good. What a place to be. I haven't told anyone. I just sit outside quietly and smoke a cigar. I have a brought a packet of them with me, and my plan is to have one a week, as a treat. I sit staring at the moon and stars. The sky is incredibly clear so the views are stunning. I think of my family at home and imagine them thinking of me. I thought about ringing Andrea but no satellite phones are available. Each week we get allocated thirty minutes' satphone time and the minutes are loaded automatically on to a phone card. People at home can purchase more minutes on your behalf and get them loaded on to your phone card too; there is also a system to send emails via laptop. No non-issue systems are allowed for communication purposes. I decide I will leave ringing Andrea; as I'm not drawing any attention to my birthday it feels like just another day anyway. I finish my cigar and head off to bed.

SUNDAY 13 APRIL

I am still waking up early and I suspect that this will continue. At the moment I know it is anticipation that is causing me to wake up, but soon enough it will be the early dawns. I head off to the gym again and then go for an early breakfast. There are three chefs for the FOB and they do an amazing job with very limited resources. The cookhouse is a large tent with folding tables in it. It can seat about 20 people at a time but most people just sit outside on the ground. The kitchen is an identical tent with gas cookers in it. The temperatures get ferociously hot so the chefs are always bathed in sweat. Their 'resources' are predominantly ten-man ration packs. This is a large box with enough food for ten people for one day. It has tins of Spam, curry and beef stew etc, as well as porridge oats and rice. Perfectly functional, but pretty bland. When resupply is available the FOB gets fresh food such as fruit, bread and eggs. As the FOB is so poorly resupplied there is not much that's fresh. The chefs have a real job keeping the food interesting but so far so good. I am lucky, as I like porridge, so that suits me in the morning.

Fried Spam, powdered egg and baked beans are not really my idea of an English cooked breakfast and not a great start to the day.

I have a bowl of porridge while sitting outside talking to some of the lads. They all seem pretty happy at the moment.

Mid-morning we have a *shura*. This is an Afghan meeting and we advertised it during the patrol around the village the other day. Down at the bottom end of the FOB, next to the HLS is a specially constructed wooden building in which we hold *shuras*. Presentation is everything, so the FOB has its own '*shura* pack' to use when necessary. There are rugs to lay on the floor and we put out bowls of boiled sweets and bottles of water.

Ade gives me a top tip – wear your pistol. Afghans appreciate symbols of power and a pistol is quite a good one. So I strap on a holster and head down.

Before long Sergeant Radcliffe leads in two elderly Afghan men. They are incredibly dignified and come and join us on the rugs. It is fantastic to see the locals up close. Bearded, with skin the colour of cinnamon, they are a tough-looking race. They both sit fingering their religious beads; one of them has a small flower that he continually plays with. The Afghans have a real appreciation for beautiful things that we in the West tend to take for granted.

We talk, via the interpreters, for about an hour. They have a good moan, which is completely understandable and I feel genuinely sorry for them. They are just farmers and all they want to do is move back out to the unoccupied compounds in the green zone and get on with their lives. With the Taliban and us in the area they can't. I explain that we are here at the request of their government but you can see this means very little to them. Unsurprising really; their system is tribal and national boundaries and government are meaningless to them. What one elected man in Kabul thinks is pretty much irrelevant.

They appreciate the sweets and water and promise to come again, next time with more people. This all seems positive and I think we have a real opportunity with the village next door. While I understand that my job is to disrupt the enemy, I also want to expand our positive effect and that will be through improving life for the locals. If I'd have known that this would be the only *shura* the locals would attend for months I probably would have tried to draw it out a bit longer.

In the afternoon we receive intelligence that there is an enemy indirect fire team (IDF) operating in the area and they are going to target a FOB. This is the enemy team that is generating the 107mm and SPG-9 rocket attacks. We put on helmets and body armour for an hour and a half and sweat it out. Literally sweat it out. The sun is baking and it is no fun sitting around in this kit. We sit, straining to hear the distant thump of something being fired. We have an unmanned aerial vehicle (UAV) on station so we spend the entire time watching activity out in the green zone. Two men are acting suspiciously off to the north-west of the FOB, about two kilometres away. They keep moving into and out of an old battered compound that has previously been used as a firing point. They carry on, blissfully unaware that we are watching them via the UAV and that, at the same time, our three 105mm artillery pieces and six 81mm mortars are all pointing at them. If something happens, the response will be quick and effective.

Nothing happens and before long the men head off and the sun starts to set. The word comes to 'stand down'. They aren't going to attack today. We all gratefully shed our helmets and body armour and head off for dinner: tinned curry, rice, spotted dick and custard. Not exactly what you're hankering after in the summer, but better than having to sort out a meal for yourself.

MONDAY 14 APRIL

I head to the gym again at 0600. The sunrise is really stunning this morning. It is amazing to watch the track of sunlight move across the desert and hit the distant mountains. I find it really quite inspirational. I can see why Islam starts its day by surrendering to the Lord. I find myself praying. I have a lot to think about and there is a lot of pressure on me. I so desperately want things to go well and I ask that we are watched over and protected. It just feels the right thing to do during such an amazing sunrise.

At midday two Chinooks arrive with another 48 of my soldiers; that's 48 paratroopers in and 50 marines out. The FOB is now filling up with paras. The balance now seems to be in our favour, so command of FOB Inkerman is transferred from Ade to me; a momentous occasion, as far as I am concerned. The two OCs and two CSMs head down to the flagpoles and we have our pictures taken shaking hands beneath our two regimental flags.

I am now in command, but I don't think this will really feel like it has started until all of my lads are here and all of the marines are gone. Being in charge of everyone and everything seems a daunting prospect. There are so many moving parts. I know that I just have to 'hold the line' mentally – don't let things overwhelm me, keep calm, keep confident. I have an expression that I use a lot to myself – 'work the problem'. This means take the evidence available and start to work through it. Don't get excited, don't distort the information, just work through it and come up with a plan. That is exactly what I intend to do.

Every evening there is a brief at 1800 hours. All commanders attend and it is used to pass information on to those that need to know. It is an opportunity for the company commander and the CSM to talk to all of the commanders and also the opportunity for specialists such as the intelligence sergeant to pass on any new information. It is known colloquially as 'prayers'. The CSM uses our first evening brief to let everyone know that the army is now in charge. The banter between the Army and Royal Marines is always good but none more so than over the different names the two services have for various things. As ever, the CSM gives a hilarious speech. He points out that HMS Inkerman is now FOB Inkerman. The galley is now a cookhouse, the heads are now toilets and wets (the marine's name for a cup of tea) are now brews. The marines take all this in the spirit it is meant.

TUESDAY 15 APRIL

I am up at 0600 and head down to the HLS. We are expecting an early flight and this should be it – all of my soldiers in and all of the marines out. I want to say goodbye to Ade and his CSM as they have been great. We sit around chatting and before we know it there is the rhythmic thumping in the distance of two Chinooks approaching. The noise gets louder and louder and they come into view, shooting by the FOB at a hundred feet and banking over the desert before flaring down on to the HLS. Just before the noise becomes deafening and we disappear in the dust cloud Ade leans over to me, shakes my hand and says 'all the best, mate; remember it's all shits and giggles until someone gets hurt'. Ade has lost men through death and injury. I quickly mull this over and understand what he means. We are professionals and this is what we joined the army to do. There will be times when we will be enjoying ourselves, especially when things are going well. But there is always the danger that someone will get hurt – seriously hurt – and we have to remember that always.

I give him a thumbs up and watch as he staggers off into the brown cloud. I move back into the FOB to get out of the downwash of the rotors, which is punishing. It is like being jet-washed with sand. I make sure I am in a position to welcome my lads as they arrive. They are all smiling and pouring with sweat as they struggle to clear all of their kit off the HLS.

I hear the helicopters increase power and then they are away. It all goes quiet and I realise this is it. I am now in charge and on my own. There isn't another company commander I can run my questions by. There is just me.

The loneliness is actually liberating. Committal, in a brutal sort of way. As there is *only me* I have to get on with it. No getting off this ride and, actually, this is what I have spent the whole of my adult life preparing for: the opportunity to lead paratroopers in battle.

With this new-found liberation comes energy and I stride

purposefully up to the ops room to see if there is any decision that can be made, to prove that I am in command.

There isn't, so in a slightly dejected sort of way I head round to the briefing area and read a book. I need to pace myself, after all.

WEDNESDAY 16 APRIL

Up at 0600, I head for the cookhouse for a bowl of porridge. I sit outside chatting to the lads from 4 Platoon. They arrived on the last flight yesterday and are really pleased to be here. Bastion was starting to grind them down, with all its rules and regulations. There is a definite 'us and them' feel between those in Bastion and those that have to go out and do the fighting. With my company group complete in the FOB and all of the Royal Marines now departed, it is time to get down to business. I have spent quite a bit of time going through my mission back in the UK but I knew I would only be able to go so far with such limited information.

Now that I am in the FOB, have received comprehensive briefs and been on the ground, I feel I am in a better position to produce a detailed plan. Sometimes you just need to be in the problem in order to understand the problem. I charge up my cafetiere mug with my favourite Starbucks coffee and head to one of the back rooms that has been converted into an office. All of the furniture is improvised and everything is covered in dust but at least it gives me somewhere to work. I realise I now need to spend some time coming up with my own plan. I sit down and conduct a detailed estimate.

The estimate is a formal process the military uses to

develop an understanding of the problem and come up with a plan. It uses seven questions to make you evaluate the environment, enemy forces, friendly forces, understand your mission and the context it sits within. It also allows you to develop options regarding carrying out your mission, enables you to score these options and finally come up with a detailed plan. The aim is to pop out the other end with a good understanding of what you have been asked to do and how you are going to do it. I need to have a detailed understanding of the ground, the enemy, the friendly forces, key risks and how I am going to mitigate them. It is a formalised, though adaptive, process. Throughout my training over the years I have been encouraged to use it in a way that works best for me. I am fortunate to have been well taught.

I get myself some blank paper, get out my notes and spend the next few hours conducting my analysis and deciding initially how I am going to tackle this tactical problem. I am mindful of the fact that flexibility is going to be the key. We are going to have to continually refine and adapt what we are doing to optimise the chance of it working. We aim for the '80 per cent solution' and then build in enough redundancy so that you can change things as you go along. Never forget, the enemy has a vote on your plan as well.

I start by evaluating B Company's mission, as given to me by the CO:

Defend the immediate area around FOB Inkerman and interdict enemy forces to the north and south in order to protect the reconstruction and development zone within Sangin.

This is quite self-explanatory. Defend the immediate area means protect ourselves. We have to ensure that the enemy is not in a position to attack the FOB. From what I have seen so far an enemy attack is not realistic anyway. The FOB is in an elevated position with good observation in all directions. There is a sangar on every corner which is manned twenty-four hours a day. There may not be a realistic chance of an enemy assault, but they have proved already that they have the capability to fire rockets into the FOB. Interdict means divert, disrupt, delay or destroy the enemy's capability before he can use it on us – or in this case, against Sangin. Effectively, we need to interfere with his plans. We are doing all of this to create the space for reconstruction and development within Sangin, which is the battle group's main effort. It is widely understood that to start making progress in Afghanistan we have to start delivering tangible progress to local people. Sangin is a town that has shown progress, from deserted streets to a thriving marketplace. The idea is to invest in this progress and assist the expansion. Our job is to create the space to allow this to happen by keeping the enemy occupied.

The marines have come up with a far simpler definition. Inkerman is known as the 'shit magnet'. The FOB and, more importantly, our presence sucks the enemy to it, like moths drawn to a light. This prevents them from continuing their journey south and causing problems in Sangin. It sounds quite simple as a mission, but I know it will be complex to achieve. For some reason known only to B Company we take a lot of pride manning the 'shit magnet'. I suppose it is the paratrooper inside all of us. He wants to be challenged and likes the idea that he is on the hardest job.

Before we all went our separate ways at Bastion I had a chance to have a final chat with the CO. He explained things quite simply with a boxing analogy. We have to keep jabbing at the enemy. This jabbing will keep him occupied and will allow us to create the opportunity for the right hook. The right hook won't be decisive – we will never 'defeat' the enemy with a single blow, but we will set him back. The more we set him back, the more we can improve the conditions for the locals and convince them that we are here to help.

I continue to work through my estimate and come up with a presentation that I want to give to all of my commanders. I now feel in a position to give them clear direction as to how I want things to progress. It has been a long morning so I go and grab some lunch before sorting out all of my notes.

At 1400 all of my commanders assemble at the briefing area. From my company everyone from lance corporal upwards is in attendance. All of the specialists – 7 RHA, logistics detachment, medics, chefs – have all sent representatives as well.

The briefing area is really useful. You can seat about 20 people and there is plenty of standing room. There is a huge map of the area propped up against a wall. The whole area is home-made, built by the Royal Engineers. It is a bit Heath Robinson, but perfectly functional. There is a corrugated iron roof about ten foot up to keep off the rain or the sun, and it is open on three of the four sides to allow in the light and the breeze.

Once everyone is there, I give them my direction. I have broken it down into points and I expect this information to be passed on to every one of my soldiers. I use the following notes:

1. The mission. I read them our mission and go through my thoughts from my estimate.

2. I explain counter insurgency. We are focused on the people and, inevitably, will have to keep reinvesting in the same areas. The analogy being used at the moment is 'cutting the grass'. If you keep grass short, it is easier to cut. If you let it grow, it is harder to cut. If we invest in an area, we can manage enemy activity. If we allow the enemy to take hold of an area, it will be harder to get him out.

3. The pace. This is a marathon, not a sprint and we have to pace ourselves. Calm down; let's keep things balanced.

4. My game plan. Our six months will be broken down into the following phases:

    i.   Handover/takeover from the marines (now complete).

    ii. Ground familiarisation/learn our environment. Short patrols that will get longer as our confidence and understanding develops.

    iii. Expansion of effect. Once we have fathomed the ground and developed our understanding, we will push further and deeper to interdict the enemy.

    iv. Maintain effect. Our resources and capacity are finite. Once we have realistically discovered what we can and can't do, we will set this as our benchmark and maintain it.

    v.   Handover to the next unit. We need to start preparing for our own handover from day one. The war will not be won on our shift, so start making plans for our handover straight away.

5. Every man has a part to play. We are all intelligence-gathering assets so people need to keep their eyes and ears open. We need to be smart in the use of our resources and assets. Get the thinking caps on and start coming up with good ideas.

6. Speed v. time. We must take the time to do things properly. There is no need to rush and no need, ever, to scrimp on drills. However, there may be times when we need to keep pressure on the enemy so we must be prepared to take risk if it is necessary.

7. We must communicate with each other. When on the ground I control all of the assets – mortars, artillery, air power – I can get them, but I have to have information to do this. Tell me your position and where the enemy is as quickly as possible. That way I can deploy the bigger assets to help you.

8. Be sensible, be compassionate. Treat prisoners carefully and understand the rules of engagement.

9. Stick to our training. We have good drills and tactics; use them. The enemy will not be able to handle a coordinated and determined company attack.

10. Care in the use of the word ambush. It has negative connotations. More often than not, we will bump into the enemy or he will bump into us.

Don't credit him by calling it an ambush – it is far less coordinated than that.

11. Rules for the FOB. There are few rules but they need to be adhered to. Hygiene is crucial so keep yourselves and your kit as clean as possible. Weapons are to be unloaded in the correct place – there is no need to walk around the FOB with a loaded weapon. Make sure you are no more than ten seconds away from your helmet and body armour. Enemy rockets can strike without warning so you need to keep your body armour and helmet close.

12. Opportunity. This will be the best soldiering opportunity of our careers. But, it's not all about 'smashing' the enemy. We have to pace ourselves and we have to be ready for setbacks.

13. Remember who we are. We are B Company. Remember our heritage and remember those that have gone before. Maintain the traditions set by the Falklands veterans. Be professional; do your best.

It is a long chat and I make it as personal as possible. I have always worked hard on my oral presentations, as I realise that they are so important. They are a sales pitch. I have to convince my soldiers that I have a plan, that it is a good one and most importantly that I believe in it. If I fumble my speech, stutter or sound unconvinced, there is the danger that they will read something into this. If they think that I don't believe in my plan, then why should they? Sometimes leadership is fairly simple – as General Slim said, 'It is just plain you'. You have to have the personality and the character to inspire people to do what you want them to do, especially when they might not want to do it. I have always believed that the best way to sell a plan is with your voice and with your personality. So I stand in front of my commanders and give them everything I've got. I am passionate about soldiering and I believe that this is our time. I can't do this on my own, though. I need them to come with me.

I can never tell after a 'speech' how much impact it has had. They are a tough bunch and they aren't going to give much feedback, but they seem happy. The questions are simple enough; always a good indicator that you have got your pitch right. They also seem pretty energised – you can tell by their demeanour: knowing little smirks and slow nods of the head. I take all of this as a good sign and let them head off to their Toms to carry the message forward.

A 'Tom' is a generic term for a Parachute Regiment private soldier. It is a term of endearment and is used by all ranks. They refer to themselves as 'Toms' and we refer to them as 'Toms'. It was enshrined in the Rudyard Kipling poem about Tommy Atkins.

I love addressing the lads, I always have done. It's such a challenge to get your message just right. As they head off, I think things have gone well so far and B Company's mission is starting to shape.

I also realise it has been a long day so I grab some food and then head back to my bed space to reward myself with a couple of hours' reading. I lie on my camp cot, shielded from the insects by a mosquito net, reading by the light of my head torch. I am pleased but I have a lot to think about. There is no one to ask advice from now. With Ade gone I am on my own. My plan is to take things steady. We will start with short patrols. Once we get a good feel we will be able to do more and more as our confidence and importantly our fitness grows. We have a lot to learn but I am really happy with our progress. I turn off my head torch and drift off to sleep. It's been a good day.

THURSDAY 17 APRIL

I am up early for the next *shura*. The '*shura* shed' is all set up and Sergeant Radcliffe is waiting by the bottom gate with an interpreter, ready to welcome our guests. Stage management is important. He will welcome them and get them comfortable and then come and fetch me. This allows me to get on with other things. The Afghans don't really stick to accurate timing, so who knows when they will show up. They have agreed to come today, at some time in the morning. I have my pistol and holster on standby, ready to sweep in like Wyatt Earp. We had only two locals attend last time so I am hopeful that we will get more today.

By lunchtime there is no sign of any locals, so I tell Sergeant Radcliffe he can stand down. The bottom gate is manned and they can always send for us if some locals do appear. This is disappointing, but as Sergeant Radcliffe points out, I shouldn't read too much into it. It is probably more of a date or time-keeping issue than a rejection.

After lunch I tuck myself away in the rear office and write my first set of orders. I have decided that I will write every set of orders out in full, but deliver them verbally. I want to write them out to ensure that nothing is missed and, also, they might become useful from a record-keeping point of view.

I am going to conduct the first company patrol tomorrow. Exciting stuff, but it is the first one, so I want it to go well. I take the time to come up with a simple and straightforward plan. This patrol will be about learning the immediate area, getting to grips with the ground and an opportunity to develop our tactics and procedures. Our basic tactics are very good but what worked in January in North Yorkshire is clearly going to need adapting for the environment here. This is all sound in theory – to take out a patrol, to learn the ground and develop our tactics, but there is a real enemy out there, and he will exploit any weakness he identifies. So I spend a good few hours planning and writing my orders.

We have good maps to plan from. They are adaptations of aerial photos so they show a lot of detail. Each photo has been 'gridded' so that we can create grid references. Every compound is shown and, usefully, each one is allocated a unique number; this will really help command and control. If a commander wants to let me know where he is, all he has to do is say where he is in relation to the nearest compound rather than take the time to come up with a grid reference. There are probably 500 compounds in my green zone area of operations.

In the afternoon I issue my orders. The commanders from 5 and 6 Platoon, snipers and the fire support group (FSG) assemble in the briefing area. I use the British Army's orders format to deliver the orders. The set format covers: ground, enemy, what you are doing, how you intend to do it, coordination measures and logistical support. All the while I use the large map board as a pictorial reference – I have drawn our route on it with a marker pen. Sergeant Radcliffe gives a very detailed intelligence brief to get things going, then I take over.

The plan is to explore an area referred to by the locals as Jusulay. Directly opposite Star Wars village is a track leading into the green zone. About 500m in, it splits and this whole area is referred to as Jusulay. The split in the track is known as the Jusulay junction. The marines had a hard time getting into this area as the enemy contested it. Both the Taliban and ourselves are conducting people-centric campaigns. They want to get their message to the people as much as we want to get ours. It makes sense for them to try to keep us away from the people. We need to establish how big Jusulay is and what significance it holds in the area.

I explain that we will patrol out from the rear gate, enter the green zone just north of the FOB and then head 500m in. We will then sweep down the unoccupied compounds to the front of the FOB, down to the Jusulay track junction before heading back through Star Wars village and in through 7 RHA gate. A very simple patrol which, on the map, is fairly short. The beauty of this patrol is that we are always about 500m from the FOB. We are in the security bubble of the FOB heavy weapons and, if needs be, we can head straight back in. I don't envision conducting a full-blown retreat on our first patrol but it is sensible to have this option. The enemy's greatest opportunity is tomorrow's patrol. It is our first one and therefore our most vulnerable. With every patrol we will gain experience and confidence. First, though, we need to walk before we run.

The CSM finishes the orders with his piece. Whilst I am in charge of tactics the CSM is in charge of administration. He covers the basics, such as how much water people should be carrying and what weaponry should be brought along but he also covers medical procedures. This all becomes much more realistic when he explains in detail how we will deal with any casualties. Sobering stuff that gets all of our attention.

The orders go well and everyone heads off reasonably happy. You can tell there is an element of underlying anxiety. The commanders now have plenty of time to think things through and brief their Toms.

I spend the rest of the afternoon adjusting my kit. It is becoming an obsession. I keep moving pouches and trying different configurations. I start to realise that I might be wasting my time. With the loads that we carry there isn't a comfortable combination, just a less painful one.

Once I am relatively happy with everything I have a chat with the CSM – we are happy with our game plan. I grab some food and decide on an early night.

Before I head off to bed my mortar sergeant comes to see me. As the title implies, he commands the mortar detachment. This detachment consists of 20 soldiers and they man three 81mm mortars and three 60mm mortars. The mortar is a phenomenal weapon, my sole heavy asset. The mortars belong to me, so they are the only guaranteed indirect fire I have. The artillery may have a troop of guns at my FOB but I don't own them. They belong to the CO. As they don't belong to me their fire isn't guaranteed – they might be on a higher-priority task. I view my mortars as a key asset.

Sergeant Philips wants to conduct a fire mission. The marines took their mortars with them and we have put ours in their place so we now need to check that they are correctly positioned and ready for accurate fire. We can't arbitrarily send high-explosive shells into the green zone – they might hit locals. At night we can fire illumination rounds and use these to check that the mortars are working correctly. It makes sense to do this before tomorrow's patrol.

So I agree and head up to the battlements to watch the display.

The mortar line – as the mortars are called – swings into action. Sergeant Philips starts bellowing out commands and all the lads respond by repeating what he has just said back to him. This is a safety check – the sergeant needs to know that the lads have understood the command they have just been given. One mistake means rounds landing in the wrong place; not an issue for an illumination task, but life or death with high explosive. I have a great view of all of the activity. I am standing in one of the command bunkers, which allows me to look down on to the mortar line and also gives me a full view of the green zone. The mortar detachment is really well drilled. It is reassuring to watch them and, before I know it, all three mortar crews are confirming they have dialled in the firing data and are good to go.

'FIRE,' screams Sergeant Philips and the lads throw mortar bombs down their respective barrels.

The mortars really fire with a boom. It's the sound of a sledgehammer hitting a sheet of steel. The mortar bombs head off on their trajectories – often up to 5,000 feet. Thirty seconds later there is a pop as the illumination round separates from its canister and three mini suns burst over the green zone four kilometres off to the north. The illumination round is really powerful and can illuminate two football pitches. That is full illumination – effectively turning night into day. With three mortars firing and the rounds spaced out they can illuminate an area about 700m by 700m.

The rounds burn for 30 seconds before plunging back into darkness. The mortar fire controller (MFC) is standing next to me. While Sergeant Philips runs the mortar line, Corporal Hickman is the actual controller of the fire. When we go on patrol Corporal Hickman will come with me and he will be responsible for calling for, and adjusting, the mortar fire.

I look around and realise that most of the FOB has turned out to watch the display. As the rounds burst initially there is a collective 'Oooh' followed by 'Aaah' as the flares start burning, as if we are at a fireworks display. It is really funny listening to 150 paratroopers all going 'Oooh' and 'Aaah'. Lord knows what the locals think in the village next door.

Corporal Hickman is not quite happy yet so he repeats the task with some adjustments.

This process goes on five times before Corporal Hickman and Sergeant Philips are both happy. Once they are happy they 'check fire' and stand the mortar line down.

After all this excitement and with the first B Company patrol tomorrow I don't know how much sleep I will get. I have a lot swirling round my mind. We have an early start so I head off to bed. I read for an hour to relax myself and then turn off my head torch.

FRIDAY 18 APRIL

My plan is to get up at 0500 but I am awake before this. It isn't nerves I am feeling, more anxiety. I really want the first patrol to go well. I keep mentally rehearsing all of the different parts of the plan and imagine how I will deal with other eventualities – such as the enemy turning up.

Just before I get up I mutter astronaut Al Shepard's prayer that he said on an 'open' microphone minutes before they ignited the engines of his Mercury-Redstone rocket, during America's bid to get a man into space. 'Dear Lord, please don't let me screw up.'

With that perfectly functional prayer I swing out of my camp cot and get all of my kit on.

Once I have checked my kit I meet my group at the briefing area. The group that accompanies me on patrol is referred to as TAC – short for company tactical headquarters. Company headquarters is my entire headquarters but when I deploy on the ground I leave my company 2IC – Captain Brett Jackson – in the FOB to run the ops room. The smaller group of people I take on the ground is called TAC.

I carry my own radio but I also have two radio operators with me. I have four radio operators in total, plus Corporal Meecham from the Royal Signals. Two will man the radios in the ops room; two come with me. Just by the nature of their jobs, the radio ops spend a lot of time with me and I am already close to them. They are commanded by a lance corporal – Lance Corporal Barker, known as 'Mad Dog'. I get on really well with him. He is incredibly loyal and tough as nails. Like a lot of 'mad dogs', he only really responds to one master. This means that he works brilliantly for me but doesn't really respond to anyone else. As the signals detachment commander he is the primary radio operator and always comes with me. He also takes on a secondary function as a semi-bodyguard for me. I know that at times I will be sucked into dealing with tactical problems. I may be more focused on my map than what is going on around me – hence why I will need someone to look out for me. This is a task we have discussed and I am reassured to have such a loyal but also such a hard individual looking out for me.

Lance Corporal Barker is on the company radio network, the same network as me. This means that there are two of us listening out for messages for me, but it also means that we have a spare radio. Communications is everything, and I have to be able to talk to the company. The other radio op carries a satellite radio. This can't be on permanently – it only works when it is static, but if we go firm (stop for a while) somewhere or we are really struggling with the company net we can always rely on satellite.

My TAC 'entourage' is big – in the region of fifteen people. There are my two radio ops and Corporal Hickman. There is then the forward observation officer (FOO), Captain Adam Greenfield from the Royal Artillery – he carries out the same function for the artillery as Corporal Hickman does for the mortars. The FOO is accompanied by two of his own radio ops, as they have to manage multiple radio nets. Then there is a fast air controller (FAC). He coordinates the use of fighter jets and the Apache helicopters. My FAC is a corporal from my Company – also called Corporal Hickman. Corporal Hickman is a side-splittingly funny, irrepressible Geordie and absolutely great value. He is never down about anything. He has also proved how capable he is, because the FAC course is incredibly demanding.

Next is a commander from my fire support group (FSG). The FSG is commanded by Sergeant Major Mitchell, known as Mitch. A real 'old sweat', he is an excellent paratrooper and an expert in heavy weapons. The FSG comprises machine gunners and anti-tank rocket operators. They man the 40mm grenade launchers and .50cal machine guns in the FOB as well as the Javelin anti-tank rockets. Although there is no tank threat in Afghanistan, the Javelin rocket is superb; with its heat-seeking warhead it can engage targets such as compounds and even an individual enemy. When on foot patrol I intend to take an FSG group, which will be about 14 people. Half will carry GPMGs and the remainder will carry rifles and spare ammunition for the GPMGs. This is a potent group due to the firepower from the GPMGs. This group allows me to put a fire support base in, freeing up the platoons to carry out attacks without having to worry about covering fire.

Behind the FSG commander will be 'odds and sods', depending on the plan; the sniper commander, Sergeant Radcliffe, an interpreter and anyone else that needs to be with my group.

The CSM has his own group. His group comprises an extra Tom to give him a hand and then the medics. He may take more manpower if the situation merits it. When on patrol TAC goes behind the lead platoon, followed by the FSG, then the CSM's group, finally the rear platoon. This isn't a rigid formation – I can change the 'order of march' as the situation dictates.

It's a big beast though, 70 to 80 people. While I concentrate on the tactical battle and often the front half of the column, the CSM tends to coordinate the rear for me. Once he knows my plan he will always be trying to look after those not in contact and ensuring that they are ready for me to use if I want to swing them into the battle. At least, that is the theory and that is what we have practised in the build-up training. It is also what we will have to do today if the enemy shows up.

I head into the ops room and have a chat with Brett. His job is to man the ops room and try to take as much pressure and friction off me as possible. He will listen to all of the radio traffic and plot the patrol's progress on the map that he has. He is also responsible for sending updates to our higher headquarters – the 2 PARA battle group HQ. This takes a lot of pressure off of me. If there is an incident Brett will start trying to get me additional assets to help with the situation. He is happy with the plan and we talk through some of the finer points.

Brett is a good guy. We haven't been working with each other that long but we have worked out a pretty efficient way of doing business.

Once we are both happy I say 'see you later', and head for the ops room door.

Just before I leave he replies, 'Have a good one', and gives me a smile. Paratroopers are as superstitious as actors. While actors use 'Break a leg' to wish people luck, we use 'Have a good one'. To say the words 'good luck' would automatically jinx everything. So 'Have a good one' is the universal way of wishing luck without bringing down a curse.

I head back to the briefing area and get the remainder of my kit on. Lance Corporal Barker is there to help me get my radio on. I buckle up my helmet and check everyone is ready. They all give me a thumbs up so I confidently stride off towards the rear gate.

I am at the rear gate for 0540 and we are aiming for a 0545 depart. There is a bustle of activity as the platoons sort themselves out and get into the order of march. The CSM is there, coordinating all of the activity and gives me a big grin as I arrive.

The lead will be taken by 5 Platoon, followed by TAC, snipers, a small FSG, CSM's group and then 6 Platoon. We will stay like this throughout, as it is a relatively short patrol. On long patrols I will have to rotate the lead platoon, as there is a lot of pressure on them – they are the most likely to meet the enemy first.

By 0545 we are good to go. The two platoon commanders check in on their radios and I let the ops room know we are heading out.

With that I tell 5 Platoon commander Wes Smart to head off. Wes is superb. Descended from circus fame, he is one of the most professional and driven guys I have met. His platoon loves him, but he is no soft touch. He leads from the front and sets very high standards.

The patrol starts to head off. I have picked this departure time deliberately; the sun is just coming up. That way we don't need to use our night vision equipment. For simplicity, doing the patrol in darkness is not an option.

5 Platoon weave out of the gate and before long their last man leans over to me and says, 'last man'. This is a universal way of letting someone know that your platoon is moving off. It is my cue to follow.

I get myself to my feet, wait until he is at least five metres in front of me, and then I head off.

Once I start moving I turn round to Lance Corporal Barker and give him a nod. He nods back, confirming that he has seen me move off. This may all sound a bit over the top but the constant checking whether someone has seen you move off is to ensure that no one gets left behind and that the patrol doesn't get split up. This may be unnecessary in the FOB but this is our drill. If you carry out a drill all of the time it is less likely to be forgotten, especially when somewhere like the green zone. My next fear, after accidentally calling in fire on my own men, is losing someone. The Taliban would love to take a prisoner. I made a speech to the company in the cookhouse in Colchester, where I made a vow that no man gets left behind. No matter what happens, if you are lost, separated or injured don't worry. Get yourself hidden, turn your radio on and wait – we will be coming back for you. So I am pleased to see that we are all doing what we are supposed to be doing, right from the outset.

With Lance Corporal Barker five metres behind me I head out of the bottom gate and hook left, following the man in front.

At first the patrol follows the edge of the FOB. We walk across the HLS, which is effectively the desert just outside of the bottom gate. The HLS is in a bowl about 200 metres across. This allows the FOB to overlook it, ensuring that the enemy don't sneak in and lay mines. Just past the HLS though, the ground starts to undulate. This causes 'blind spots', small pockets of land that we can't see into. This is a worry. Not so much when we are on foot, but more for vehicles that transit into and out of the FOB.

South-east from the HLS there are a few compounds but they are mainly unoccupied. Amazingly, there is a large Bedouin tent with a camel hobbled just outside. I can see all of this as the patrol starts to head north, staying in the desert.

Heading north, just past the HLS, is a local graveyard.

The graves are all clustered around a small hill. Each grave is a simple affair – just a small mound, a cluster of rocks and then some decorative ribbons that flutter in the wind.

The lead element of the patrol has walked straight through the graveyard. This won't have been a deliberate act – tactically, it makes sense to dominate the high ground. The little hill that the graveyard is on is an obvious point of elevation and I can see that 5 Platoon's commander has pushed some machine guns up on to it. I don't want to criticise the platoon commander so early on in the patrol, but I don't want people walking through the graveyard. I doubt the locals will be impressed. So I make a mental note to brief everyone, when we get back in, to avoid it.

The patrol continues north up the desert and 200 metres past the FOB we come to a huge compound. Our next-door neighbours. This compound is at least 300 metres long and 200 metres wide and seems to house multiple families. Glancing through the large open gates as I pass by, I can see that the inside of the compound is broken down into a series of smaller compounds. The walls are at least ten metres high and the whole place looks very secure. There are kids running around inside and some indifferent-looking men cast us the odd glance as we pass.

Once we have gone past this huge compound the lead platoon swings left and starts to drop down from the desert towards the 611, the road that passes in front of the FOB. It is still early so there isn't any traffic yet.

On the other side of the 611 is the green zone. Initially there is a row of fields, before a large drainage ditch and then a tree-line. The tree-line is 150 metres into the green zone and is effectively the first piece of shelter. But 5 Platoon are well drilled and treat this wide-open field as a threat. Being out in the open with the nearest cover 75 metres away is not where you want to be if the enemy shows up. So they place machine guns out covering their front and I watch as one of the sections sprints across the field and gets itself into the tree-line. This section's job will be to clear the immediate area and then get itself set up to cover the remainder of us across the open ground. We can see up to the tree-line; their job is to make sure they can see beyond it.

All of these drills are slick but time-consuming. I don't want to rush the pace as we are finding our feet, but I glance at my watch and realise that in the last hour we have covered about 300 metres. I can still clearly see the face of the sentry and the sangar that is providing overwatch. Never mind, this is all a learning experience.

Wes gets his whole platoon over and pushes them forward to create some space. We now have a lot of firepower up in the tree-line so there is no need for the mad dash across the fields. Wes gets on the radio and lets me know it is all secure so I cross the 611 and lead my group over to the tree-line. I am amazed at how much the ground changes in such a short space. It is striking how different the green zone is when you compare looking at it to being in it.

Once we have all crossed the open ground we swing left and start heading north-west. We are moving in an anti-clockwise loop around the FOB. We are sweeping through the same compounds that we cleared with the marines but it all looks so different. Different time of day and different direction makes it all look new.

The sun is getting higher and local activity is starting in the fields. I watch with fascination as men of all ages leave the Star Wars village and head into the fields. I suppose this is them 'off to the office'.

At the same time, traffic begins to build on the 611. Rickety old cars start bumping up and down on the rough, undulating track, throwing up small clouds of dust. No one is paying us much attention.

We are now in the belt of compounds to the front of the FOB and we get a bit of momentum going. It is still quite stop–start though. The lads are doing all of their drills correctly and, to some extent, all of us are staring into every bush and fold in the ground imagining that there are Taliban there. It creates a lot of tension in your mind and I can feel the sweat start to drip from under my helmet.

We might be going a bit quicker, but the pace is painful. We take five paces forward, stop; kneel down, five paces forward, on and on. With 40kgs of kit on, there is tremendous pressure on the thighs and knees. It is preferable tactically to kneel down as you can still see quite far, but a lot of people are opting to sit down to relieve the pressure.

I am next to the drainage ditch and I follow the tree-line. This is early in the tour and the temperatures are only around 30C but already I am thinking how nice it would be to strip off and get in the water.

As I approach a bend in the drainage ditch I notice that the lads are passing a hand signal down the line. Just past the bend a soldier will point to something on the ground. Once he gets the nod from the guy behind he moves on. As the next soldier in line comes level to where the last soldier has just pointed he points. Thus we can point out a potential obstacle or hazard to the guy behind.

I look up to see the soldier in front of me pointing at a

diesel generator thumping away next to an earth mound. I nod and then approach. As I get closer I realise that the mound is actually a well and the generator is powering a water pump to irrigate the fields. The water is pumped into a holding tank and from there it flows into numerous irrigation channels. The crystal-clear, inviting water is flowing out of this metal tank into channels made of baked mud. It is incredibly intricate but ruthlessly simple and I am quite fascinated by it. I'm not entirely sure why this is being pointed out as a hazard though – until I approach the well.

It takes my breath away. It is four metres in diameter and as I look over the edge the well drops down 20 metres before it hits the water. I hadn't expected it to be so deep. What immediately strikes me is that if any of us were to fall in, we would be dead. A 20-metre drop would knock the wind out of you and with 40kgs of kit on you, you would sink immediately. There is no way to get all of our kit off in a hurry, so you would just disappear into the murky gloom. What a thought. I make another mental note that this needs to be passed on to everyone as a warning. There is no problem spotting these wells in daylight but at night, on NVGs and with the pumps silent, you would stand a good chance of stepping into one.

I realise I am making a lot of mental notes so I pull out a notebook which is in a pouch on the front of my body armour and quickly jot them down.

Brett comes up on the radio and informs me that intelligence has indicated that the enemy are out and about and that they are in the vicinity of Jusulay. They are trying to put something together and are going to try to have a go at us.

This sharpens our attention and people start kneeling

instead of sitting and also actively seeking out cover when we halt. Even a small hole or fold in the ground is better than nothing.

The locals are still working the fields so I wonder if the enemy really are around. The locals are great survivors and there is no way they would let themselves get between the enemy and us.

Wes lets me know that he is at the Jusulay junction, which is our next turning point. I give him the go ahead to make the next left turn towards the 611 and Star Wars village.

We cross the 611 and then head up a small, dry wadi that heads to the heart of the village. The village is pretty quiet, which makes sense. All of the locals are tending the fields, so we don't have anyone to talk to. I would like to know why the elders didn't come to the last *shura* but I have no one to ask.

We pop out of the village and head in through 7 RHA gate. As soon as we have unloaded our weapons the Toms head back to their accommodation and the commanders head to the briefing area.

Brett is there to meet us and he has kindly filled up my coffee mug. I tell him he will go far in this man's army and take a grateful sip. I know I should be rehydrating with water – nice, chlorinated, warm water – but I can't turn down a good coffee.

We go through a patrol debrief, which is standard. Brett has to send off a report after every patrol so he has a set series of questions, as does Sergeant Radcliffe, who is trying to develop our intelligence picture.

I wrap up at the end with the points from my notebook and some overall thoughts, all of which are positive. At this stage we are slow and very deliberate but I feel this is under-standable. It's all about 'small steps' right now.

After we have finished and everyone has headed off I strip off down to a pair of shorts and fill up a solar shower. The sun is quite warm so I lay out the bag in the sun to warm the water and clean my rifle and pistol. Once I am happy that all my kit is squared away, I have a shower.

There is a showering area next to the briefing area. This is just a hole with a wooden pallet over it and a small pulley attached to the wall. You sling your shower bag on to a hook, winch the bag up above your head and then off you go. The run-off goes into the hole.

The problem is that the FOB sits on solid bedrock. The holes for both the toilets and the showers only go down a few metres before they hit rock. This means that drainage is incred-ibly slow. The showering holes are full of stagnant water, which encourages mosquitoes. Plus they stink – who knows what people have been throwing down there? The CSM has already spotted this problem and is going to have fresh holes dug.

For now, though, I enjoy the bliss of our outdoor show-ering facility and while the water might not be nice to drink, it is nice to shower in.

As most of us have been on patrol there was no breakfast; instead, we are having brunch. I manage to hold off until midday, as I know I will be hungry later if I eat too early. I head over to the cookhouse tent and grab a bowl of corned beef hash, one of my favourites. I sit out in the sun chatting to some of the lads and feel really content.

The six months' journey in front of us seems very long at this stage. I have to break it down into chunks to make it manageable; in one large lump it feels impossible. I realise

I have to take each day as it comes and each challenge as it presents itself. Effectively, take the rough with the smooth. For now though, it feels good to have cracked a patrol, had a coffee and a shower and to be sat here with a nice bowl of corned beef hash, talking to the lads.

I spend the rest of the afternoon wandering around the FOB talking to people. I am still discovering hidden nooks and crannies and the lads are already being enterprising, making furniture out of wire and planks and generally trying to make their own little area feel like home.

6 Platoon has its own area, 4 and 5 are next to each other. They all want their own space and there are already home-made signs up stating what belongs to whom. This is all healthy activity as far as I am concerned and it is best to leave them to it.

It's been a long day. I go into the ops room to see how things are going with Brett before heading back to my camp cot. I feel a relaxing read is in order. As I lie there in the glow of my head torch I realise how lucky it is that the enemy didn't show up today. I could do with a few more patrols like this so that we can learn the ground and practise our movement. A series of 'inoculation' patrols to get us used to the environment, before we have to use our battle tactics. The enemy will have a different plan of course. For now though I am happy so I turn off my head torch and drift off to sleep.

FRIDAY 18 APRIL

I am woken at 0545 by one of the radio ops. He says that I am needed in the ops room. So I pull on a T-shirt and shorts and head round to see what is going on.

We have received a set of orders for an operation we are to carry out. The operation is called Op Loam. Op Loam is a standing task carried out when necessary. It is a vehicle convoy to the FOB to deliver stores.

Now that 2 PARA is in command, the quartermaster (QM) has had every FOB do a stock check of ammunition, rations, emergency water and other essential stores. Based on the returns that he has received, the QM has now decided that he wants to top up the FOBs so that they are self-sufficient for six weeks, especially with food. This makes sense, as helicopter resupply is never guaranteed. The use of the helicopters to conduct the changeover from marines to paras has meant that the FOBs haven't been resupplied with essential stores during this period, so in some areas we are getting dangerously low.

Op Loam also gives the battle group HQ the opportunity to plan and control a large, complicated, but relatively straightforward operation.

I start to read Op Loam orders, which have been sent electronically to the ops room. Op Loam starts at Bastion where a vehicle convoy in excess of 20 vehicles will be strategically loaded with the required stores. The vehicles will be a mixture of transport trucks, with shipping containers on board, and protection vehicles. This convoy will head deep into the desert to avoid obvious routes before coming in to our battle group staging area. A staging area is just a secure location to sort yourself out and reconfigure before conducting the next phase of an operation. Our staging area is at another FOB ten kilometres south of Sangin, FOB Robinson. FOB Robinson is a huge FOB used for logistical resupply as well as a patrol base. From FOB Robinson,

Operation Loam will split into smaller convoys that will deliver stores to the individual FOBs.

I read that I am to expect a ten-vehicle convoy into my FOB the following night during darkness.

B Company's role is to deploy out and secure the 611 up to, and including, the Jusulay track junction. This will allow our part of the convoy to move rapidly from Sangin, straight down the 611 and into our FOB. They will unload the stores, sort the vehicles out and then stay for the day before heading out again the next night.

This all looks relatively straightforward and Ade had briefed me on all of this, as these operations happen quite frequently. I realise that I have all day to plan this and I decide to give orders the following morning before heading out tomorrow night. I will come up with my plan this afternoon.

I want to check my rifle so after breakfast I head down to the HLS. The HLS doubles up as a range when it isn't in use with the helicopters. All of the platoons are rotating through the range and they are conducting 'check zero'. This is where you confirm, by firing rounds, that your rifle will hit what you are aiming at. Our rifles get knocked about all the time and it is easy for the sights to lose their zero, hence why it is worth checking.

I settle down behind my rifle and work through a string of 20 rounds before going forward to check my target. I am happy – the bullets are landing where I want them.

I then head over to see what the snipers are up to. I have a real affinity with the snipers and have always been a huge fan. They are very good soldiers and incredibly dedicated to their job. They are, effectively, professional hunters and as a hunter myself I enjoy their company.

They are test-firing the new .338 sniper rifle. An awesome weapon, this rifle is really accurate and has significant range. I have a personal stake as well; my previous job had been in defence procurement and I had helped bring this rifle into service.

I have a chat with Corporal Berenger and before I know it he asks if I want a go. Do I ever? I tuck myself behind this behemoth and fire five rounds, all of which are made quite pleasant to shoot by the suppressor that is fitted. I am really impressed with its accuracy.

Once I have had my fix of shooting I head up to the ops room, re-read the Operation Loam instruction and then go to the back office to come up with a plan and write my orders.

This takes a few hours and before I know it, it is mid-afternoon. I decide to go for another walk around the FOB and end up back with the snipers. Corporal Berenger has put in an observation post (OP) above their accommodation that looks out to the north of the FOB, into the green zone.

I join the snipers on the roof and spend the next hour watching locals through the powerful sniper telescopic sight. The scope is amazing and I find myself sucked into searching the hedgerows trying to spot hidden enemies. It is fascinating to watch the snipers as well. They are quiet, methodical and focused. They are on the roof to catch that fleeting opportunity. The opportunity to get a 'confirmed kill'. I can't fault their dedication but I am also concerned that they are getting sunburn.

As I head off to evening meal I realise how lucky I am

to have such professional people under my command. People who are happy to sit on a roof, in blistering sunshine, staring through a scope for four hours, all in the hope that they can see the enemy. You have to admire them.

SATURDAY 19 APRIL

I issue my orders before lunch to the commanders from 5 and 6 Platoon, plus the Royal Engineer sergeant. They don't take long, as this is all quite straightforward. It is basically ground holding and all of it will happen 500 metres from the FOB.

The company is formed up at 1700 hours and I head out with 5 and 6 Platoon, TAC and a Royal Engineer detachment. We head out of the front gate and sweep down the 611. I push 6 Platoon over to the drainage ditch in the green zone and they parallel the rest of us, who move along the 611. The lead is 5 Platoon, followed by the Royal Engineers, who are sweeping for mines. We are not so concerned about anti-personnel mines as there are so many local people walking up and down the road it would be hard for the enemy to target us and not them. We are more concerned about a large anti-tank mine that will only go off when it has a lot of weight put on it, such as a large truck with a shipping container full of rations on the back.

I think I may have overestimated how long this is all going to take. I based my time calculations on the last patrol but within twenty minutes, 6 Platoon are at the Jusulay track junction. They clear an unoccupied compound and then set themselves up. It is a good position to defend themselves from and they dominate the track junction. They will stay there until the operation is complete.

Now 5 Platoon break left off the 611 and move into a dilapidated compound on the edge of Star Wars village. They will do the same as 6 Platoon – defend and dominate.

TAC is combined with the CSM's group so there are 20 of us. I plan on stopping short of the track junction and providing depth to the two forward platoons who are now dominating the junction.

I spy a small compound with a little well that looks about right. We will be 150 metres short of the track junction and I can see the compounds being occupied by 5 and 6 Platoon. Perfect. Of course, all of this activity is in full view of the FOB so I am fairly content that we are safe.

The CSM goes forward with his crew and sweeps the area. Once he is happy I move the whole of TAC in.

There are two small buildings and an open courtyard. The buildings look in good condition and the well has the obligatory generator pumping water. The water flows down a 100-metre long baked mud irrigation channel into the neighbouring fields. This looks a nice place to spend the night, so we all grab ourselves a bit of space, the CSM places out sentries and we settle down. It is only 1800 hours.

Our activity has generated a lot of attention from the locals. It looks like most of the village has turned out to watch and they are fascinated by our activity. A crowd of about 20 drift over to our location. By this point I have one of my snipers on the roof of one of the buildings to extend how far we can see.

One of the elders steps forward and informs me that the building is a mosque. I apologise profusely and tell Lance

Corporal Smith to come down. The locals say they don't mind as long as we don't go in the building but I think it best if we have no physical contact with the building at all. They seem to appreciate this.

I decide it is time to deploy our secret weapon – Pashto speakers. I have three Toms in the company who have spent the last nine months learning Pashto. It's not what they wanted to be doing; they were selected based on educational assessments and they have all done really well.

I lean over to Private Cutler and tell him to have a go. So he moves over to a cluster of young men and starts talking to them. He stutters at first but you can see it coming back to him. The locals stare at him transfixed. They can't believe a westerner can speak their language. More and more locals start to drift over to listen in fascination to Cutler speaking. It is brilliant. At one point he cracks a joke and they all start laughing, which I take as a huge success.

The CSM and I drift over and join in the conversation with an interpreter. This is a *shura*, as far as I am concerned. They promise to come to the FOB for a chat.

The meeting starts to break up so I walk back to my kit and sit down.

Suddenly all of the locals line up and an elder starts calling out prayers. It is instantaneous and all of them join in the final prayer before the sun sets. It is amazing to watch. Incredible how quickly the atmosphere goes from a laugh and a joke to serious prayer.

I decide to put some mosquito repellent on, as we are near water. As I smear the cream on my face I realise that my actions look similar to the ones that they are carrying out. A couple of the young men are watching me with curiosity. You can tell that they can't work out why I am joining in with them.

Once prayer is finished they all start to drift off. It is Saturday night – the weekend – so everyone is milling around. It has a real weekend feel to it, but as the sun sets they all head back into the village.

I wrap myself in a lightweight blanket and sleep for a couple of hours before I am woken by Lance Corporal Barker. The convoy will be here at 0300.

The convoy rumbles by at 0315. There is no need for us to stay out any longer so I tell everyone to head back in. I am back in my camp cot by 0430. Our interactions with the locals have been very positive and the locals have agreed to come to a *shura* on Tuesday. I just hope they show up. I am thankful that, again, the enemy left us alone. We could still do with a few more 'dry runs' before it goes live.

SUNDAY 21 APRIL

As most of us were out late last night the FOB has a fairly quiet feel to it. I am up at 0800 and go down to the bottom of the FOB to talk to the Operation Loam guys. As I start to walk down, I take in the whole scene and realise that it is a fantastic snapshot of life in the FOB.

Corporal Jang, my company clerk, is sitting in the shade reading his Bible. A chubby lad from the FSG is circuit training out in the sun.

The JCB is moving pallets of bottled water into one of our own shipping containers. The water needs to be locked up as the lads keep stealing it, as the water from the borehole is so heavily chlorinated it is quite hard work drinking it.

Bottled water going missing is understandable, but we can't allow it to happen.

The bonnet is up on one of the Land Rovers and two of the mechanics are working on the engine.

There are hammocks strung up between the Op Loam vehicles and the drivers are gently swaying in the wind. They are all shattered. It is a 31-hour ordeal for them to get to here and they have to do the same to return tonight.

All of this activity brings a smile to my face. It feels good to be here and good to be in command.

I have a chat with Ian, the Op Loam commander. He takes these patrols in his stride but I don't envy him. I would rather be on foot in the green zone than driving around the desert and towns running the risk of hitting a mine. I tell Ian I wouldn't want his job. He tells me he wouldn't want mine. Fair one. So we agree to keep our respective jobs and I leave him to get some more sleep.

We all head out again at 1700 hours to secure the Jusulay junction. This will allow the convoy to get away. It is very slick this time, as it is the same plan as before, plus people now know what they are doing. We don't go to the same locations, so as not to set a pattern, but the overall plan is similar.

The convoy heads out at 2200 so we are all back in by 2230. No hanging about this time.

MONDAY 22 APRIL

I get told that the 'helicopters are inbound'. I am expecting the CO on a visit. I put on my body armour, grab my radio and head to the front command sangar. Lance Corporal Barker meets me there.

The HLS is pretty open and the reason why the RAF is so reluctant to fly in to the FOB is the amount of time they have come under fire when on the HLS. The procedure when we expect helicopters is to go to full manning in the sangars. The front fire support sangar has both the .50cal and 40mm grenade launcher manned and they set up a Javelin ready to go in its bay. The mortars and artillery get themselves ready to fire on to known enemy firing points and I move forward to the command bunker and meet my MFC, FOO and FAC. By being together in the command bunker we are ready if an incident occurs. At the same time, the FSG board stripped-down fire support Land Rovers and head to the far side of the HLS and take up positions covering the desert. Once all of this is in place we are covering 360 degrees and are, hopefully, dissuading the enemy from firing. Of course, the Chinook is still an incredibly attractive target. But this preparation does mean we will have a very rapid response if something does happen.

The twin Chinooks flare on to the HLS and disgorge their contents amid a mass of brown dust and furiously working soldiers. It is all hands to the pumps to unload the helicopters as quickly as possible. The longer the helicopter sits on the ground the more vulnerable it is. Sergeant Train is my HLS commander and he has a work party of twenty guys to get things done as quickly as possible.

Once the Chinooks are gone I see that the CO has arrived and that we have sacks of mail. This is good news.

The CO has a big grin on his face and seems pleased to see me. I talk him through my plan for the day.

I start in the ops room. Once we have both got a brew we go to the briefing area and I take him through a very detailed brief based on my findings from my estimate. It is useful to expose him to my thinking. I need him to have confidence in my plan and also, this is a chance to have a second set of eyes look at my thinking. He may spot things I haven't. He is happy though and he then takes me through his initial findings based on the battle group's first couple of weeks in Afghanistan.

After lunch I give him a guided tour of the FOB and this turns into a rolling 'walk and talk' exercise. We spend all afternoon walking round the FOB and having detailed discussions about how we see the tour developing. He is keen that we 'walk before we run'. He wants us to build our confidence and experience before we get more ambitious. I am in complete agreement. He is also keen that we generate battle group level operations. The risk at the moment is our lack of initiative – effectively, we are tied to our FOBs. Generating operations at the battle group level by bringing two companies or more together for specific operations will alleviate this. The challenge, as always, is finding the manpower.

I am struck by how relaxed he seems. I haven't stage-managed any activity for him and he seems happy with this.

In fact he is having such a good time he decides to stay. He was originally going to be collected by helicopter but after a chat on the radio in the ops room he gets it cancelled and organises for the Viking armoured vehicle troop to come from Sangin and pick him up tomorrow.

The commanders gather for the 1800 brief, or 'prayers'. At the end of the brief is a slot for anyone to speak and the CO takes the opportunity to address the group. He gives some positive feedback on what he has seen so far and talks about some of the plans that are developing. All of the proposed battle group operations involve B Company, so we are happy. We would hate to be left out.

After dinner he spends the rest of the time chatting to the lads.

TUESDAY 23 APRIL

For the Vikings to come into the FOB we have to carry out the same drill as for Operation Loam. To keep things simple, I plan to use all of the same people from the previous patrol. I grab the platoon commanders and quickly go through the plan. They are happy and I don't envision us being out that long.

I have a final chat with the CO. It has been a good visit. He seems on good form and seems happy with what the company are up to. He is keen to start 'expanding our footprint' so he wants me to start taking longer, deeper patrols as soon as is practicable.

I say goodbye and head out the front gate to conduct another patrol to secure the Jusulay junction. This is starting to get a bit boring but at least I am getting to practise my command and control procedures.

We secure the junction. The Vikings pass by, nip into the FOB and pick up the CO. This whole procedure takes all of ten minutes so before I know it the Vikings are heading back out and the CO is waving at me from one of the turrets.

As we head back in I realise that I have enjoyed seeing him. It was handy to run my thinking by someone else. It was basically a sanity check. He has given me some further direction, so it is now a matter of getting deep into the green zone and putting pressure on the enemy. The enemy can't be allowed to continually bring the fight to me; I have to take the fight to him.

Once back in I sort myself out and then conduct a hasty planning session. I am taking a patrol out tomorrow. Once happy with my plan I write my orders and then grab some lunch. Straight after lunch I issue the orders to the platoon commanders before spending the rest of the afternoon going through my estimate again. I want to capture what the CO and I discussed while it is still fresh in my mind.

Just before heading off to bed I realise that I hadn't heard if the locals came to the FOB today for the *shura* we discussed on Saturday. Brett and the intelligence cell would have covered it in my absence.

I go to the ops room and ask if any locals showed up. They didn't. Maybe our patrol activity down to the Jusulay track junction put them off?

WEDNESDAY 23 APRIL

I am woken at 0100 hours and asked to come to the ops room. I am informed that my patrol needs to go out later than planned. My intention was to patrol from 0500 to 0900hrs but I am told I need to go out from 0900 to 1200hrs. I am not particularly happy with this. First, it is very prescriptive without any explanation and second, it will be scorching by midday.

I decide to get on the radio and speak to headquarters. They explain that they are trying to sequence activity across the battle group area of operations so that they don't have to deal with multiple incidents at the same time if something happens. Effectively, they are taking baby steps, the same as us. This seems fair enough but I am not taken with the idea of being out at midday. Never mind. We will just have to get on with it. At least I don't have to get up at 0400.

I get up at normal time and after breakfast I head to the ops room. There seems to be a lot happening on the radio. There seem to be incidents going on all over the place. Both Kajaki and FOB Gibraltar are in contact and there has also been an incident with an unsuccessful suicide bomber in Gereshk.

I start to think about our patrol and decide that I will cancel it. If there are multiple incidents there is a strong chance that the medical evacuation helicopter will be tied up and I don't want to run the risk of not being able to evacuate a casualty. Although they will always come for a high-priority casualty, it still seems like a risk that I don't need to take. So I 'roll over' the patrol; we will instead do it in twenty-four hours' time.

Twenty minutes later the order is given over the radio to reduce all patrolling to a minimum as the helicopters are tied up. Welcome confirmation that my thought process is sound at the moment.

THURSDAY 24 APRIL

I am up at 0500 and get myself sorted to go on patrol. I am getting slicker at sorting myself out – armour on, webbing, daysack, shake the shoulders to seat the load, try to tuck the cables for the radio and the hose from my water bladder away before taking the first, staggering steps. It takes a while to tune out the discomfort in my shoulders.

We leave the front gate at 0600. I have 4 and 5 Platoon today. This is 4 Platoon's first time out as part of a company patrol and I am keen to give them a run out. The plan is to push back towards Jusulay and head deeper into the green zone this time. I believe that the enemy have a psychological line that they don't want us to cross. I am going to keep pushing until it becomes obvious where that line is. We can then try to work out why they have drawn the line there.

It is a slow start again. By 0650 we have only gone 400 metres. After this, though, we start to build up some momentum and 4 Platoon is quickly gaining confidence.

I decide to start changing formations. I need to get a feel for how complicated this is to command and control. It makes sense to do it now. We have received strong intelligence that we will be left alone for the next couple of weeks. The Taliban's main effort is the poppy harvest and they are putting everyone to work. This would tally with what we are seeing on the ground. We are not directly involved with the counter-narcotics programme, so we let them go about their business. No need to disenfranchise even more people. There are a lot of 'fighting age males' helping with the harvest. Intelligence indicates that these men are the ones we will be fighting in two weeks' time.

I swing the platoons up so that they are parallel and start to sweep through belts of compounds. I have instructed the guys to search compounds as they see fit. They don't have to methodically clear every compound, that would take us the whole six months. If one of the compounds gets their interest then they should conduct a proper clearance by searching it thoroughly otherwise they should conduct general searches as they are moving along.

The guys are patrolling well and they look really professional. They are carrying out their drills correctly. In clearing one compound, 4 Platoon discovers flight boarding passes to Pakistan and doctors' prescriptions for a surgery in Quetta. These look out of place in a battered old compound in Helmand, so they bag the items and we will send them back for the intelligence specialists to deal with.

We are now deeper into the green zone than we have ever been before and it amazes me how much it differs from the initial fields in front of the FOB. The sun glints and reflects on the numerous streams that seem to criss-cross everywhere. The greenery is rich and lush and the birdsong echoes around the compounds. At certain points this could be the English countryside – nice babbling streams, wheat swaying in the breeze, willow trees with their toes in the water, fennel growing out of the stream banks. And poppy; poppy fields as far as you can see. Incredibly, most of the poppy fields are bounded by marijuana plants. I can't believe it – the only things that grow really well in this country are drugs.

The other thing that strikes me is how many men are out tending to the poppies. There are people everywhere and they stare at us with a mixture of curiosity and indifference. I'm not surprised; we must look like aliens to them. Except for the younger men, the ones we think look like the 'fighters'. They glare at us, seething with anger.

It is a good patrol and I enjoy it. The lull created by the poppy harvest is a godsend for us. The platoons are getting slicker on the ground and I am having the opportunity to practise command and control. We are also generating intelligence. We have the opportunity to talk to the locals and by the time we get back to the FOB we receive intelligence that the enemy were watching us today. They are not happy with where we are getting to but they are being told to focus their efforts on the harvest. Psychologically, I am glad that we are frustrating them but it also feels like we are kicking a hornets' nest. Inevitably, before long, they are going to react.

FRIDAY 25 APRIL

I have the first example of expectation management. Two helicopters arrive early in the morning and after I have watched them depart from the command bunker I head back to the ops room. I am excited about getting some mail and I have watched all of the sacks being brought up into the FOB.

Once the mail is sorted I get a few letters and that is it. My family have all sent parcels and, foolishly, I have built up my hopes that they will arrive today.

Mail has such a morale-boosting effect. You can literally feel spirits lift when mail comes in. Mail is a link with home that reminds you that people are thinking about you. I sit in the ops room and watch happy signallers opening their parcels. Haribo sweets are very popular, as are other items such as biscuits – basically, anything that won't melt in the heat. Everyone seems to be receiving toiletries as well, especially wet wipes. Obviously, word hasn't got through yet that the well provides us with enough water to have as many showers as we want.

I am incredibly grateful for the letters but it still leaves me a little deflated. I stomp off to the gym to throw some weights around. I will try not to get my hopes up about mail in the future.

Mid-morning I get a message to meet Sergeant Radcliffe down at the bottom gate. We have a 'walk-in'– a local with intelligence who has just 'walked in' and is happy to share it with us. I am fascinated to meet such an individual because he is taking a huge risk. He will be made an example of, if the Taliban find out.

The walk-in is called 'Wally' and is a fantastic source of intelligence – the marines briefed us on him. He hasn't been to the FOB since we have taken over as he was told to give us some time to settle in. He is far younger than I expect, maybe sixteen. He is short with very dark cinnamon skin and very aquiline features. He has a jovial face and smiles a lot. Plus he pathologically hates the Taliban. We don't know what they have done to him or his family to create such loathing but it is clearly evident.

He confirms my pet theory about the lack of enemy activity. He explains that last year the Taliban treated the locals appallingly, they made them conduct the harvest whilst they concentrated on attacking coalition forces. This resulted in the harvest taking far longer than it should have done and the wheat being planted later than it should have been. This meant that the wheat wasn't ready for the winter. As a result the locals suffered. If you combine this with reconstruction and development in Sangin, the result is that coalition forces are starting to look like the good guys. So the direction from the enemy's higher command in Pakistan is to leave us alone and focus on the harvest – they need the revenue from the drugs. Once the harvest is complete they can switch focus back on to us. Wally thinks we have two more weeks' grace before the harvest is complete.

I realise that we need to make the most of this opportunity and explore as much of the ground as possible. During training we call this 'walking the range'. Before a live fire training attack the safety staff walk up and down the range to ensure that they understand all of the safe arcs and to identify which directions people are likely to fire in, thus 'walking the range'. As far as we are concerned, the enemy are letting us walk the range at the moment. The better we understand the ground the better it will be when it does kick off.

I wish Wally all the best and tell him to come in as much as possible without compromising his safety.

I take out a patrol in the late afternoon. The temperature is definitely getting warmer. By now there is no breeze and you can feel the heat clawing at you from the ground. The baked mud radiates heat.

I send the Vikings north from the FOB to some high ground looking over the green zone. At the same time I take 4 and 5 Platoons back down to the Jusulay junction. I make it look like we are carrying out the same drills as for Operation Loam. I get the platoons to go firm, as if we are getting ready to stay out the night in anticipation of a convoy. Then, on my command, the two platoons suddenly get up and push north-west at speed, straight in to Jusulay. The idea is to generate a response from the enemy. We get 1.5km into the green zone before I get everyone to go firm.

Nothing happens. It is clear that the Taliban are not going to get involved until after the harvest. We receive intelligence that some fighters are asking permission to attack us but they are told to get on with their work. The only other comment we receive is how big the patrol is.

We head back in at 2000hrs, very sweaty and all pretty tired. Late patrols are draining and it is the first time I have really seen the heat have an effect on us. People are lethargic and slow, like they are walking through treacle.

Once back in the FOB I shower off and sort out my kit before crashing gratefully into bed.

SATURDAY 26 APRIL

I realise that we have had quite a demanding week so I put in a rest day. There will be no patrolling today so people have a chance to sort themselves out. This goes down well.

I go to the gym early in the morning. This sort of defeats the object of a rest day, but I just enjoy training.

There isn't really much else to do. The platoons are doing their own thing so I spend most of the morning in the ops room. Brett has been sent some cookies which he kindly shares with all of us. We make some good coffee and all sit around talking.

Brett takes the opportunity to pin me down and work out the patrol programme for the next ten days. We work on a ten-day cycle and we have to send this to battle group headquarters. I get Sergeant Radcliffe to join us and between the three of us we work out a matrix of where we will go and who will be involved. I start to mix things up. We will begin to conduct a mixture of company-level patrols involving two platoons, individual platoon-level security patrols and mobile patrols involving the Vikings.

In the afternoon I grab Lance Corporal Barker and we head down to the deserted ANA compound. We set up a makeshift range and spend a pleasant hour shooting our rifles and pistols. I always enjoy shooting.

At the commander's evening brief I have to give my first bollocking. A couple of soldiers have lost items on patrol. Nothing serious – a magazine and some medical kit – but it is the principle. Professional soldiers don't lose kit. There have also been reports of stealing. This can't be tolerated. In such a close environment we all have to trust each other. The last thing we need is a few 'magpies'. Plus, I am concerned that the perpetrators will be identified and dealt with 'internally'. I don't want any kangaroo courts. So I let everyone know that we need to up our game. I can't say I enjoy doing this but it is necessary. We have to set high standards.

SUNDAY 27 APRIL

I decide to take out as many commanders as possible to conduct a ground familiarisation patrol using the Vikings. We will head out into the desert and then go north to a dominating position looking over the green zone. I haven't been out in the Vikings before and after a detailed brief from James – their grizzled troop commander – we head out. James and his troop are five months into their tour, so they really know what they are doing.

I am struck by how good the Viking armoured vehicle is; it is really powerful and the ground it can go over is impressive. It comfortably tackles ditches and steep banks. The downside is the dust they throw up. It is horrendous and before long we all look like sand men. I am fortunate to be in a turret and I feel quite 'cavalry' with my goggles on and a scarf wrapped round my face. Tally ho ...

We drive ten kilometres north and stop 500m opposite the power station. This power station sits just off the 611, in the green zone, and provides electricity to most of the surrounding area. It is also a known staging area for the enemy. We all clamber out of the vehicles and take a detailed look through our binoculars.

We then head further north and stop opposite a large village called Putay. Putay marks my northernmost boundary. As I stare out across the whole of my area of operations, the enormity of it sinks in. It is massive – probably 100 kilometres and stretches as far as the eye can see. I can just make out the FOB through my binoculars. There is no way we can dominate it. All I can do is jab at the enemy. I am heartened by one thing, though. Once the enemy have got the harvest out of the way he will focus on me. I don't necessarily have to worry about finding him. From everything I have been told he will come and find me. I find this bizarrely reassuring. As I stare out over kilometre after kilometre of green zone, I realise that it wouldn't be that much of a challenge for him to stay hidden in there.

I am also struck by how peaceful everything is. Putay is affluent for these parts. The compounds look well kept and here the 611 is even tree-lined. There are men harvesting everywhere. There must be 100–150 'fighting age males' to my front. James leans over to me and hands me a set of laser binoculars. 'Have a good look at those blokes,' he says. 'In two weeks' time that is who you are going to be fighting.'

It's hard to believe that in a couple of weeks' time this whole place will be a battlefield again.

Once we get back in I plan and deliver my orders for tomorrow's patrol before heading off to bed.

MONDAY 28 APRIL

I am up at 0500 and go through my normal routine. Today we are going to patrol up to and clear compound KA917. All of the compounds are allocated target numbers and KA917 is probably the most infamous. It is a compound three kilometres directly north from the FOB, in the green zone. It is the most used firing point for the enemy – it is where they launched the SPG-9 rockets from when I first arrived. Ade has pointed this out to me in great detail and told me his company had never made it up there to clear it – the enemy had always attacked them before they got close. It is clearly another psychological line that the enemy has drawn. I feel we have enough experience now and it is time to be a bit bolder. So we are going to go up there and clear it.

I am using 4 and 6 Platoons today and we head off at 0600 with 6 Platoon leading. The route takes us straight into the green zone and then we will start to hook right, leading directly to KA917. I have studied the route through the 'ship's binos' and I am pretty happy with it, right up to the last 700 metres. This is open ground that we will have to cross before we can get on to the compound. My plan is to stop short of this and evaluate the situation. If things are looking good we will carry on. If we think the enemy are around, I won't commit to an essentially suicidal approach over 700 metres; we will work out another way. It is a flexible plan that I can adjust once we are up there.

We are finally getting some speed up; 6 Platoon is moving really well. I think we are all getting a bit more comfortable with the procedures. Within an hour we are one kilometre short of the target compound. I decide to slow things down at this stage as, according to Ade's advice, we shouldn't have even made it this far.

Eerily though, we haven't seen any locals, a strong sign that the enemy are in the area.

I implement 'bounding overwatch'. This is where I get one of the platoons to go firm and get into a position to provide covering fire. Once they are set, I get the other platoon to push forward and then they set themselves up in overwatch. We then continue this 'leapfrog' motion forward. It works well and means that we are always poised to support each other.

The platoons are continuing to search compounds and things begin to get interesting. We are in an area where a marine lost his life during the last tour, when his Viking hit a mine. We discover a Viking door hidden in a compound. It is too heavy for us to carry back in, so I ask permission from headquarters to 'deny' it. Permission is granted – headquarters agree with my logic that we don't want the technology of the door armour falling into the wrong hands.

As part of my company group I have a detachment of Royal Engineers. This comprises ten soldiers from 9 Squadron – the Airborne Engineers. These guys are serious grafters. They accompany every patrol and when they are not on patrol they are usually undertaking some kind of construction task in the FOB. They are commanded by a really good guy, Sergeant Dale. A relaxed, easy-going commander, his guys work really hard for him. They might be grafters, they might all be highly technically proficient but they have one love, and that's blowing things up. Nothing makes an engineer happier than being given permission to slap explosives on something.

I call Sergeant Dale forward to have a look at the challenge. After some pensive scratching of the chin and mental arithmetic he decides that he will place two bar mines on it. A bar mine is a Cold War mine. Looking like a piece of lumber, it is packed full of explosive and is powerful enough to blow up a main battle tank. On patrol, each engineer carries half a bar mine.

I pull back as they technically place four halves of bar mine on the Viking door. Theoretically, this is enough explosive to blow up two tanks. This might seem overkill on an armoured door but I don't want to question his logic. We all tuck ourselves behind cover a hundred metres away and marvel at the huge explosion that sucks the air from our lungs. Sergeant Dale's calculations are correct – the door is vaporised.

At this point an elderly man drifts by. I send Sergeant Radcliffe over with an interpreter to ask a few questions. The man says that there are no enemy in the area.

We get to the edge of the open ground. Now that I am here I can see why it is open ground. It is effectively a swamp, so only loose grass has grown in it.

It is decision time. Cross the open ground or head back? We haven't been generating intelligence, so I decide we will go for it. Leaving 4 Platoon as a covering force I tell 6 Platoon to push forward.

They fan out and head straight across the open ground. It is a worrying time for me and even more so for them. You do not want to be out in the open if the enemy decide today is the day. There is no way round this though – the compound is surrounded by open ground.

They start jogging and before I know it they are at the other side. I breathe a sigh of relief.

They start an initial sweep of KA917. I think to myself 'check this out, we made it all the way up here, further than the previous company'.

Dave, the platoon commander, tells me that he has security out and they can cover me if I want to bring my group over.

I jog across the swamp and join Dave at the entrance of the compound. I want the guys to conduct a really thorough search of the compound so I give direction to Dave and Sergeant Dale and let them get on with it.

I am just having a drink of water when a shout goes up.

'We've got something,' shouts one of the Toms. He has found bundles of switches and wires – it all looks like 'bomb making components' so Sergeant Radcliffe bags it.

Then a really excited shout goes up.

'RPG!' One of the engineers has found an RPG warhead in a pile of sawdust. This is a great find.

Not long after, Dave comes to see me to say that they have found a bunker in the next compound. 'This is going well,' I think to myself.

Dave takes me round to show me the bunker. It is really well built. There is a 'rat run' – a narrow tunnel under the compound wall which leads into a well-constructed T-shaped bunker. The bunker has perfect observation on to the FOB, which we can see prominently off in the distance. I am impressed with its construction and sighting.

I have a chat with Sergeant Dale and, unsurprisingly, his suggestion is bar mines and plastic explosive. I give him the go ahead. He places some bar mines on the bunker and a lump of explosives on the RPG warhead, setting a fuse so that they will all go off together.

We pull back and sit around laughing and joking as the whole lot explodes. The bunker is a collapsed mound of mud and the warhead is gone.

These discoveries have been really good for morale, hence the good atmosphere. I know we aren't going to win this by removing individual warheads but it does feel we have got one over the enemy. Plus, it has instilled a degree of competition in the lads – they all want to find things now. Good news, as they will carry out their search drills properly.

I give the command to head back in. I realise we have been out for five and a half hours. This is a long time and I have run out of water, as have a lot of people. I think we all got sucked into what was going on.

We keep it together though; I think everyone is on a high from the finds. I get a real sense of pride as one of the Toms goes by carrying a GPMG. He really looks the part. Shoulders and head up, machine gun in his hands, a big grin on his face. It's been a good patrol. We were in the enemy's back yard and we destroyed some of his kit.

By the time we get in it has been a six hours forty-five minute patrol. This is a long time in this heat. I have a strange mix of sensations and emotions. I am euphoric as I consider the patrol a real success. I also have a headache and

I have lost my appetite. I am really dehydrated. I can't face evening meal so I concentrate on drinking as much water as possible before going to bed. I am shattered, but really proud of the lads. They did well today.

TUESDAY 29 APRIL

I am still suffering from the patrol yesterday, as are a few of the lads. It is dehydration and it takes a while to get myself sorted it. Warm, chlorinated water is not that nice to drink but I keep forcing it down.

Today is the first platoon-level clearance patrol; 5 Platoon will go out and sweep the green zone to our front in a close, anti-clockwise arc.

I go into the ops room to listen to the patrol on the radio. I am also well positioned to move into the command bunker if needs be. Once 5 Platoon heads off it quickly sounds like they are moving well. It is good to watch how Brett plots their progress on the large map in the ops room and sends updates to headquarters. I realise that I could be watching the patrol from the fire support sangar so I head round there and watch them through the 'ship's binos'. They are moving well and I can see that Wes has good control over them. The locals are utterly indifferent and we are generating no intelligence.

After two hours they are back in and Brett debriefs them. All pretty straightforward and it is good to get one of the platoon-level patrols done.

I receive a warning order that the battle group is planning a three-day operation ten kilometres south of Sangin. Details are sketchy at this point – it is just a warning, but B Company will be involved, which is good.

I still feel rough so I decide to sit in the company office and rehydrate. It gives me time to mull over yesterday's patrol again. I am still euphoric. As a commander it feels great when it all comes together, like an orchestra that you are conducting and everyone is playing the right notes. The company suddenly becomes one large organic being, and its movements are synchronised and fluid. Commanding it becomes a drug. I consider the patrol a success. We are moving into areas that would have previously been contested and we are destroying the enemy's equipment. I realise the challenge we are going to face though. There are a lot of 'fighting age males' in the area and everything seems to indicate that in two weeks' time they will make the transition from farmer to fighter.

I am just heading off to bed when the CSM comes to see me. He explains that most of the company is suffering from dehydration. The patrol yesterday affected 4 and 6 Platoons, plus me, and the patrol today has affected 5 Platoon. I cancel tomorrow's platoon-level patrol and instigate another rest day. We need to take things steady at this stage.

WEDNESDAY 30 APRIL

I feel much better today. I am awake at 0520 and decide to get up. I can feel that I am rehydrated, so decide to go down to the gym and do a quick session. I have a shower and then chat to the lads before brunch at 1030.

After brunch I take my signallers down to the ANA compound for some pistol drills. We didn't do much pistol shooting during training, so I take the opportunity to take them through some drills that I know. We all like shooting pistols. After firing 300 rounds we sit around in the briefing area cleaning our pistols and having a chat. It is these sorts of moments that I have always enjoyed most in my career – the banter with the blokes.

In the afternoon I decide to make some phone calls on the secure phone. This is in the ops room and is encrypted so that the participants can talk normally to each other. I chat to the CO. He still seems on good form and happy with the way things are going. I then have a chat with the battalion second in command, Jacko. One of his tasks is to plan and coordinate all of the tactical activity within the battle group. The CO comes up with the plan, the 2IC makes it happen. Jacko is happy as well and talks me through some of the bigger operations they have planned. All of them involve B Company, so the lads will be happy.

MAY

The poppy harvest means that the enemy are still distracted, giving us breathing space to continue to settle in and learn the area. The atmosphere is building, though. This 'phoney peace' can't last for ever and when it breaks we have to be ready. My challenges become more complex, as battle group operations are planned for this month, making the challenge of balancing manpower even more acute. I have to have enough fighting power on the ground but there also need to be enough people remaining in the FOB to guard it. I continue to learn that command is often about making trade-offs; I have to take risks. My job is to ensure the risks are as small as possible.

THURSDAY 1 MAY

I am still concerned about the dehydration within the company, so decide to send out the Viking troop on a patrol. Not all of the commanders got out on the last one so it makes sense to get the remainder out while we have time. This also means that I don't have to send out a foot patrol.

I brief James and he is happy. He will do what we did the other day to orientate the rest of the commanders. It will also be useful to see if they generate any enemy activity.

I get called to the ops room as I have a call on the secure phone. It is HQ telling me that we will be getting helicopters today: fantastic news. The bad news is that they will be two Sea Kings, which are a lot smaller that Chinooks, therefore I will have to prioritise what I want on board. That is a simple decision – we want mail. I have picked up on the fact that a lot of people try to come to Inkerman. It is seen as the FOB to get to – a nasty, dangerous FOB. We are already calling this 'Coming to get the Inkerman T-shirt'. I have no problem with this but when it comes to a decision of sight-seers over mail, mail wins. The downside is I have to bump off the padre. Padre Alan is an excellent guy and really popular with the lads. He is the most professional padre I have ever met. Unfortunately, it is all or nothing – people or mail. So I bump them all off.

The helicopters arrive mid-afternoon and as I watch them depart from my position in the command bunker I really hope I get some mail. We haven't been here very long but already mail means everything.

By the time I get back to the ops room the mail is sorted and I have done well. I have some parcels. Andrea has sent me some bags of Starbucks coffee and Mike from Edgar Brothers has sent a huge box of magazines and T-shirts for us. Plus a new belt. Good man.

I realise that you don't need much out here. It is very similar to the jungle – you need two sets of everything. That way you can wear one, wash one. Simple. We all need some luxuries, though and mail always lifts the atmosphere in the FOB.

I am just getting ready to head off to bed when one of the signallers comes from the ops room and tells me that I am wanted in the north sangar.

I walk round to the sangar above 6 Platoon's accommodation and climb up the narrow ladder. Waiting for me is one of the corporals and a Tom who is on sentry.

They brief me that they have been watching suspicious activity off to their front about a kilometre away. There are a cluster of compounds in an area designated KA8 and there are a lot of men around there for this time of night. They have also seen them moving cylindrical objects around. Very suspicious. I congratulate the Tom on his observation and diligence and head straight back to the ops room.

I have a chat with Brett and immediately change the patrol programme. I have planned to take a company-level patrol out tomorrow, so it is easy to change the task around. I get the platoon commanders to come to the ops room and we talk through the new plan. It is pretty similar to what we were going to do anyway – instead we will now concentrate on KA8, where the activity was seen.

FRIDAY 2 MAY

We depart at 0800 hours with 6 Platoon leading, my group then 4 Platoon. I haven't deployed the FSG yet as I am holding them back. I want the enemy to think this is all I have got before I add an additional 15 guys with machine guns.

The lead platoon heads straight out from the front gate and over the fields to the drainage ditch. I have realised that the fire support sangar is directly above us and they can cover all of our initial movement. There is no need for bounding overwatch at this stage.

The drainage ditch, 6 Platoon discovers, is now dry. The other day it was a two-metre wide torrent; now it is empty. The locals must have diverted the water. The ditch is a couple of metres deep and leads all the way up to KA8. Perfect – 6 Platoon pushes on and we all follow in what is, effectively, a perfect trench. The added bonus is that it is all in the shade. This trench becomes even more reassuring when we receive intelligence that the enemy is watching us and is going to try to mortar us. It will provide good cover.

We soon arrive at KA8. I deploy 4 Platoon into an overwatch position and then send 6 Platoon in to clear the compounds. It was a 6 Platoon sentry that watched the suspicious activity so it makes sense for them to conduct the clearance.

They quickly discover another RPG warhead, hidden in a building next to the 611. Sergeant Radcliffe and I push forward to take a look and with the aid of a set of laser range-finding binoculars we work out the enemy's plan. The RPG-7 rocket has a fuse set to self-destruct after 800 metres if it hasn't hit anything. This is the Taliban's preferred method of using these weapons against us. They effectively get them to explode above our heads. It is also their preferred way of engaging a helicopter when it is on the ground – it is far easier to get an RPG warhead to explode in the vicinity of a helicopter than to hit it directly.

From the building the warhead is in you can see the HLS, behind the FOB. It is also 800 metres away. Very clever.

I tell Brett all these details by radio and ask him to get permission from HQ to blow up the warhead. There are certain rules about who can blow up what. The engineers are allowed to blow up enemy ordnance. If there is the remotest suspicion it is a booby trap then we have to get in an ammunition technical officer (ATO); the bomb disposal expert and his team. This doesn't look booby-trapped. It is lying on a hard earth floor. In fact, it looks like it is going to be used soon.

Strangely, HQ say that permission is denied. We are to make a note of its location and then leave it. Once a bomb disposal team is available they will be sent to the FOB for us to escort out and they will deal with it.

This is utter madness and I am furious. I can't in all conscience leave an RPG warhead. What if it is fired at the FOB or a helicopter? What if it injured one of my soldiers? I understand the reasoning but this clearly isn't booby-trapped. When I speak to 6 Platoon they tell me that a local pointed out the warhead to them and that he said he had just moved it – he was worried that his kids were playing near it.

I pass on all of this to Brett and get him to try again, but to no avail.

I am no rebel but I realise I can't leave it. I have a chat with Sergeant Dale and he says that he can get rid it with a liberal amount of explosive. I give him the go ahead.

We all pull back and it is quickly dealt with. They use a small amount of explosive so as not to damage the compound and it gets rid of it very efficiently.

I pull back to have a chat with the CSM – I have visions of being relieved of command for disobeying orders already. I know that as long as I can justify my actions I should be all right and I am clear in my own mind; I made the right decision. First and foremost, my job is to protect my soldiers and leaving RPG warheads lying around would not be doing that. There is also the reality of being 'the man on the ground' too. HQs don't have the full picture; they often can't 'see' the problem. My view is that I am the ground commander, so it is my call. None of this helps my stress levels though.

Fortunately, the CSM soon has me laughing when he discovers that 4 Platoon, who had been feeling a bit left out as they haven't found anything, have done a really thorough search and turned up ... a load of rubbish. First they spotted a 'landmine' that turned out to be a plastic pot, then some 'bomb-making equipment' that was actually wire and an old meter. The CSM then found a 20cm toy AK-47, so he uses this to rip into 4 Platoon. 'Ooh, look what I found, an AK!' he is chanting at them. They are not amused, but it certainly eases my tension.

We head back in and I sort myself out. Once sorted, I plan tomorrow's patrol and then deliver orders after lunch.

That night I am summoned to the ops room for a phone call. 'Here we go,' I think to myself.

It is Kev, the commander of 9 Squadron Engineers. He doesn't sound happy. For some bizarre reason Sergeant Dale has put on his daily report back to his HQ that he has blown up an RPG warhead. Obviously my report doesn't mention this and, as far as battle group headquarters are concerned, the warhead is still out there. I explain to Kev what happened and why I couldn't leave it. He is genuinely sympathetic. He politely tells me not to do this again and then tells me not to worry about it. He will sort everything out at his end. Obviously I don't want a bomb disposal team wasting their time coming to my FOB for a non-existent RPG.

I am grateful for his help but I am still pretty annoyed by all of this.

SATURDAY 3 MAY

Another company patrol, this time with 4 and 5 Platoons. I am up at 0600 and sort myself out ready to depart at 0700. We are getting bolder now and our endurance in the heat is coming on. I want to push deeper into the green zone directly opposite the FOB. This is the area the enemy are most likely to use to get into a position to attack us; we need to go deeper than the bubble provided by the FOB.

We head out of the front gate and move straight across the open ground, 5 Platoon leading, my group, then 4 Platoon. The lead platoon has really picked this up quickly and is moving very professionally.

We head north-west through the initial battered compounds and then press further. There is harvesting activity everywhere, so I don't envision anything happening but we have to remain vigilant.

I want us to push up into an area designated KA2, which is a kilometre beyond Jusulay.

After the initial belt of battered compounds there is another belt, 400 metres beyond. On the edge of KA2 the compounds are unoccupied, battered and full of human waste. The terrain then changes.

There is a well-developed track being used as a road and a study of my map reveals that this track leads all the way down to the Jusulay track junction. The area is really lush – we are only two kilometres from the river Helmand and the trees overhanging the track effectively screen it from view.

There are a lot of people in this area; children playing, people waiting by the side of the track for transport.

We keep pushing forward and the area opens up, almost into a village green. The area looks quite affluent. The compounds are large and well made, the walls are intact and there is no sign of battle damage. There are vines growing up the compound walls and lush fruit trees growing within. For some reason it reminds me of an Austrian mountain village. It must be the wood piles and the open green with a stream gently meandering down the middle of it. We like nicknames, so I decide this will be called Austrian village. The aerial photos have given no indication how nice this place is.

We have a chat with some of the locals. We are pointed in the direction of the village elder and Sergeant Radcliffe goes forward to have a chat with him. He tries to convince him to come to the FOB for a *shura* but the elder can't see the point – he doesn't need anything. Fair enough; we let him know that the offer stands.

The village seems clean and content. We have a look around the surrounding area but it is getting on so I decide that we should head back. We will use the track and follow it down into Jusulay. There is so much vehicle and people traffic on it I doubt the enemy would be able to plant a device solely for us.

Brett comes on the net. He says that James would like to bring the Vikings out to Jusulay and prove some crossing points into the green zone. He wants to check whether he can get the vehicles over certain drainage ditches. The fact that we are beyond Jusulay means that he can do these trials without having to worry about the enemy; we will provide security for him. I give him the go ahead and we start heading back towards Jusulay.

By the time we get there James and his troop have arrived. There is something very reassuring about a large, powerful armoured vehicle with a .50cal machine gun on top.

James clambers down from his vehicle and we have a quick chat. He is happy with the routes he has proved so we agree to head back in. He offers us a lift but I think it will take longer to get us all on board than walk back. I decline the offer and continue back towards the FOB.

Once inside, we go through the normal debrief. Sergeant Radcliffe is very pleased with the patrol. We learnt a lot today about a village we knew nothing about.

It was another long patrol, though. Five hours and forty-five minutes. I decide that we will send the Vikings out again tomorrow to give everyone else the chance to rehydrate. Over five hours is a long time to be patrolling with 40 kilos of kit on in 35C heat.

SUNDAY 4 MAY

I am up at 0550; it is a combination of early nights and the light. There isn't a great amount to do once the sun has set so I am finding myself going to bed earlier and earlier.

I am told that we are getting helicopters today, which comes as a surprise. At 1130 I am in the command bunker chatting to my gang. As the aircraft begin their approach we start to scan the green zone for anything suspicious. I look over to my left and I can see the snipers manning their position, straining through their telescopic sights. Nothing happens though and the helicopters unload and head off.

I decide to go to the stores and have a brew. Most of the sergeants tend to congregate there. The stores are run by Sergeant Payne, another old sweat from support company. I make myself a cup of tea and join them. The sergeant from 6 Platoon, Sergeant Robertson, starts chatting to me. I have known him my whole career. He is an engaging Scot who loves his blokes; he really cares about them. He tells me that the lads know about the decision that I made the other day to blow up the RPG warhead. Word has spread about the decision I had to make and they are impressed that I would make this kind of decision when it comes to their safety. I really appreciate the feedback. I ask all of the platoon sergeants how their lads are and everyone seems pretty happy at the moment. The only real concern is the heat. Not much we can do though but get used to it.

MONDAY 5 MAY

As seems now to be my default, I am awake early and head down to the gym. I always do my best thinking early in the morning, so I find myself wandering back to the accommodation with a mental 'to do' list. I need to email the pay department about the lads' pay. Corporal Jang, the company clerk, deals with pay issues but he is hitting some 'inertia' with those back at Bastion. I think it best that I get involved. I need to speak to Sergeant Radcliffe about a format for the intelligence briefs and speak to the CSM about cleanliness in the FOB. I find, from the moment I get up until the time I go to bed, I always have something to deal with. That is the nature of the job but the list seems to be growing.

The temperature is really climbing. One of the snipers has loaned me a small weather station that they use when calculating shot data. I am becoming obsessed with measuring the temperature and at midday it is now hitting 38C. I find myself starting to worry about being out in this kind of heat and I am not convinced that I can get used to it.

In the afternoon I am asked to come to the ops room. We have received orders for a forthcoming brigade operation – Operation Oqab Sterga (Op OS).

The plan is to coordinate a large number of intelligence-gathering assets and put the Taliban under pressure over quite a large area. We will then measure the response and use this information to prevent the enemy gaining the initiative once the poppy harvest finishes.

At this stage it is a huge operation with a breath-taking number of moving parts. B Company is heavily involved and there is tactical activity up until the end of the month. 2 PARA will be concentrating ten kilometres south of Sangin.

I spend the afternoon reading through all of the detail and coming up with some provisional plans. The operation is in five phases, so I work out a loose plan for each one, predominantly based around who will be involved. The more I work through the plan the more questions I have so I end up sending a long list of questions back to the battle group 2IC. There isn't much more I can do until I get the answers, so I spend the rest of the afternoon chatting to the lads in the ops room.

TUESDAY 6 MAY

I can't believe what a nightmare we are having. Another of my worst-case scenarios has started – diarrhoea and vomiting (D&V). It seems to be the curse of the British Army when operating abroad. If you consider the state of the FOB it is hardly surprising. For the last two years close to 200 people have lived in a very small area. Who knows where people originally went to the toilet? It is in the dust – old, dry faeces. As you walk around you ingest it and before you know it people are struck down. It spreads like wildfire and the symptoms come on so quickly. Last night people were lying in bed and suddenly they would throw up or soil themselves. Inevitably this spreads around the eight-man rooms.

By the time I get up twenty people have been struck down. They don't just feel ill either; they are utterly felled by it.

We group sick people into a reinforced building that we have had constructed towards the bottom of the FOB. This was a brainwave of the CSM in case of a mass casualty situation. It can house twenty people and is constructed from Hesco. He nicknamed it 'the Priory' and by morning it is almost full. Once the lads are struck down they pick up their camp cots and move to the Priory. It becomes the walk of the damned.

I go down to see the lads, but talk to them from a distance. I desperately can't afford to get this. The CSM is running around trying to get things stabilised. He calls an emergency meeting of the platoon sergeants and quickly puts measures into place. We close the cookhouse and go on to individual ration packs. The kitchen will be deep cleaned.

The doctor is having a workout as well. He has had to give so much plasma to people as they are dehydrated that we have had to put in an emergency request. I have asked that the environmental health team (EHT) come out as well and have a look at the FOB.

In the afternoon we patrol to the Star Wars village. I find it an incredible place – it really does look like a movie set. It is good to watch the intelligence cell talking to the locals. Those that they speak to confirm that there are Taliban in the area but they aren't going to be interested in us until after the poppy harvest.

I notice there are faeces everywhere in the village and wonder if the village is to blame for the D&V outbreak.

In the afternoon a Chinook comes in with the plasma

and the EHT. The EHT team has a really good look around and talks to people and quickly concludes that we have been doing all we can considering the living conditions in the FOB. I find this reassuring. The CSM has been working really hard to enforce hygiene standards.

That night I am in bed and the CSM suddenly gets up and walks out. He returns ten minutes later.

'Sir, are you awake?' he asks. I let him know I am.

'I'm really sorry,' he says. He has just thrown up, fortunately not in our room. He drags his camp cot out of the room. He has been cursed, as we are now calling it.

It's a nightmare.

WEDNESDAY 7 MAY

The D&V continues to spread. We now have 30 people crammed into the Priory. It looks like a Dickensian workhouse when you walk by. I really want to see if the lads are all right but I don't want to go near the place. I can't afford to be laid up for four days. So I stay 20 metres back and have a quick chat with the CSM. He looks terrible; haggard and gaunt.

As part of the preliminary phases of Op OS the Viking troop is due to head out to the east and see if they can generate some enemy activity. For vehicles to enter or leave the FOB, mine clearance drills have to be conducted. As we can't see into the area past the HLS, it would be easy for the enemy to place a mine there without us knowing.

I have a chat with James before they head off and agree that my lads will conduct the sweep for mines to speed up his departure.

A team of eight lads heads out and starts to conduct the sweep. They quickly discover something suspicious. One of the corporals crawls forward, has a look and brushes some sand away with a paint brush. It looks like a small anti-personnel mine.

They let me know in the ops room. I put in a request to headquarters for a bomb disposal team. I am told I will have one within the hour. I can't believe how quick they come out. I am impressed with the lads. They are obviously doing their drills properly.

It is only a small mine but a Taliban tactic is to place a 500lb bomb under a small mine. When you blow up the little mine, the big one goes off and takes out anyone who isn't far enough back.

Within the hour the bomb disposal team arrive by Chinook. They are a really slick crew commanded by Warrant Officer Gary O'Donnelly. He quickly heads out, with my guys providing protection. After an hour he confirms it is a mine and blows it up. There wasn't a 500lb bomb underneath it, but the mine would have been big enough to blow up one of our vehicles. Warrant Officer O'Donnelly and his team are picked up later on and before he leaves he congratulates the lads on finding the mine. It is a sharp reminder that the enemy is out there and targeting us.

FRIDAY 9 MAY

The D&V is still spreading. Fifty people have now been affected. The sword of Damocles hangs over all of us. Fortunately, a few people are out of the Priory but they are too weak to do anything. I agree to the doctor's request that once they are out of the Priory they can't be used for anything for a further four days. This seriously depletes my available manpower.

I still manage to muster enough people to take out a company patrol. We head off in the Vikings towards a desert village called Zard Regay, which sits ten kilometres to the east of Sangin.

It is eerie, as there is a sandstorm blowing – you can only see ten metres in any direction. We are dropped off in the desert a kilometre from the village and walk in. The Vikings circle round to the other side to act as a block. Due to the sandstorm the villagers haven't seen or heard us coming, we just appear out of the dust. We quickly sweep through the village but most people are sheltering from the storm. We don't find anything. It looks like Zard Regay is a 'motorway service station'. It sits on the Sangin wadi with 'high speed links' in various directions and is set up for trade.

Just as we are leaving one of the Vikings fires a burst from its .50 calibre machine gun and races off. James informs me that a 4x4 has seen us and is trying to speed off. The Vikings encircle it and bring it to a halt. They quickly find out why the driver is trying to flee: he has 120kgs of opium on board. I seek advice from headquarters and I am told to let him go. I find this breath-taking but after a brief argument with the ops officer I am again told to let him go. So much for the counter-narcotics programme. I know that we aren't directly involved but even I struggle to believe that this is for 'personal consumption'. I suppose it is best not to alienate anyone else – we will have enough 'enemies' to deal with without upsetting armed people by removing their livelihood.

The journey back is grim. One of the Vikings is

struggling and we chug back slowly, each vehicle trying to follow in the tracks of the one in front. The mine found yesterday has got everyone a bit spooked. I am in the commander's turret and I find myself imagining what it would be like to hit a mine. It's horrible; I can feel the fear rising in me, so I quickly think of something else. We get back at dusk, caked in dirt.

SATURDAY 10 MAY

I get up early and I realise that I need to have a bit of time to myself as the D&V problem is grinding me down. I grab a spare sniper rifle and head down to the range, enjoying the time to myself having a shoot. I like the discipline that is required to shoot well. I fire 25 rounds and this cheers me up.

I head back up to the accommodation and make myself some breakfast. We are still on individual rations, as the cookhouse is shut. Everyone seems to be enjoying being on rations; I suppose it is the variation. I have a meal bag containing sausage, omelette and beans which is very good. The new ration boxes are quite enjoyable. The old ones used to contain 'Lancashire hot pot' and 'pork cassoulet' – lamb stew and pork stew. Now there is chicken tikka and I plan on having chicken arrabiata for dinner tonight. There is even a sachet of tuna to have on hard biscuits. All very nice.

Enough people are mustered for a 6 Platoon patrol and they escort me down the 611 to Patrol Base (PB) Downes. PB Downes is two kilometres west of us, towards Sangin, and is manned by the Afghan National Army (ANA). I haven't had the opportunity to meet the ANA commander yet and we have scheduled a meeting.

At 0900 the ANA commander arrives, sweeping down the road in a Humvee with a huge Government of Afghanistan flag flying.

The meeting is really good. Commander Karim is ex-mujahideen and fought under General Dostum, an infamous warlord. Karim is tough as nails and all he wants to do is kill Taliban. We quickly establish a good rapport. He explains that he usually fields 20 men to patrol into the green zone. I explain that I usually deploy 90 and that I have three 60mm mortars, three 81mm mortars and three 105mm light artillery guns. His eyes light up. Now he wants to work with us! I can see he is mentally working out how many Taliban he can kill with that lot. He pathologically hates them.

He agrees to an immediate joint patrol. I want to get an Afghan face on our patrols as quickly as possible. We agree some coordination procedures for how we will work together in the future and he gives me an ANA radio, so we can communicate with each other. This has been a really productive meeting.

I come out of the meeting room and 6 Platoon are ready to go. There are also 20 ANA soldiers. They look like a cut-throat bunch of mercenaries; rifles on shoulders, belts of ammo wrapped round them. They look up for a fight, though. They agree they will follow us through Star Wars village before heading back.

It is great to watch this patrol. The ANA leave the patrol base as a right rabble. Once 6 Platoon push past them, they switch on. They immediately started mimicking us – holding their rifles properly, spacing between men, kneeling down when not moving. It is good to see.

SUNDAY 11 MAY

There isn't much manpower available for patrols so I send out the Vikings to conduct a patrol into the desert and to the north of our AO. I give Brett the chance to head out so I control the ops room while he is away. I am utterly engrossed in a book called *Al-Qaeda* by Jason Burke. I am finding it fascinating, but also useful. It not only provides an informative window on my enemy's mindset but, importantly, it also describes what his motivations are. Will it help my planning and decision-making? Time will tell. I appreciate a few hours sat in the ops room, reading.

I spend the afternoon writing orders for Op OS. The first phase which involves us is rapidly approaching. I deliver the orders at 1830 hours and most people seem content. Not all of my questions have been answered by HQ yet, but I have enough to work off.

MONDAY 12 MAY

Despite the nightmare of D&V I still have to mount patrols in order to fulfil my mission. We manage to pull together a patrol of two platoons but a lot of people will have to step up into the next rank as 4 and 5 platoon commanders are down with the curse, so the two sergeants are in command. This is where our training comes into its own. At every level we train not only to do our own job, but also the next level up. We call it 'step-up' and every training exercise will see commanders being 'killed' and their subordinates having to take over from them. I am also fortunate that the sergeants are very good and more than capable of commanding their platoons.

We head out at 0600hrs and push west of the FOB into the green zone. I am trying to patrol in an area east of the 'Austrian village' designated KA5.

It is a nice time of day to be out and we make good progress. As we push past Jusulay we start receiving intelligence that the enemy are watching us. I get the patrol to halt and I find myself next to a very nice cluster of compounds – lush grape vines and good walls. I am measuring the locals' affluence by the state of their walls at the moment.

The atmospherics continue to build and we are told that 'Hamzah' is set up and ready to ambush us; he is waiting for his commander. This looks more promising.

I decide to wait and see what happens. I realise I am holding us here so that they can attack us. Why? Because I am very confident in my soldiers' ability to take the enemy apart. We are ready for this now. If I am to achieve my mission I have got to start disrupting the enemy's plans. I need to get him to come to me, in order to keep him out of Sangin. I am genuinely confident that the Taliban are going to get the shock of their lives when they first engage us.

So we wait, and nothing happens. After forty-five minutes we move off. I start the platoons doing bounding overwatch and I control the movement.

We then hear that they have lost us. I decide to help them out and loop the patrol back the way we have come. It is still quiet. The enemy aren't going to play today.

Back in the FOB I have a solar shower, write up a weekly commander's assessment and then finalise my plans for Op

OS. We will secure an objective south of Sangin by a combination of helicopter and Viking drop-off. We will relieve the ANA who are in the vicinity and provide cover for them to clear the town of Tambelah. We will then return to FOB Inkerman.

Orders keep arriving for Op OS, the latest version is 75 pages. There is an incredible amount of detail but large chunks of information are missing. I end up having to type out a whole list of questions again to Jacko. The op does look good though and I am looking forward to getting out of the FOB for a while.

TUESDAY 13 MAY

The day has a hot, close feel to it and I am finding myself in an intolerant mood. I get some answers to my questions but I get the impression that the plan is a 'work in progress'. I think that Op OS will go one of two ways; either it will be cancelled or they will tell us that we are already late.

We are kicking our heels a bit, 'waiting for the off' and you can sense there is a bit of tension.

The oppressive heat and claustrophobia start to hit me today. We live so close to each other that things are bound to grate. I keep hearing people moaning. The lack of enemy contact is leaving people disappointed – they just want to do their job. The D&V is grinding people down and some are starting to let their standards slip.

The doctor seems to have appointed himself the health and safety executive representative for the FOB and comes to see me with a new issue every day. I think he is missing the point somewhat.

The CO has sent around an email that I find myself agreeing with; there is obviously moaning from all over the battle group. He reminds us that we are on operations and with that goes a degree of discomfort. After a while you have to accept what you have got and remember those that have gone before have gone with less.

So I feel a bit cagey. I need some time to myself, which is impossible. I need people to up their game. I never envisioned that I would have to give out so many disciplinary chats. The bulk of the lads are doing a great job; it is the lowest common denominator dragging us down. I pretty much do a bollocking a day at the moment – hygiene, dress, facial hair, FOB tidiness etc. Hence the lethargy, it just saps you, like a force pulling you down. I hate to say it but we need a contact now to settle everyone down.

WEDNESDAY 14 MAY

More waiting for Op OS. It is complicated pulling such a big operation together – most of the brigade is involved. The plan keeps changing as new factors emerge. Rightly so. These kind of ops need to be intelligence-driven and I find it reassuring that battle group HQ is evolving the plan as the situation develops.

So we sit here and wait. It has a 'waiting to go over the top' feel to it. I am still not convinced it will happen, though.

THURSDAY 15 MAY

Today is the start of Op OS for us. I sort out my kit and finalise our plans, fully expecting to be told it is cancelled.

The plan is for the Vikings to take one of the platoons and my group off into the desert and drop us off tonight. We will insert on foot while my other platoon is inserted by helicopter, meeting up with us on the objective, a village called Chinah. We will then conduct clearance operations.

The plan is still 'fluid', as is who is on the patrol. The lads are still being struck down with D&V.

At 1430 hours, 5 Platoon and my group load up and head off in the Vikings. The op is on.

We move off into the desert and past Zard Regay, heading deeper and deeper south. The scenery is fantastic, rolling rocky desert and it feels good to be out of the FOB. I am glad that the waiting is over and the doing has begun.

My original plan was to stop the vehicles three kilometres' short of Chinah and wait until darkness before moving in. As we approach, I realise this will not be feasible. There are people everywhere.

James and I take the chance to recce the route in. He parks his vehicle on a hill and we both stand on the roof looking through binoculars.

We change the plan. We will head back into the desert, find a quiet location and 'lie up'. Early tomorrow morning they will drive us forward, drop us off three kilometres from the objective and we will walk in under cover of darkness.

We head off and find a suitable area nine kilometres away. There is no one for miles. James 'circles' the wagons and then the wonderful routine begins. There is hot food, courtesy of the onboard water boiler (you just float meal pouches in it). I find myself a spot next to the vehicle and sit down to eat my dinner. It strikes me how clean the desert is. As the sun sets I lie back, using my daysack as a pillow and feel really happy. This is more like it.

FRIDAY 16 MAY

I am woken at 0200 and we get back in the vehicles to be driven to the drop-off point.

We all clamber out and wait for the vehicles to go before sorting ourselves out. There is too much noise and dust to do it with the vehicles there.

It feels a bit unnerving, listening to the sound of the vehicles disappearing into the distance. We are now alone.

We get sorted out and then move off, stopping just outside the village. We then wait for H-hour.

On H-hour – 0430hrs – 4 Platoon arrive by Chinook and land 1,500 metres to the east. The remainder of us sweep through Chinah and then link up with 4 Platoon on the other side. Chinah is only 20 compounds and once the locals realise what is going on, they leave. I feel very guilty watching these families pour out of their compounds with a few hastily grabbed items and head off up the road.

We thoroughly search the compounds but find no evidence of enemy activity.

We leave the village and push down into a large gulley with an inviting little stream meandering through it. I get us laid out so we can defend ourselves and it is then a competition to find shade. The temperature climbs but we have nowhere else to go. This is where we were told to go firm. The heat just sucks the energy out of us and you can sense the inevitable lethargy creeping in.

Fortunately the Vikings return at lunchtime dropping off water, rations and fresh batteries. I have a quick chat with James and ask him to go on the scrounge for me. He has to go to FOB Robinson to refuel so I ask him to try to grab me a book to read. I realise that there is going to be a lot of waiting around on this op.

Mid-afternoon the CO's convoy of vehicles arrives. I brief the CO, then head back to the lads.

James returns with some supplies. He has found a book for me and also brought a box of 25 Cuban cigars: very generous and slightly surreal. They come with the compliments of a US Special Forces commander that he has been talking to in FOB Robinson.

Once the sun starts setting things became a lot more bearable. The moon comes out and it is so clear and strong that I can read by it.

The CO and I have a chat on the radio and he briefs me on what he wants doing tomorrow.

SATURDAY 17 MAY

We are up at 0230 hours. The moon is still amazing and there is no need for any night vision. We head off north, ready for the next phase of the operation – another town clearance.

As we leave the outskirts of Chinah we pass the CO's vehicles and then head off.

By 0430 we are at the next location and ready for H-hour. We are now moving into C Company's area, so they have sent out a platoon to link up with us and provide some local knowledge.

We quickly clear the next two villages, Towmrah and Khoman, before continuing to head north towards FOB Robinson.

I am pretty certain that we aren't going to get any enemy activity. There is just nothing to indicate that they are interested. At this stage I am more concerned with the heat and the lack of cover. The next phase of the operation sees us going firm next to a bend on the 611 road for the next two and a half days. We are providing security on a vulnerable stretch to allow an Operation Loam to resupply FOB Robinson.

We follow a canal out of Khoman and hit the 611. It is now midday and the heat is horrendous. I get everyone into cover while I conduct a quick reconnaissance; there is no point in us all moving around.

Our luck holds. There is an abandoned fort round the corner from our current location on the edge of the hill overlooking the 611. The fort is not very big but it is secure and there is cover. I leave 4 Platoon in an orchard next to a canal and take 5 Platoon up to the fort. The C Company platoon covers the rear, using a tree-line for shade. It isn't perfect, we are more spread out than I would like. My reasoning is that the heat is going to cause more casualties than the enemy, so we will just have to make do.

We come up with a plan that sees the platoons conducting local patrols in their own designated sectors; nothing further than 500m. I leave them alone to get on with it.

There isn't that much room in the fort so my group moves into a goat poo-filled cave. It stinks but it is sheltered and we spend the afternoon sweating it out and chatting.

Mid-afternoon there is suddenly a burst of fire, followed by another burst. Two Taliban have appeared 200 metres away and fired two or three rounds at 4 Platoon. A Tom armed with a light machine gun managed to get a burst off at them before they ran away. I accompany a 4 Platoon clearance patrol but we can't find the gunmen. We find the 'rat run' they have used but the gunmen are long gone. It is a good reminder that there is an enemy out there and I am impressed with the lads' restraint. Everyone is so desperate to fire their weapons that I am amazed they didn't all fire.

Late afternoon the CO arrives on the 611 in his vehicle convoy and I wander down to have a chat with him. He explains that Op Loam has been brought forward and that they will be through tonight. We will then be able to move into FOB Robinson in the morning. He seems refreshed and we have a pleasant chat. He is impressed with the lads' restraint as well.

SUNDAY 18 MAY

We are all up at 0450 and head off to FOB Robinson. It is only two kilometres, but we are all a bit tired.

D Company is in FOB Robinson and they are pleased to see us. The company commander, Mike, is a really good friend of mine and it is great to catch up. I figure we will be here for a while so we grab ourselves a cup of tea and are just having a good natter when I am told that a Chinook is on its way to pick us up.

I am a bit disappointed. I wanted to spend some time with Mike – and the facilities are far better at his FOB than mine. I wanted some decent food!

It's funny though. As I run off the back ramp on to the HLS at Inkerman I have this sense of coming home. It may be a complete dump but it is our dump and I have kind of missed the old girl. A few days' away has got all of us sorted out.

Brett is there to welcome me and it feels good to be back. I give him a quick rundown on the operation before heading to my bed. I managed to grab a can of Mountain Dew at FOB Robinson and as I sit there cleaning my weapon I think through the op and I am pleased with the company's performance. The lads are doing really well and the little time away seems to have sorted out some of the tension.

Personally, I am feeling ready to meet the enemy now. I am confident about my ability to control all of the moving parts.

I am also paranoid. My stomach feels odd and I am really worried that I might be getting the curse. That's all I need.

MONDAY 19 MAY

I am up at 0345. My stomach is not good. It doesn't feel like D&V, more 'New Delhi belly'. I head down to the toilets to sort myself out.

I don't feel too bad. I am sure I am a bit run down and I am definitely dehydrated. I just feel a bit 'loose'.

I am deep in thought as I wander back into the accommodation. Just as I walk through the door a stray cat shoots out from under my bed and runs through my legs.

It scares the life out of me. So much so that I let out an involuntary, guttural, high-pitched scream that wakes up the whole of company HQ. The CSM jumps up and asks me what's going on. Once I tell him, I can hear most of the company HQ giggling. They are clearly impressed with the OC's girly scream.

I drink a load of water and manage to doze off again. I get up at 0615 and send some emails.

I need to sort myself out quickly, so I grab one of the medics and the CSM and have a chat with them. They take my statistics and all is fine – they think I have pushed myself too hard on Op OS. They don't think it is D&V but the medic gives me some antibiotics just in case. I don't want to see the doctor as he is a bit over-exuberant about bedding people down.

I feel a bit of a hypocrite. I keep telling the lads that if they have D&V they must go sick, as it is so contagious they need to be segregated once they have it. I don't want to over-inflate my own self-importance but I realise that I can't afford to lie on my camp cot for four days. There are issues that only I can deal with; I am going to have to get on with it.

What I also notice is how unclean the FOB is. Now that I feel ill I am hypersensitive to all the dust and muck that swirls around. I am just going to have to take it easy.

I deliver orders for a patrol tomorrow and one for the day after. Fortunately, Brett sits in. By the end of the orders I have almost lost my vision. I feel terrible; the squits are really dehydrating me. I grab him and say change of plan. He hasn't led a patrol yet so he can take out the one tomorrow and go into Star Wars village. He is really happy with this as he hasn't had the chance to get out and at least I can now get some rest. There is a big local op in two days' time to support the counter-narcotics special forces and I need to be ready for this one.

TUESDAY 20 MAY

I have a very relaxed day. I try not to stray too far from the toilet. The toilets are horrendous; a two-metre deep trench, almost the same length, with improvised wooden toilets above them. With the number of people using them, the heat and the flies, it really is a challenge going down there. We still have to carry our helmet and body armour everywhere, so getting that on to walk down is a pain. The toilets are right at the bottom of the FOB, to keep them away from the accommodation, so it takes a couple of minutes to get there; not great when you are concerned about your ability to hold things in.

The fact that I can control things is what convinces me it isn't D&V. I spend the day staying in the shade, reading and drinking water.

By early evening I am starting to feel a lot better and I decide that I will be all right for tomorrow's patrol. I will review the situation in the morning and if needs be, I will cancel or change the patrol. I should be all right though.

WEDNESDAY 21 MAY

I get up at 0500hrs and fortunately I don't feel too bad. My stomach seems to have settled and I feel good enough to go out. The thought of getting 'caught short' with full patrol order on is not a good one.

I sort out my kit and clean my weapon. I am really

concerned about my stomach but it feels too late to cancel now.

I take a few minutes to review my plan on the huge map board in the briefing area. I am always trying to visualise the plan on the map and convert it into what might be the reality on the ground. I want to really see in my mind's eye potential problem areas and try to think through what I will do if something happens. The last few weeks have been a gift to us, as the enemy have allowed us to explore most of the area which I am seeking to dominate. I doubt this gift will last.

The plan is quite straightforward. I am trying to create as big a 'footprint' on the ground as we can. This means covering as much ground as possible. My presence is either going to draw the enemy on to me, or drive him away. Either way, it will achieve what I want. The patrol has two groups. Two of the platoons and my group will go out on foot and patrol in a large clockwise loop outside the FOB's security bubble, while the Viking armoured vehicles will go in an anti-clockwise loop. I can adjust the plan on the ground – either keeping us on our respective loops, or we can climb into the Vikings and get a lift back.

I am ready for 0600hrs at the side gate. Slipping out through the side gate should allow us to pop into the village and enter the green zone unimpeded. It should also allow us to talk to some of the locals, which I think is important. They may have information on the enemy. Today could be the day that the harvest is officially over.

At 0610 we are all good to go, so I give the word and we head out. There isn't much activity in the village. I have 6 Platoon leading and they cover the ground in a steady manner.

We enter the outskirts of Jusulay and continue pushing west. The poppy harvest has created some wide open spaces, so we have to exercise caution when crossing them, though 6 Platoon is ensuring they always have some form of cover before pushing anyone forward. Good drills. I am taking this all in and sending continuous updates to the ops room about our location and progress.

We seem to be generating more interest than normal and then the strangest thing happens. All of the locals disappear. One minute there is normal activity going on in the fields – farmers and their young lads moving around and tidying up the old poppy stalks then, suddenly, there is no one around. This switches us all on. Something out of the ordinary, it is definitely a 'combat indicator'.

The sun is up and the area is as striking as ever. The poppy harvest has really cleared a lot of ground and it is only the tree-lines that are breaking it up. Incredibly, the next crop is already in the ground and the first signs of the wheat are starting to push through, giving the initial impression of rolling English countryside.

I realise that things don't feel right. The lack of locals is really odd.

The ops room informs me of intelligence they have just received. Haji Aka, a local enemy commander, has been heard telling people to start using satellite phones. An interesting development and one we haven't heard before. I find my mind drifting again as to how they have got – and how could they afford – satellite phones? They aren't cheap. Another 'combat indicator'?

By 0745 we are about two kilometres from the FOB. The lead is still with 6 Platoon; 5 Platoon is just behind

TAC. The lead follows a tree-line to skirt round some open fields. They are in the process of moving in a large right curling 'U' shape. My group is moving along a bank next to an irrigation ditch just behind them. As I look over to the right I can see lads from 6 Platoon carefully moving forward when suddenly the quiet is shattered.

A huge amount of enemy rifle fire opens up from the tree-line. There is a good six-second opening burst from multiple machine guns directed straight into the lead element of 6 Platoon. My position is perfect to see what is happening so I dive behind the bank and start scanning the tree-line.

Inevitably, it is hard to see exactly what is going on but a tremendous firefight is ensuing in both directions. The lads are really putting some fire down and my group is well positioned to help. I crawl a bit higher up the bank to get a better view when an RPG-7 comes flying overhead and lands in the field 50 metres to our left. This refocuses my attention and I crawl back behind the bank a bit. Lance Corporal Barker has identified the enemy position so he gives a really good target indication to let us know where they are. My group starts firing and while this is going on I pull out my map and start to try to make sense of what I think is going on. It is all happening quickly and I don't have enough information to allow me to use my mortars and artillery.

Enemy fire is going everywhere and there is enough fire passing over our heads to keep us behind the bank. For the moment I need to stay out of it and let 6 Platoon get on with their battle. I have all the assets keyed up but I can't start using anything until they tell me what is going on.

The huge weight of fire from 6 Platoon appears to break

the enemy's attack and after five minutes it all goes quiet. I sit for a minute taking it all in and decide that the best bet is to push forward and find out what has happened.

Just as I begin moving forward there is another huge burst of fire. The enemy is trying to outflank us, but 6 Platoon have moved a gun group to their flank to cover this threat. They have just got themselves set up when two enemy walk straight in to Lance Corporal Jenks and his gun group. They are cut down with a burst of fire from the GPMG.

The ops room comes up on my radio and reminds me that the Vikings are available if I want them. At this stage I think this is a great idea but I am mindful of how far they can get into the green zone. After I study the map I decide to push them forward to the east of the FOB about two kilometres from our position, my plan being to cut off any retreating enemy. It will also give us something 'firm' to move towards.

My intention is to push forward. If the enemy attack us and we start to withdraw, he will take this as a psychological victory. I intend to always push into the enemy after an attack and withdraw – if necessary – on our terms. I'm not about to hand him an easy PR coup.

I give the go ahead for the Vikings to push out and I decide to push TAC forward to see what is going on. The firing has stopped and 6 Platoon is in a good position of all-round cover.

As I begin to push forward I come across some of the lads and the further I push forward the bigger their grins get. The lads are beaming. Each one is stoked and you can see the confidence oozing out of them. They are justifiably pleased with themselves. Each one I pass I give a congratulatory comment. Just a 'nice one' or 'well done'. The adrenaline is flowing in all of us, so I make the conscious effort to calm myself down. At this stage my FAC informs me that we have an F-16 coming on station.

He comes in low, with his afterburners on; an incredible display of brute force. The afterburners are ferocious and the low height he comes through at makes us all cheer. I can see the pilot's helmet! The F-16 does another transit through the area but he can't see anything. The enemy, as ever, seem to have blended into the background.

I arrive in the centre of 6 Platoon to an amazing sight. Dave, the platoon commander, is absolutely covered from head to foot in mud. The way the enemy ambush was configured the initial fire had been directed at his group. He dived into a mud-filled drainage ditch, fortunately unscathed. He is in good spirits, if not slightly shaken by the whole thing. He seems more disappointed that his rifle is full of mud.

The next strange sight is the dog handler, his Alsatian – Rab – and two Toms. They are also covered from head to foot in mud. I go over and ask them what happened.

The dog handler explains that Rab is a failed attack dog. He was not aggressive enough so he was retrained as a patrol dog. Patrol dogs sniff out the enemy, follow blood trails etc. Rab is clearly still aggressive, he has started biting Toms in the FOB, which the lads all thought was a good effort. As aggressive 'dogs' they like a fellow aggressive dog.

Under fire a patrol dog is trained to lay down, while an attack dog is trained to go straight at the threat, that is, attack.

In the green zone, movement is often easiest in the streams and canals.

View to the rear of the FOB.

Afghan graveyard overlooking the 611 road and the green zone beyond.

The resilient Afghan locals.

The amazing agricultural fertility of the green zone.

Reaching the River Helmand and a long way back to the FOB.

Issuing orders in the briefing area.

A Pashto speaker talking to the locals while we secure the Jusulay track junction.

Helping with the harvest: A local showing me how to collect the resin from the poppies.

The range behind the FOB: The snipers 'check zero'.

Above: Myself and my ever loyal signaller Lance Corporal Barker.

The lads working hard to unload a Chinook as quickly as possible.

Securing the enemy command and control node outside of Musa Qala.

My FAC calls in Apache attack helicopters in Musa Qala.

Unfortunately for the dog handler Rab defaulted to his original training as an attack dog, rather than his patrol dog training.

When the enemy initially fired, the dog handler was behind Dave and they both dived into the drainage ditch. Rab on the other hand had other ideas – he wanted to get amongst the enemy. So while the handler was desperately trying to stay in cover, Rab was dragging him out of the drainage ditch and straight towards the enemy fire. With panic setting, the handler started to scream for help.

Two Toms spotted what was going on and they both dived on top of Rab, getting bitten in the process. What a scene!

I can't help but start laughing. Three bleeding mud men. I look at Rab and he can tell he is in trouble. His ears are dropped and he looks very sheepish. I have to admire the handler's loyalty to Rab though. Despite considerable risk to himself, he wouldn't let the dog go.

We switch back to the job in hand. The lads sweep through the surrounding compounds and find a large chunk of flesh and a huge blood trail. I doubt whoever has received that injury will survive it.

I speak to Dave and tell him we are going to push on. He needs to get his lads sorted as quickly as possible and get moving. If the enemy are still out there I want to keep the pressure on.

Soon 6 Platoon are moving again and they quickly come across an old, white-haired local, just sitting there quietly taking in all of this. Amazing; I assume that Darwin's theory has weeded out those that don't know how to take cover properly. He is friendly enough and I get one of the interpreters to have a chat with him. He explains that there were eight Taliban. He saw them come back after the firefight with three casualties and one dead. They were loaded into a white Toyota pickup truck and driven off.

We continue to push forward and quickly meet up with the Vikings. James is an old hand at this and he is grinning like a Cheshire cat. He has watched the tension building in the lads due to lack of enemy activity. Like the experienced warrior that he is, he hasn't commented – he knew it would come.

I walk up to James and he gives me a comforting slap on the back. At this stage I realise that we are quite vulnerable while climbing into the vehicles and the huge fear that we leave someone behind is ever-present. The Viking troop is very experienced and it is quite comforting to be under the protection of their .50cal machine guns. The CSM sorts things out and quickly informs me that we are all accounted for and ready to go.

I climb into the commander's turret of my vehicle, clip on a radio headset and tell James to get me out of here. It feels great to be in the turret as I can see the countryside. There is the added benefit of a nice cooling breeze.

The Vikings are powerful vehicles and we are soon covering the ground. The rhythmic sway of the vehicles and the seclusion of the headset allows my mind to relax and it suddenly dawns on me that this is it, our first contact. I remind myself to stay focused but I realise that I have a huge grin on my face. The lads were awesome today.

I am just starting to gather my thoughts when suddenly we are approaching the rear gate. I look up in time to see the soldier manning the sangar – Lance Corporal D-P – giving me a huge grin and pumping his fist in the air. I give him a big thumbs up as we sweep back in.

The vehicles come to halt in the middle of the FOB and I take my time clambering out. Space is tight in the back and there is always something to get caught on. The atmosphere amongst the lads is electric, a confident excitement that comes from a job well done; all of the tension and frustration instantly flushed away. Before any of this can go to their heads, the NCOs are all over the lads and herd them off like the proverbial sheepdogs, back to the accommodation to clean their weapons and sort out their kit.

I head up to the ops room and Brett is there to meet me with a big cup of coffee. I know that I am dehydrated and I know that this won't help my stomach but I can't say no to a nice cup of cafetière coffee. Brett helps me get my patrol kit off and listens intently as I give him a quick rundown of what happened. I give Brett enough information to send off to our higher headquarters before moving round to the briefing area.

I strip off my kit, clean my rifle and recharge my magazines, while chatting to the CSM. We are both really pleased with the lads. They performed exactly as they should have done. No one over-reacted, no one got carried away and no one from our side got hurt.

After a quick solar shower I am pretty much sorted, so I decide to sit in the briefing area and gather my thoughts. It dawns on me that this is the first time since the Falklands War that B Company, 2 PARA, has been in a proper 'contact' battle. As paratroopers we put the 'Crew of '82' – as the Falklands veterans are known – on a pedestal. They are a true generation of warriors. They went down to the Falklands and, with minimal support, achieved incredible results. I think that we are now some way to joining those hallowed ranks.

I realise that a lot of the physiological effects that I had read about are correct. I had a sense of tunnel vision, especially when looking through the sight of the rifle. I had a sense of auditory exclusion – I couldn't really hear all of the fire. I also had the sense of time speeding up. The contact was at least five minutes but it felt like five seconds. Most notable, though, was the huge dump of adrenaline. I could literally feel myself feeding from it – I could have gone for ever. Now I am back in the FOB I can feel it wearing off and a gentle sense of fatigue is creeping in.

The CO rings in the evening and asks for a blow-by-blow account. He is really pleased with the company and he asks me to pass on his congratulations to the lads.

We later hear from intelligence sources that after the initial contact the Taliban commander was asked if he wanted reinforcements. His reply was priceless, 'Don't send reinforcements unless they want to die'. Brilliant, we have definitely had the desired effect.

What a good day. The tension is easing as the lads realise that there is an enemy out there and he wants a fight. Our training does work – everyone did what they were supposed to do. In fact, our training works really well.

For now, though, I am just happy that it all went so well and I am so proud of the job the lads have done.

WEDNESDAY 21 MAY

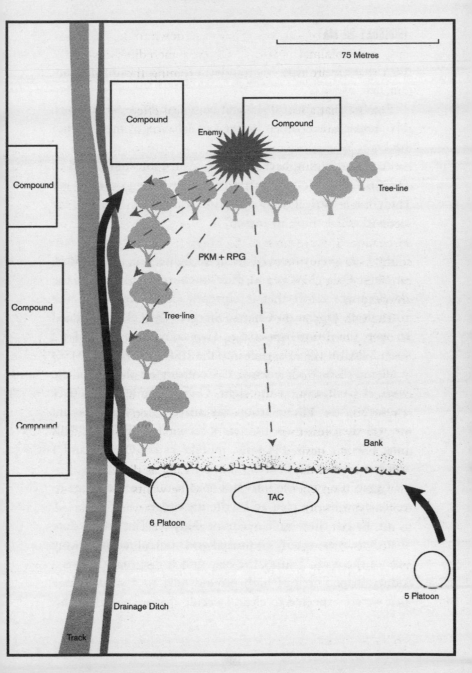

THURSDAY 22 MAY

I am awake really early. My mind is still swirling with emotion; our first contact.

I go to the gym at 0515 and have a really good workout. My stomach feels much better and I have got my strength back.

As I am heading back from the gym, I am summoned to the ops room. We have just received a warning order to get ready for a battle group operation tomorrow. 'No rest for the wicked,' I think to myself.

There is an enemy force of about 40 fighters on the outskirts of Musa Qala (MSQ) and their intention is to disrupt the development effort that is currently occurring within the town itself. Operation Ghartse Sterger (Op GS) is designed to stop this from happening. Two companies (B and C) from 2 PARA will air assault into the 1,500-metre wide MSQ wadi and disrupt the enemy; C Company on the left of the wadi, B Company on the right. Once the initial objectives are secure, the Viking troop will arrive to resupply us and we will then move on to clear a secondary objective. This time I won't make the same mistake as on Op OS and I will put a book on board.

I grab the available info and head round to the office to come up with my plan and write my orders.

As always, there isn't much intelligence. The orders state that there is an enemy command and control facility on my side of the wadi. I study the map and realise that there is a kidney-shaped area of high ground next to a small village that we are expected to clear. I decide that we will clear this high ground first. I will then set up a fire support base and systematically clear the village.

At 0930 hours I deliver my orders. It is a flexible plan as there isn't much information on the enemy and not much information on the ground. In this situation a flexible plan, something that we can adjust on the ground, is definitely the best option. This op looks like it will be interesting though – there is definitely an enemy out there and the poppy harvest is officially over.

We are desperately hoping for a helicopter and some mail today. The last one was on 13 May and the next one isn't due until 29 May. We were taken off the last Op Loam and we are actually starting to run low on supplies. Due to the threat to the HLS, the RAF is reluctant to fly in here so we get significantly less than the other FOBs. This is starting to affect the lad's morale. I type out a long email to Jacko. Fortunately he takes it in the spirit that it is meant. I am not one to complain or cause problems. He says he will look into it.

I spend the afternoon sorting my kit out and then go to bed early. Yet again, I am not convinced this op will happen. I doubt we will be able to get the helicopters.

FRIDAY 23 MAY

I am woken at 0030 by one of the signallers. The op is on. There is the normal sense of sombre anticipation combined with middle-of-the-night lethargy. We quietly sort out our kit, the reality of facing a group of 40 enemy starting to sink in.

The anxiety and sleep are soon blasted away with the sound of the Chinooks approaching. It is 0100.

You can't beat a short, sharp, low-level helicopter ride, with all the lights off, to get your adrenaline pumping.

The helicopters land and we all clamber on board. I am standing up in the middle with the dog handler and Rab – firmly muzzled – just in front of me. As we get on board the internal red lights are on but as soon as we take off, they turn out all of the lights. I flip down my NVGs and look out of the open back ramp at the ground whizzing by 50 metres below us. You can feel the tension on board; we are all nervous. The flight will only be a couple of minutes, as the objective is only 15km away.

The shout goes down the aircraft 'Two minutes', we are two minutes from the objective.

The RAF crewman lowers the back ramp. The aircraft has really built up some speed now.

'One minute' is shouted down the line. We all start rocking and getting ourselves ready to go. I can feel the adrenaline coursing through my veins.

From the open back ramp I can see red tracer randomly streaming up into the air. The enemy can hear us, but can't see us. He is shooting wildly into the sky.

I feel a wave of fear wash over me. I do not want to be shot down. I immediately lean forward and start stroking Rab and saying 'It's all right,' to him. The act of thinking about someone, or something, else distracts my own emotion.

'Stand by' is bellowed out and I am instantly focused, staring out of the back ramp.

The Chinook thumps down on to the ground and we

are off. I can see everyone shouting, it looks like a tribal roar and I find myself joining in. We surge off the aircraft like a swirling organic mass.

The noise, the dust and confusion is disorientating but I run for a hundred metres and dive down on to the ground. Lance Corporal Barker crashes down beside me.

The helicopter starts to lift off and I can see the mini Gatling gun spewing fire from the front door. 'Christ, I hope he knows what he is aiming at,' I think to myself.

Fortunately the enemy has not worked out where we are and as the Chinook departs, it all goes quiet.

We expand our security perimeter, ready for the return of the Chinook. It has gone back to pick up another load of people.

I push us out to a very wide circle and within minutes we can hear the Chinook coming back. We are all scanning through our NVGs, trying to see any enemy.

The Chinook shoots into the middle of the secured area and disgorges its next load. The engine speeds up and it again lumbers away over our heads. The gun is firing again and I really do hope he can see all of us; I have no idea what he is firing at.

The Chinook is just pulling away when the pilot fires his chaff. Molten globules of burning magnesium, designed to blind and confuse the enemy, rain down on us. There is a collective shout of 'FUCK' as the magnesium lands among us. We all have to rip our NVGs out of the way as the intense light causes them to flare out. The screens just go bright green. The chaff also destroys our natural night vision. Brilliant.

FRIDAY 23 MAY

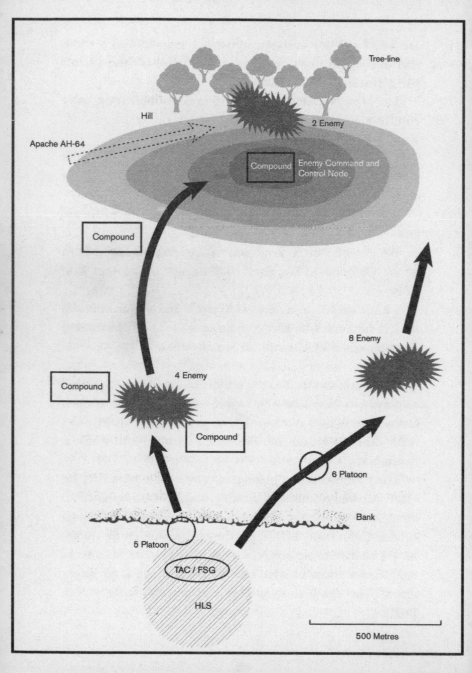

'Really helpful,' I think to myself. I get on my radio and quickly check with all of the call-signs that no one has been hit by the chaff. Amazingly, no one has.

It is all quiet, so I think it best to use the time to sort things out.

The second Chinook lift has delivered more soldiers and a quad bike with trailer. The quad has a 60mm mortar on board and spare ammunition.

The CSM needs some time to get everyone into the order of march and get the quad in the right place, so I give him some time and stay out of the way.

Before long he lets me know that we are all sorted. I tell 5 Platoon to start to advance towards our initial objective – the kidney-shaped high ground.

The ground is a mixture of rolling, rocky desert and widely interspersed compounds. It is very quiet and a really clear night so we can see a long way with the NVGs. The MSQ wadi is one kilometre to our left and we are heading north, 5 Platoon, TAC, 6 Platoon, CSM's group with quad and then a fire support group.

We are pushing forward steadily, having to stop every now and then for the quad bike to negotiate obstacles. Wes suddenly comes up on the net. The lead section of 5 Platoon has identified four males, 100 metres to their front and they are armed with AK-47s. They are standing in a cluster staring up at the sky, obviously trying to work out what all of the helicopter activity is about.

Wes asks me what I want him to do.

I am just starting to think about this when there is a huge burst of fire to my front and a big gunfight ensues.

The armed men had heard some noise and fired at the lead section, so there is no decision to make now.

We are on a false ridge just short of the high ground I want to take so I tell Wes to push on. The four enemy are quickly dealt with; those that aren't cut down fall back to a compound on top of the objective.

We continue to move and we start to come under fire from a compound on the high ground. I can clearly see enemy muzzle flashes through my NVGs. Rounds are flying all around us and I can hear and sense bullets whizzing by me.

Wes gets a good fire support base in and continues to push forward while I decide to swing 6 Platoon round to our right flank. I am concerned that the enemy will start trying to reinforce.

This turns out to be a sound decision. As 6 Platoon gets level with my group they see eight enemy trying to come in from our right flank. Good use of the gun group shatters this lot, but two manage to escape and pull back to a tree-line on the other side of the objective.

At this point an Apache joins us. Corporal Hickman runs up to me and starts relaying messages to the pilot. I tell him that we have seen two enemy pulling back into the tree-line. The pilot quickly identifies them with his thermal imagery and says that it looks like they have set themselves up in a position to ambush us.

I get Corporal Hickman to start the procedure for bringing in fire from the Apache and tell 5 Platoon to go firm and switch on their marker beacons. That way, the Apache can see where we all are.

The Apache keeps orbiting and lets me know that he can see all of the flashing marker beacons. Do I want him to fire?

Corporal Hickman informs me it is 'danger close'. This means that my soldiers are within the recognised safety distance for the 30mm cannon. The enemy is only a hundred metres to our front. Danger close means that the pilot cannot guarantee the safety of the troops and it is, therefore, my call to make. As the commander on the ground I have to take responsibility for the fire.

I double-check with Wes that they are all firm and tell Corporal Hickman to authorise the pilot to carry on.

Wes's platoon is formed up in a line running east–west and the enemy are just north of us. The pilot comes in parallel and just in front of the lead platoon, hovers, and then opens fire with the 30mm cannon.

It is breath-taking. A guttural, rhythmic thumping that oozes power. I have never seen or heard an Apache fire this close and it is staggering. No one will walk away from it. The pilot fires three long bursts of fire and then wheels round to a new position.

There is a pause as the pilot scans the area. He then comes up on Corporal Hickman's radio and says, 'Scrub two enemy'. I ask Corporal Hickman to check. 'Have they gone?' The pilot confirms that they are well and truly gone. They are, literally, vaporised.

At this, 5 Platoon quickly push forward and take the high ground. They clear the compound but it looks like the enemy have managed to withdraw.

I push the FSG forward and they set up their GPMGs. At this stage we are taking quite a lot of fire from both the north and the west.

I request the Apache again but I am turned down. C

Company is also in contact over on the left-hand side of the wadi and the Apache is now supporting them.

The CO is collocated with C Company so I send him a sitrep and then try to get a better understanding of what is going on. We are taking fire from most directions to our right flank but I am not convinced the enemy knows where we are, due to the darkness.

I configure the company into all-round defence. There is a distinct lack of cover so we will end up more spread out than I would like. The FSG are on the high ground and they are well set up. I put TAC just behind them, next to the compound, as the elevation on the hill gives me good observation in most directions. Just behind us is 5 Platoon, on the reverse of the hill; a bit exposed. I keep 6 Platoon even further back in a set of compounds one hundred and fifty metres to our rear.

We are sporadically engaged for the next couple of hours and as I plot each contact on my map it is obvious what the enemy is doing. They started from the north and are now systematically working round us in a clockwise direction, probing our layout and defences. He is pushing in, getting contacted, pulling back and repeating this pattern in a half-circle. Very clever, but he hasn't found an opening yet. At first light though, we will lose the advantage of darkness.

Dawn begins to break and we get our first look at Musulmani, the small village we are expected to clear.

Sergeant Radcliffe comes over with some good news. We have found and cleared the enemy command and control node. In fact, we are standing on it. The small compound on top of the hill has radio rebroadcast equipment and phones in it. That would explain why the enemy were falling back to it.

Just as dawn begins to break a heavy machine gun fires a huge burst straight at us, sending most of us sprawling. He then starts firing at the Apache. I try to get a better view and rise up from behind the small mound I am sheltering behind and I have a huge burst fired straight at me. I roll down the small hill in a heap realising that I hadn't really thought that one through. I look up to see Lance Corporal Barker laughing at me. Fair one. Close call.

The FSG suddenly comes up on the radio. They can see 20 enemy 1,500 metres off to their front, moving towards our location.

I request the Apache but again I am turned down. I turn to the FOO and ask if there is anything else. He says that the 105mm artillery at FOB Inkerman is in range. We call in a fire mission and watch with great reassurance as round after round of high explosive breaks up the enemy's advance.

The CO comes up on the net and asks why I am using artillery. I tell him politely that it is because he won't give me the Apache. I am told that the Apache has had to leave to refuel. He then explains that there is significantly more activity on our side than C Company's. The CO is collocated with C Company and he suggests that he might bring his command group over to my side to help coordinate the battle. I politely suggest that we are fine but he is not buying it. He tells me that if we get any more groups of 20 or more enemy he will come over to 'assist'.

We continue to take sporadic rounds until 0600 and then it all goes quiet. I am back on my little hill, scanning the tree-line to our front with my ACOG rifle sight. The enemy suddenly opens up again with a long burst of fire. I can't see how many there are, but I can see the puffs from their weapons firing. I give a target indication to the FSG and snipers and they immediately put down masses of fire into the tree-line. The Apache arrives back from refuelling and now that it is daylight it is easy for him to identify us and see the direction that we are firing in. He wheels round and starts hammering the tree-line with his 30mm cannon.

The CO wants to know what is going on and how many enemy there are? I give him a situation report and tell him I think there are about six to ten enemy.

This tit-for-tat firing continues until 0930 when it all goes quiet. I think the enemy have worked out that there are a lot of us and they can't have failed to see how much fire-power we have.

I decide that it is time to send out a clearance patrol and sweep through Musulmani. I leave the FSG on the hill and take 6 Platoon down into the small village.

The guys are just trying to clear some compounds when an RPG is fired at us. It clips a wall just over a metre above my head, showering me in dust and explodes in a field fifty metres to my right. Lance Corporal Barker and I raise eyebrows at each other – that was close.

After that it all goes quiet. We finish the sweep and head back to the hill. We spend the rest of the day seeking as much shade as possible and sweating it out. Most of us use the old enemy command and control compound but the FSG tough it out in the sun. Fortunately the Vikings arrive mid-afternoon so we have plenty of water.

Just before last light I receive radio orders for the next phase, which will commence tomorrow morning. The CO's group will join B Company and we will push two kilometres to our north and clear the next village.

SATURDAY 24 MAY

We get up at 0200 hours and depart at 0300. The CO's group has crossed over the large wadi and he joins us as we head off.

The movement is a bit stop–start as the quad bike is struggling to negotiate some of the obstacles.

We arrive in the next village without enemy interference and immediately head for another piece of high ground. Same plan as before: secure the high ground, put in a fire support base and then conduct a detailed clearance.

At first light an even better hill, with a large compound halfway up it, presents itself off to the east. I send 6 Platoon over to secure it and once they are firm the rest of us will join them. It looks as if most of the villagers have left as we only see a few people.

The FSG push up the hill to establish overwatch while the rest of us push into the large compound. It is the length of a football pitch and subdivided into three smaller compounds. It is lovely. The walls are decorated; there are small fountains, flowers, vegetables growing and there are subterranean rooms that are cool and furnished. We are all very pleased with this. The CSM allocates each group an area and then we conduct a further clearance of the village. It is all quiet.

We spend the rest of the day conducting a patrol programme. The FSG stays in overwatch and I send out platoon-level patrols to dominate the local area.

Mid-afternoon a lone sniper opens up on the FSG. Corporal Berenger immediately tries to identify the firing point. The sniper is good – he is firing from 600 metres away in strong winds and the rounds are accurate, the FSG are scrambling for cover. The sniper earns the begrudging respect of Corporal Berenger, which is some achievement.

I send out 6 Platoon to try to find the sniper. He isn't stupid, once he sees the patrol approaching, he hides. The platoon has a good look around but they can't find him.

As the platoon is returning the sniper opens up again. Lance Corporal Jenk's section is the last one in. He has just led the front half of his section down the hill behind us when the sniper opens up on the remaining half. The Toms on the hill dive for cover. Lance Corporal Jenks sees that his Toms are stuck and without even thinking he charges back up the hill under fire. There is a whole group of us watching and we all start cheering him on. He safely makes it back to his Toms and then coordinates their fire. In pairs they run down the hill, Lance Corporal Jenks being the last man in. It is a tremendous act of selfless leadership and courage.

I head into one of the underground rooms and make myself comfy. It is carpeted with huge cushions so I have a fantastic sleep before being summoned round to see the CO. He is just next door in the middle, inner compound.

He explains that brigade has deemed that we have achieved our mission. The enemy has been smashed up and the command and control node destroyed. The plan is to extract us by Chinook tomorrow. Good news that we have achieved our mission, but I feel a bit disappointed. I fancied staying a few more days in this luxurious compound.

SUNDAY 25 MAY

I wake up having had the most amazing sleep. The carpet and the cushions were just wonderful. I get up and wander outside to have a chat with James. The Viking troop is parked just outside and they are starting to work out how they are going to get back to Inkerman. They have been tasked to clear an old Soviet trench system further down the wadi and they don't have a huge amount of fuel.

At 0700 we say farewell to our luxury villa and head off into the desert. The Chinooks are extracting us from a desert HLS two kilometres to the east.

By 0800 we have secured the HLS and the CO heads down for a chat. We spend the next hour having a really good talk. He is justifiably proud of this operation. This is the largest battle group operation that 2 PARA has been in since the Falklands. It is also its first air assault. I like the thought that we are now part of the regiment's history.

We sit and wait. We receive intelligence that the enemy has worked out that we are extracting. Fortunately, James and the Vikings are still here, so they widen the protective circle and make sure that nothing is close enough to shoot at the helicopters.

At 1000 two Chinooks arrive. Due to the amount of people we now have, they will have to conduct two trips. As they come in I fully expect to see something fire at them. Fortunately, the enemy hasn't been able to get close and we are soon on our way.

The flight is awesome. It is the lowest-level flight I have ever been on – we are literally hugging the ground. Before

I know it I am running off the back ramp back into Inkerman. Yet again, I have the reassuring sense of coming home.

I walk up the inside of the FOB and Brett is there to meet me, with a smile and coffee in hand. I dump my kit and start chatting to him. I can hear the helicopters returning with the remainder of the lads.

I watch as the Chinooks flare on to the HLS when suddenly there are a series of explosions and the .50cal in the front sangar starts firing. I grab my radio and sprint up to the front sangar. The enemy have fired three RPGs and machine guns at the Chinooks. The sangars have identified the firing point and are returning fire.

Down on the HLS it is chaos. The Chinooks are so noisy and throw up so much dust that when they are on the ground they have no situational awareness. Sergeant Phil Train is supervising the HLS and he is in the process of guiding the quad bike out of the back of the Chinook when the RPGs start landing. The crew of the Chinook are oblivious. Sergeant Train waves off the Chinook but the crewman in the back doesn't understand the message. The crewman gets the hint when he sees the Toms running for cover. The crewman's eyes bulge and he screams into his headset for the pilot to get out of there – just as Sergeant Philips is gently driving the quad off the back ramp. The pilot 'pulls stick' and the Chinook shoots up. Fortunately, Sergeant Philips revs the quad and it shoots off the back ramp, smashing into the ground from two metres up.

As soon as the Chinooks are out of the way I start the mortars and artillery on to the enemy firing points. They are still shooting at the FOB but the heavy fire soon silences them.

Once it has gone quiet I head back to the ops room and

tell Brett all about the op. I then move round to the briefing area and sort myself out. I clean all of my kit and have a lovely solar shower. The operation has gone very well and I am really proud of us all. It was a gritty battle and classic Parachute Regiment: a surprise assault and then shock action to shatter the enemy.

I am sitting there gathering my thoughts when one of the signallers runs round. 'Sir, you're needed in the ops room quickly,' he says and heads off.

I nip round to meet a sea of grim faces. The Viking troop has been in rolling contacts for hours and they have just had a mine strike.

I stay at the back of the ops room listening to James give a situation report over the radio. He is describing a grim scene. The front cab of one of the Vikings is split in two. He then says that he has one serious casualty and one of his marines has been killed.

The blood drains from our faces and the room falls silent. The Viking troop lives in our FOB and we have grown really close to them. It is like losing one of our own and we are devastated.

Communications are really bad and James is struggling to get through to HQ. I realise that we are probably closer geographically to him than headquarters so I step forward, put on a headset and sit down. I need to help and I hope that James might find my voice reassuring.

Brett and I then sit there and help BGHQ coordinate the casualty evacuation and recovery of the vehicle. It is a horrible hour and a half and I feel so sorry for James. It takes the sheen off a superb Op.

Once the incident is sorted I head back to the briefing area.

Late afternoon the Viking troop arrives back. They are really upset. They only have weeks to push before they head home. I have a chat with James and ask him if it would be all right if I speak to his troop. He says that would help.

I have never had to do this before and I realise that pre-packaged officer rhetoric won't help at all. So I am honest. I tell them how desperately sorry we are for all of them. I tell them how close we feel to them and it feels like we have lost one of our own. It is horrible having to do this and I hope that I have communicated the message correctly. I then leave them to their grieving. As I walk back up the FOB I feel really sad. Looking at their devastated faces is one of the hardest things I have ever had to do.

MONDAY 26 MAY

After the op I am keen to put some rest days in. The lads worked hard and the D&V finger of fate is still floating around the camp. I am up early, so head to the gym. Post workout I am planning a nice relaxing day. I am summoned to the ops room. Jacko – the battle-group 2IC – is on the secure phone and wants to talk to me.

He starts with a huge compliment calling me the 'Lord of War'. He has seen gun camera footage of our assault on the command and control node from the Apache and he tells me how good it looks. He also lets me know that the op has made it into the *Sunday Mirror* under the heading 'Paras Blitz the Taliban'. The lads will be really pleased.

Then the bad news. The CO wants to keep the pressure on the enemy so I have to mount patrols every day for the next few days. I try to argue my case for letting the lads rest, but to no avail.

We head out at 1300, which is just madness. It is so hot that not even the locals are around. We head out towards Jusulay and then I get the whole patrol to go firm. I get 5 Platoon to conduct a sweep of our right flank and then 4 Platoon to sweep our left flank. This works well, as it allows one platoon to be in the shade while the other is moving. We generate no interest whatsoever from either the locals or the enemy. I spend a good hour talking to Lance Corporal Barker while sheltering next to a refreshing-looking stream.

After two hours we head back in. The lads are starting to suffer and we have a heat casualty. Fortunately he can walk but we have to share out his kit.

Once in I quickly issue orders for the next day then try to rehydrate. I don't feel too bad and I think my body has really adapted to the heat. I head off to bed early as I reckon the next few days are going to be a challenge.

TUESDAY 27 MAY

We leave the back gate at 0615. This patrol makes far more sense – we are going to clear the firing point that the enemy used the other day to engage the Chinooks. I need to get this area secured as the RAF is now even more unhappy about landing at the FOB. We are due a resupply flight on 30 May and we really need it; the last one was on 13 May.

We head off into the desert and then do a large left hook down to an area designated KA8 which is just on the edge of the green zone. There is a large compound with a building which was used to fire RPGs from, the other day. The compound is quickly cleared by 5 Platoon, then I leave 4 Platoon outside as security. The compound and buildings are very nice and I climb a ladder to the roof to get a better view.

As I get on to the roof I have to smile. At one position on the roof there is a cut-out in the compound wall. It allows you to see the FOB perfectly and, when we measure the distance with laser binoculars, it is exactly 900 metres. Very clever – this distance allows you to use the RPG as an airburst when it self-destructs.

I have a chat with the engineers and they come up with a novel and very out-of-character suggestion. I thought they would want to blow up the wall. In fact they have found some bricks and a ladder and they suggest bricking up the hole.

It is a brilliant idea and much less likely to alienate the locals. Quite soon we are all in hysterics as they fill the hole in – this really appeals to our sense of humour. I call it 'reverse denial'. Once finished we get an interpreter to write a note. It says simply 'We can see you, do not remove the bricks from this hole or you will be shot'. It works; the bricks are never removed.

As we start to head back in we take a heat casualty. Fortunately the deep drainage ditch that leads back to the FOB is empty. We all get into it and try to use the shade to make our way back. We take it slowly and, fortunately, the casualty can walk with assistance. The heat is really starting to take its toll.

THURSDAY 29 MAY

Our third patrol in a row. We depart at 0645, this time with 5 and 6 Platoons. We push in to Jusulay then hook right, until we are about two kilometres into the green zone. We are just short of the 'Austrian' village. I line the two platoons up on two belts of compounds that are 200 metres apart and run east to west. I put in a thirty-minute soak period to see if we generate any interest. We are getting dicked – slang for the enemy watching you – but he can't seem to generate anything.

I then push us forward, sweeping down the belt of compounds for a kilometre before hooking left and sweeping back in through the Star Wars village. We are back in for 1100hrs.

The cumulative effect of the heat is really starting to bite. There is a general malaise, people are slow, shoulders dropped and they are struggling to stay alert. Every step is a challenge. I am desperate to let the lads recover but my orders are clear – keep getting out there. I find this annoying as it doesn't seem to be serving much purpose, but there isn't much I can do.

In the evening I have a chat with the CO on the phone and he starts to understand my point. I am really concerned that I am going to lose people to the heat. Once someone becomes a serious heat casualty they are sent back to Bastion and we don't see them again. He agrees that I can put in a rest day on Saturday. He then drops in the good news. We should be getting helicopters tomorrow. Word about a resupply spreads quickly and you can feel the mood lift within the FOB. I can see Toms grinning and the banter increases. I catch the odd whisper or snapshot of a conversation as I wander around … 'Have you heard the news? Helis tomorrow'. It is amazing how quickly news spreads. We just have to hope that they do actually come.

FRIDAY 30 MAY

We receive orders that we are going to receive an airdrop tonight. We haven't had supplies for so long they are going to parachute pallets of rations and stores into the desert for us to retrieve. This sounds straightforward but it is in fact a complex operation involving 80-odd people. We are also expecting helicopters late morning.

Due to the last attack on the Chinooks I now have to send two platoons out into the green zone to provide security to the HLS.

At 1100 two Chinooks arrive with more soldiers for the FOB and a tonne of mail. A whole tonne of mail! It is fantastic and morale shoots through the roof. Very quickly there are happy people staggering around the FOB with armfuls of boxes whilst chewing mouthfuls of Haribo sweets.

It is quickly like a 'show and tell' in the ops room as we open our parcels and show each other what we have got.

I have loads of letters. I decide to keep them and open one each night in bed before I go to sleep; that way I can space them out.

I spend the afternoon planning and discussing the air drop with Wes and Sergeant Train. Sergeant Train, as our 'air' commander, will mark out the area for the drop while Wes and 5 Platoon will provide security. They will escort two large trucks out to retrieve the 20-odd tonnes of stores we are expecting. The drop zone is three kilometres away, out in the desert. I decide that I will let Wes and Sergeant Train run this one while I stay in the ops room. They don't really need me.

The air drop team head out at last light. This allows them

to do their initial mine clearance in the light before heading off to the relative safety of the desert.

The air drop quickly turns into a farce. Sergeant Train is diligent and methodical, laying out an easy to identify drop zone out in the desert. There are low gusts of wind so he requests the aircraft to come in at 2000ft; that way, the pallets are in the air for less time and won't drift as far. The Hercules comes in at 5000ft and drops the pallets way off the release point. Most of the pallets miss the drop zone by two kilometres; one of them misses by five kilometres. Poor 5 Platoon and Sergeant Train spend the whole night retrieving them.

SATURDAY 31 MAY

I finally manage to put in a rest day for the lads. The air drop last night has kept a lot of people up all night and the lads now need a break. I get up at 0500hrs to meet Sergeant Train just as he is arriving back. He is covered in sand, tired, but still grinning. He explains what has happened before supervising the unloading of the pallets with the CSM.

Within the hour the situation gets even dafter. The CSM comes to see me. There were four pallets in the air drop last night: two with rations, which are useful, but two contain stores that we haven't asked for and can't use. They have sent lubricants and spares for vehicles we don't even have at the FOB and a load of engineering stores we can't use. To add insult to injury they put fresh food on one of the pallets – fresh bread, frozen chicken breasts and fruit. The vehicle lubricants have spilled and ruined most of the food. For some strange reason, we all just start laughing. Thankfully we had mail yesterday and most people received some luxuries. I am sure we would not be finding this all so amusing if we hadn't.

I spend the rest of the day lazing around reading a book and watching DVDs on a laptop. We all need a rest. Battle group headquarters is in the process of moving from Bastion to Sangin. I am sure once they are settled the CO will be pushing for another operation so I am keen to get us rested and 'keep our powder dry'.

JUNE

At a higher level it appears that this tour is going well. The brigade is mounting large-scale operations that are keeping the enemy off balance and generating useful intelligence. The tour is going very well for 2 PARA. The air assault operation was superb and prevented the enemy from destabilising Musa Qala. Battle group headquarters is now in Sangin, allowing it to focus the reconstruction and development effort. All the while, C and B Companies continue to disrupt the enemy. There is a feeling that the tour is gathering momentum.

Morale within B Company is sky high. We have been 'blooded' and the enemy came off worse. The stress and the tension have evaporated now that shots have been fired in anger. We have been in battle and I think all of us have increased in confidence because of this.

SUNDAY 1 JUNE

I am trying to keep an active presence but minimise our activity in order to let the lads recover.

I am heading up from the gym when I have a brain-wave. I immediately find Sergeant Radcliffe and ask him if he knows when a Vehicle Check Point (VCP) Operation was last conducted in our area. Those of us with Northern Ireland experience know all about these. You establish a cordon, place out protection then 'spring' out on to the road, stop the traffic, talk to the vehicle occupants and search the cars.

Sergeant Radcliffe thinks that the last time anything like this was done was in February when the Afghan Army used to be in the FOB. They would just randomly stop traffic on the 611.

I send for Wes and his sergeant. Sergeant Marshall is an impressive character; tough but compassionate. Wes and Sergeant Marshall drive their platoon hard but they get good results. With Sergeant Marshall's wealth of Northern Ireland experience he understands exactly what I am after. We will use the VCPs as an opportunity to push out key messages and hand out leaflets.

The vehicle checks start soon after 0700hrs when 5 Platoon pops out the front gate, establishes security then stops traffic on the 611. The interpreters and intelligence cell do all of the talking. The cars soon back up, so it is easy to spot anyone acting suspiciously.

The platoon does four twenty-minute VCPs and it seems to work well. The intelligence cell get a good feel for where people are travelling to and from, and why.

I am really pleased with this as I think it is quite creative. I write up a commander's assessment and then send it off as part of our daily brief to HQ.

In the evening the CO rings and we have a good chat. He tells me that the brigade commander has read my comments on the report that I sent off and had rung the CO to say what a good idea the VCPs were. This will go down well with the lads. The CO seems on good form and happy with the way things are going. They are still mid-move to Sangin at the moment so he is content to leave us to it.

MONDAY 2 JUNE

I receive a message that the ANA commander, Karim, would like to come to the FOB for a meeting. He arrives mid-morning and we have a really long chat at the briefing area. He is as impressive as ever and has a really good grasp of what Afghanistan needs right now. His view is that it is all about education. You have to start educating the children if Afghanistan is to have a decent future. I am in complete agreement; there are no short-term fixes.

His intelligent and insightful comments on Afghanistan's future are in sharp contrast to his views on the Taliban and how to deal with them. For the locals that help the Taliban he takes on a Mafia boss approach. He has told the locals, through an imam in the local mosque, that if they harbour the Taliban, and if any of his men are hurt or killed and he finds out they are involved he will kill them, their family, their livestock and blow up their compounds. This causes some raised eyebrows. While this approach may not sit comfortably with us, his is an Afghan approach and their culture certainly respects strength.

In the past he has been mujahideen and we have a long chat about fighting the Soviets under General Dostum. It is fascinating. Their approach was brutal and uncompromising. They blended in with the people and the terrain, swooping down to attack as opportunities presented themselves. He talks of picking off Soviet resupply convoys and we listen with macabre fascination.

I have Sergeant Radcliffe make up some gifts for him and we send him away with as much kit as we can spare – surplus rations, candles, pads, pens etc. He seems very happy and I am pleased with the talk that we have had. It is still early days, but I am keen for us to start working together. We need to get into a position where we are supporting him, not doing everything on our own.

TUESDAY 3 JUNE

I push a platoon-level patrol into Star Wars village to see if they can talk to the locals and develop our intelligence picture. The patrol doesn't really achieve much. The weather seems to have really shot up and it is hitting 45C at midday. Even the locals seem to be lethargic from it and spend most of the time seeking shade. The patrol encounters only a few people and they are unwilling to generate any conversation.

I am in the ops room making notes on a neurolinguistic programming (NLP) book I am reading at the moment when we receive a fast ball. Operation Granite will be coming to our location tonight. This is effectively a mini Operation Loam. It will only be coming to our location, so it is much easier to coordinate. We will receive four shipping containers of stores, mainly comprising rations and engineer stores. I am desperately hoping there is some fresh food as we haven't had any for weeks.

I decide to make the security of the Jusulay track junction a platoon task to minimise the manpower burden. I pick 6 Platoon and Dave is happy with the task.

I spend the afternoon making notes on NLP. It is a subject I am fascinated by and I am determined to use the opportunities I have out here for self-improvement: I have the time to study and carry out practical exercises. It all fits within a personal subject I am keen on – warrior improvement. I have spent a long time preparing myself both mentally and physically to go into combat. I believe a warrior has a passion. He accepts that this is his calling and strives to be strong. He is analytical, courageous and – most importantly – he wants to lead. There is no greater honour than leading men in battle. He is committed and takes pride. He has a code, one that the knights of old would recognise. He strives, always, for self-mastery.

The word warrior does not sit as comfortably with the British as it does with other countries but I feel it offers more of an explanation as to who we are than the word 'soldier'. As the samurai knew, the professional warrior tries to develop himself every day. Having engaged with the enemy I am keen to continue to develop myself both mentally and physically. I feel we can call ourselves warriors because of the experiences we have been through but it is an edge that needs continual sharpening. Unless we learn from the experience it will quickly fade.

Operation Granite arrives at 2230 and I am hanging around outside the ops room when I suddenly hear my name shouted out. It is the company commander from D Company – Mike, from FOB Robinson. His lads are responsible for the convoy and in a healthy display of leadership he has decided to ride in the front vehicle. He also wanted to come and say hello after our last chance for a good catch up was cut short.

It's great to see him. We grab a cup of tea and head round to a quiet corner so we can talk out of earshot. We have a good 'vent' and let off some steam. It is reassuring that we are experiencing similar frustrations, frictions and pressures. On the flip side, we are both loving company command. I give Mike a blow-by-blow account of the air assault, which he is interested in.

Before we know it his driver comes to get him. It has been wonderful to catch up and as he heads off I realise the truism about the loneliness of command. I am close to my CSM and 2IC but I am conscious that I am the company commander. Sometimes I have to bottle things up as it wouldn't be appropriate to say them out loud. It was nice to be able to talk to a fellow major who is going through a similar experience. I drift off to bed feeling better for talking to Mike, but also feeling quite lonely.

WEDNESDAY 4 JUNE

I am woken at 0100 and asked to come to the ops room. A US Special Forces team has been operating five kilometres north of our location. One of their vehicles has hit a mine. No one is injured but they are keen to recover the vehicle and we are the closest unit to assist.

I shake myself awake, make a cup of coffee and wait for their arrival. The team arrives at 0200 in their remaining three vehicles. We quickly make our introductions and head up to the ops room to work out what we are going to do. Within an hour we have worked out a good plan. They will lead four of my vehicles up to the damaged vehicle. I will send out three of my Land Rovers and our recovery vehicle. They are happy to lead the convoy but I decide to put my most experienced mine-searching team in to assist. We work up the plan and then I back-brief it on the radio to HQ. They will then send this on to brigade HQ.

The convoy assembles and the vehicles are all running, lined up at the back gate, ready to go. We then get the message from brigade that they want us to wait until further notice. We all head off to bed.

I am up fairly early to see if there are any developments but at this stage the direction is to wait to see if there are other options. Sensibly, they do not want us to return to the site of a mine strike.

I spend most of the morning chatting to the US SF, who are a good bunch. It's good to see some Americans. We are all on this together but, due to the way each country has been allocated a sector of Afghanistan, we rarely cross over. The only others I have seen were at Kandahar. The Americans are invariably positive; they moan far less than the Brits.

We refine our plan and talk the usual soldier talk – kit and tactics. They have very impressive vehicles and they operate in a very different way to us. They drive around until the enemy engage them and then call in aircraft to destroy them. They are impressed that we go out on foot and 'hunt' the enemy.

In the afternoon I manage to phone Andrea on a satellite phone. We are already crafting plans for R&R, which seems incredible really. The time is flying by. I am sure I will be ready for a break when the time comes.

THURSDAY 5 JUNE

We head out on patrol at 0900 and it is already 40C. It is unbearably hot, but we struggle on. We could go earlier but then we would miss the locals. We need to talk to them to gather intelligence.

A local 'walk-in' has told us that the Taliban have placed IEDs in the large drainage ditch we have been using so we are going to clear it.

The clearance is conducted by 4 Platoon, working methodically up the drainage ditch searching for any evidence of IEDs while 6 Platoon and my group provide outer protection.

The ditch is clear and we head north-west up towards KA8. I want to check on the compound where we bricked up the gap in the wall.

The compound is as we left it so we put a VCP on the 611, stop some cars and talk to the locals.

A lot of locals are fleeing the area at the moment. The US SF team currently in my FOB have been conducting operations up near Putay and the 'bombing campaign' has got them all spooked. As we talk to them we find out that they do differentiate between British and Americans, which is interesting. They can spot the differences in uniform and equipment and also in our different approaches.

We receive intelligence that the enemy is watching us but they don't do anything.

After two and a half hours we head back in. Hot, but at least we have had a chance to talk to some locals and we have received some useful intelligence.

I am just enjoying my post-patrol shower when I am summoned to the ops room.

Battle group HQ has received credible intelligence that the Taliban have anti-aircraft kit in the AO and are preparing it for use. We are given three grid references and the order to clear them now. They need clearing now, or no helicopters.

I issue hasty orders, try to get as many fresh people on the patrol as possible and then we head back out at 1545hrs. It is still really hot but the nature of this op has people buzzing. The first grid reference is two kilometres away and we get out there and clear that one quickly.

We push on, but it is obvious that we are slowing down. The heat is sapping everyone. We push on another two kilometres and clear the next one. Nothing there, either. We then receive intelligence that the enemy are out there and getting ready to ambush us. This is not good as most people are running out of water. I try to push things on as quickly as possible but the heat is causing slow progress. Eventually we clear the third grid – nothing there either – we then start to head back in. Fortunately, despite the indicators, the enemy decide not to hit us. This is good for us: we are all so drained that a two-hour gun battle would have been hard graft.

We get back in after four and a half hours, absolutely shattered.

After my second refreshing shower of the day I have a sudden burst of energy. I spend an hour and a half planning the next ten-day patrol matrix. I am buzzing – it must be the adrenaline. I find that I just can't turn my mind off. I go to bed at 2230 but can't sleep. I get up again at 2330 and sit outside looking at the stars. Afghanistan has the most amazing sky at night. After a while the adrenaline wears off and I am shattered, so head off to bed.

SATURDAY 7 JUNE

I award a well-earned rest day after yesterday's activity. We schedule brunch instead of breakfast so that people can have a lie-in and leave the platoons alone. The only direction is to try to rehydrate, ready for tomorrow's patrol. In the afternoon I deliver orders and then leave the lads to it.

SUNDAY 8 JUNE

I am up at 0600 and sort myself out. The company patrol departs at 0700. I have 4 and 5 Platoons out on the ground today. This patrol has been tasked to me by battle group headquarters. They have received intelligence about enemy activity in the area and they want me to check it out. We are to go out and clear specific compounds which may be being used by the enemy.

I follow 5 Platoon, which departs by 7 RHA gate, and 4 Platoon leaves via the ANA gate. We then meet in the green zone and 4 Platoon joins the rear of our patrol. This method gets us all out on the ground quicker. We push north in a direct line to the eastern end of the area designated JA2.

On the way out we are out in the open and about to cross a small stream when two older locals approach from a track to the right on a motorbike and approach the middle of the patrol, which is my group. They are coming directly towards me so I flag them down at distance. They both get off the motorbike and seem friendly enough. The rear of the two is holding a bundle so I gesticulate for him to open it. He carefully unwraps the bundle and produces a dead baby. It is quite a distressing sight. At this point one of the interpreters arrives and chats to them. They are on their way to the graveyard to bury the baby. I offer my condolences and they move on.

I stop the patrol at the end of JA2 and order a ten-minute break. It is a glorious morning and the views are impressive. JA2 looks like a much more affluent area; there are vegetable gardens and widely-spaced large compounds. I sit for ten minutes in the shade chatting to Sergeant Train, who is just behind me. Everyone seems in good spirits so once we have had a break I reconfigure the patrol into 'two up', with 4 Platoon on the left and 5 on the right, and start the sweep.

We advance through JA2 chatting to the locals and stopping to search the allocated compounds. All of the compounds we have been told to search have a common theme – they have guest annexes. It looks like the annexes are being used as enemy bed-down locations.

The CSM comes on the radio to point out an occurrence that we haven't seen before. The occupants of compounds we are passing are lighting smoky fires. From a distance this provides an obvious marker for the enemy to track our progress.

Sergeant Radcliffe dips in to the next compound that lights a smoky fire and chats to the occupants. They deny anything untoward.

JA2 is probably the nicest part of the AO we have been to so far. Nice compounds and different crops – they are growing tomatoes. The occupants seem friendly. It also appears more liberal as the woman aren't covered up or herded back into the compounds when we approach.

We get to the end of JA2 and hook left to start to head back to the FOB. This reconfigures us in to 'one up' with 4 Platoon leading, then my group with 5 Platoon behind and off-set. Brett comes on the radio and lets me know that there is intelligence that the enemy are preparing to attack us – they don't have any ammunition but they have a 'big thing'. We assume that this means an RPG.

By 1100 it has really warmed up. We are all keen to get in as quickly as possible so 4 Platoon takes the most direct route to the FOB, which is two kilometres away. This will take us through KA1A, which is opposite Star Wars village.

Corporal Baillie's section is leading 4 Platoon. His route through KA1A takes him down a narrow alley between two compounds up to a track. The track leads to the Jusulay track junction, 200m off to his left.

Once at the end of the alley Corporal Baillie pauses at a drainage ditch with a log over it before deciding to push Private Murray with his GPMG over to the other side of the track. This will provide cover over the open ground to the left. Private Gamble – a Pashto speaker – moves opposite

Corporal Baillie while Private Cuthbertson and Sapper Little move directly behind.

Corporal Baillie looks to his right down the alley and sees a local approaching. The local has just appeared, potentially from a doorway and is already only 20 metres away. He tells Gamble to go over and speak to him and instructs Murray to cover Gamble.

Gamble and Murray get up from kneeling, approach the local and with smiles on their faces try to start a conversation.

There is a huge explosion.

From my position, 150 metres away, I haven't seen any of this, but I hear the explosion and think to myself 'Oh, they have brought an RPG up'.

There is a burst of fire from off to the left and I send 'Contact, RPG' on my radio to our ops room.

It then goes quiet. My group is behind a ditch, waiting to cross a hundred metres of open ground to our front which will take us to the back of the alley where 4 Platoon is.

The silence continues so I assume the best and wait for an update. We then hear the first shouts for a medic.

The CSM charges forward with his group of medics and asks if he can move up to 4 Platoon. I make sure that people are in place to cover his crossing of the open ground and watch as he races off.

After a couple of minutes I realise I still haven't been told what is going on so I decide to move over and have a look for myself.

I run across the open ground with my entourage following and stop at the back of the alley where the rear end of 4 Platoon is currently waiting.

I still can't get a feel for what is going on and the lads direct me up the alley.

I start moving up the alley. There is still a lot of dust and debris and the distinctive smell of high explosive.

About halfway up the alley I see Lance Corporal Du Plessis (always known as D-P) bandaging Sapper Little's arm. I ask them if they are all right and think to myself 'Thank the lord for that, at least it is just an arm injury'.

I then look up the alley and see a scene of utter carnage. The local that Murray and Gamble approached was a suicide bomber. As they got close he detonated himself, hitting Murray, Gamble and Cuthbertson. The force of the blast threw Corporal Baillie into the ditch.

Murray, Gamble and Cuthbertson each have at least two people working on them, a medic and one other. They have had their kit cut off and there is medical kit everywhere.

I am almost overwhelmed by what I am seeing. I can feel time slowing down and my hearing is beginning to go.

David True – the platoon commander – runs over and starts trying to tell me what is going on, but I can hardly hear him.

It is at this instant that I truly understand leadership. It is about all those that you command. At that single moment they all need you more than you need yourself. Your feelings, your emotions, your thoughts are utterly irrelevant; it is theirs that are important.

A voice inside my head booms, 'If ever there was the moment to do your job properly it is now' and I am instantly back in the moment.

I turn to David and ask him where his security is. With lads down and others working on them, he is thinly stretched.

I turn behind and call for Corporal Berenger. He runs

up and I tell him to take people from TAC and secure the open ground to our east. He grabs some lads and purposefully moves off.

Corporal Baillie then appears. He quickly lets me know that he is securing the right flank. It is incredible. He was blown off his feet but he has got straight up and immediately and correctly thought about security.

I realise that I need to be in a position to influence so I push left, kneel down just short of Cuthbertson and detach myself from the situation. I have got to stay calm.

Sergeant Sykes joins me and we both gather information for the ops room. Brett is already piecing together what is going on and has called for the medical helicopter.

I keep watching the scene and sending reports to Brett. The CSM and the medics are doing an amazing job but the lads are in a bad way.

I am told that the helicopter is twenty minutes away.

I then get told that the enemy know that we have casualties and they know that we will have called for a helicopter. The RPG team is still out there and ready.

The ground opposite the alley is perfect for the helicopter. It is wide and open.

I look at the injured lads and the medics, working like men possessed. The guys are in a bad way but they are alive. They need to be evacuated as quickly as possible. In a terrible instant I realise that I can't bring the helicopter in to this location. If it was shot down an already terrible situation would be made ten times worse.

I make the hardest decision I will ever have to make. I tell Brett to tell the Chinook to use the HLS at the FOB and to deploy the FSG in their vehicles to come and collect the casualties. All I want is to bring the helicopter in to our location, but I know that I can't.

Sergeant Major Mitchell is already listening on his radio and is ready to come and help. We have a chat on the radio. To do the correct drills to get vehicles out of the FOB takes thirty minutes. I can't ask him to skip these drills, they are lifesavers. I just ask him to come as quickly as he can. He says he understands.

The FSG are incredible. With complete disregard for their own safety they drive straight out. No checks for threats, they just motor. Within five minutes they are pulling up at our location.

Murray, Gamble and Cuthbertson are loaded on to a vehicle with Sapper Little. A medic and Sergeant Train climb on as well. The lads are still receiving CPR.

At this stage an Apache arrives on station so I get Corporal Hickman to ask the pilot to look after the vehicle convoy.

I am staring at the ground and realise that I am looking at a severed leg. It is the lower right leg of the suicide bomber. As the lads cut-off kit is being thrown in a vehicle I point the leg out to the CSM. He goes and picks it up and is about to throw it in a vehicle when I point out it is the suicide bomber's.

'Do we need it?' he asks.

'Not really,' I say and he throws it back in the ditch. All very surreal.

Mitch gives me a thumbs up and the four vehicles race off, the Apache low overhead, following their route.

With the lads gone I try to slow things down. I tell people to pick up all of our rubbish – don't leave any medical wrappers for propaganda victories.

I look at my watch and realise it is gone midday. We have been out a long time.

There isn't anything we can do from here so once we are all sorted we start to head back to the FOB.

I keep listening to my radio. The injured lads are at the FOB in five minutes and the doctor and every medic is there to meet them down by the HLS. Five minutes later the Chinook arrives and the pilot asks if the HLS is secure.

I can't give her that guarantee. She says not to worry and flies straight in. Minutes later the lads are off.

Brett lets me know that they are on their way and we keep plodding back in.

It is only fifteen hundred metres to the FOB but it feels like fifteen hundred miles. We are all out of water, it is hot and we are all to some extent in shock. It takes ages.

We move in through 7 RHA gate and the gunners are just fantastic. As I get in to the FOB I can see that they are all there to help us off with our kit. They are sitting people down in the shade and giving them drinks. It is a very kind gesture. Their friendly, sympathetic faces mean a lot.

Once we are all back in I let Brett know and then ask 4 Platoon to gather round. I have to say something. All I can do is let them know that they did a great job on the ground and that the lads are now in the best possible place. Once I get news I will let them know. I finish by telling them to go and get themselves sorted because tomorrow we go back out, we will find who has organised this and we will kill them.

I then start to walk up to the ops room, Lance Corporal Barker walking just behind me. He asks if he can say something.

'Of course,' I reply.

'I don't know how you did that, sir. I have been an OC's radio op for ten years and I don't think that I have ever seen anyone stay as calm as you were out on the ground today,' he says.

All I can say is 'Thank you'. I am so grateful for my leadership epiphany and his words mean a lot to me.

Brett meets me at the ops room. There is no update on the lads yet. I strip off my kit and dump it in the corner. Cunliffe, one of the signallers, is really upset; these lads were his best friends

Within an hour the CO is on the radio asking me to clear the ops room so he can speak to me alone. Our secure phone isn't working. I ask everyone to leave. Once I am alone I put the headset back on and let him know that we can talk.

He tells me Murray, Cuthbertson and Gamble have all died.

I can't speak; I just stare at the radio in front of me. I default to 'voice procedure'. He asks if I understand and I just reply 'Roger'.

He explains what happened and I just keep replying in the affirmative. We agree to speak later on.

I take a moment to gather my thoughts and then walk outside. Everyone is staring at me.

David True walks over and I tell him the news. He asks if he can be the one to tell 4 Platoon. I agree and I watch him walk off.

I then wander around the FOB and let people know. Everywhere I look people are upset – word is spreading already.

I end up sitting with Sergeant Train. He is really upset, as he was working on one of the lads. He tried so hard but he couldn't save him. It is horrible. He is really beating himself up but there was nothing he could have done. I try to console him.

I speak to all of the medics and they are the same as Sergeant Train. They are upset because no one survived, despite their best efforts. From the size of the explosion I doubt anyone could have survived.

Late afternoon we conduct a patrol debrief. We need to capture information as quickly as possible so that the rest of the brigade can be informed about a potential change in enemy tactics. All of the commanders gather in the briefing area and we go through the patrol in fine detail. This is horrendous for Corporal Baillie and 4 Platoon. We all have to relive it again so that we can create an incident report. Hopefully, the report will save lives.

I spend the remainder of the afternoon writing up various incident reports, eulogies and press releases. The time is tight and Nick, the adjutant based in battalion HQ, helps me through the process; this is not something we have trained for. Eulogies are written from right across the company and sent off to HQ.

At dusk I wander round the FOB. I can see small clusters of people consoling each other. We are all going to have to find a way to deal with this.

Come nightfall I feel spent and I need some space, so I climb up the ladder on to the roof of the building next to my bed and sit there looking at the night sky.

I know that I am going to have to compartmentalise this. I run through all of the decisions I had to make and I believe that they were right. I can take some solace from this. I think that everyone performed magnificently on the ground. The level of everyone's medical training shone through.

Although the lads didn't survive, I think people's drills were superb. I think the FSG were incredibly brave coming straight out – we know that mines have been placed out the back.

I feel strangely detached, like an observer. I can't shift the thought of the fallen lads being back at Bastion on their own. They were such wonderful young men, fun and full of smiles. Now their lives have been snuffed out by a coward.

The enemy spotted a weakness. We have been pleasant, polite and have tried to engage with the locals. The enemy realised that they can't take us on at range so they have worked out a way to get close.

The company is in shock but we will bounce back. We have been ordered to take a patrol out tomorrow to escort an incident exploitation team to the site. They need to gather information. This will be brutal and is being used as a way of getting us 'back on the horse'. I am not sure I agree, as we are all so dehydrated from today that there is a strong chance the horse will collapse.

As I sit on the roof I try to gauge how and what I am feeling. I feel empty and hollow. I have three soldiers dead. I never believed we would suffer like this. It is a bad day for B Company.

Before climbing down my thoughts turn to the lads' families and friends at home. I offer a prayer to them. What an awful day.

MONDAY 9 JUNE

I manage to sleep and wake up fairly early. I lie there and have to remind myself that this isn't a dream, three of my soldiers are gone.

A Chinook arrives early morning with the CO, RSM, Padre Alan plus a bomb disposal team and a Royal Engineer specialist team. The two teams will be gathering as much information as possible on the incident to develop our own counter procedures.

I quickly brief on today's patrol. It is very simple. Patrol out to KA1A, secure the incident site, and allow the teams to do their work before patrolling straight back.

There are a lot of people dehydrated from yesterday so I want to keep it as short and as simple as possible.

We leave mid-afternoon and patrol out quickly, with 4 Platoon securing the incident site; some of the lads are clearly upset. The outer perimeter is secured by 5 Platoon.

Initially I stay on the fringes while the specialist teams go in and do their work; I just sit talking to the signallers. The banter is light-hearted and jokey; false humour to hide our feelings. Fortunately Padre Alan is with me so I can chat to him.

Once the teams have carried out their search we are allowed to enter the 'cordon'. The CO asks me to walk him round the area and talk him through what happened.

I walk him round the track junction, pointing out where the lads had fallen and what happened. I am struck by the blast damage to the compound walls. It must have been a large amount of explosive.

Once I have talked him through the incident I manage to break away as I need some time alone. I walk back down the alley and once I am on my own I look round the scene again. I am struck by the feeling of time. I can't believe it happened only yesterday, it feels weeks ago. I offer a prayer to the fallen lads and their families before making my way back to the junction. Lance Corporal Barker has, discreetly, waited for me. My ever-loyal bodyguard, he could sense that I needed a moment alone and waited at the corner of the junction, all the while keeping an eye out for my security.

As I walk over he hands me a steel ball bearing, slightly chipped and covered in blood. The suicide bomber must have wrapped the device in ball bearings to increase the effect. Now that Lance Corporal Barker has pointed them out I can see the scars on the walls from where the ball bearings have hit.

Then 5 Platoon radios that during their rummaging around they have found an RPG warhead hidden in a tree. Fortunately, I have the bomb disposal team with me so they quickly go over and deal with it.

The discovery of the RPG confirms what intelligence was suggesting yesterday. There was an RPG team out there and they were in a position to shoot the Chinook if I had brought it in to this location: confirmation that it was the right decision to use the alternate HLS.

We patrol back in and sort ourselves out. The two specialist teams are picked up and the CO, RSM and padre stay. I have a long chat with the CO. We discuss how we deal with what has happened and how to continue to move the tour in the right direction. Once we finish I leave him to sort out his kit and I head off to the ops room.

I come back to the briefing area and take a seat. I find myself sitting on my own, feeling even more dehydrated and run down. I realise that the 'vision of hell', which is the only way I can describe the scene from yesterday, is burned into my mind. Every now and then the image is just there and I find myself staring at it with a slight sense of fascination and nausea.

Fortunately, Thorpy arrives and breaks me out of my

trance. We have a good chat and I tell him how drained I am feeling. He kindly points out that it must have taken a lot out of me, staying that calm during a crisis situation. This is much appreciated.

In the evening I make myself some food then drift off to bed. It feels like another long, surreal day.

TUESDAY 10 JUNE

I am awake early and I realise that my mind is dwelling on the 'scene', so at 0545 I go to the gym. I am run down and I know that I should take it easy but I need to do something to take my mind off things.

Mid-morning the CO and his party head off. The Chinook arrives and I wave off the CO and welcome the brigade commander.

Brigadier Mark Carleton-Smith (known affectionately as Mark C-S) has come to visit with the 2IC from the Engineer Regiment and two captains in tow. The writer Sam Kiley is also with him. The brigade commander is impressive and popular, so it is good to see him.

I take the group up to the briefing area and once they are settled I talk them through a tactical area brief followed by a detailed brief on the suicide bomber incident. They are all interested and ask very pertinent questions.

I then take the brigadier on a tour of the FOB, pointing out things and identifying the myriad of challenges we face. The two captains spend a lot of time taking notes.

I drop the brigadier off with 4 Platoon. They have all gathered round a small fire and he just naturally sits down with them and starts talking. I leave him to it.

About an hour later I come back and the brigadier is still chatting to the lads. You can see they are enjoying his company.

He politely breaks away from the group and asks me what I would like him to do. This is rather flattering, as brigadiers normally tell majors what to do. I ask him if he would mind speaking to the whole company as I think they would like to hear from him. He is happy to oblige.

Thirty minutes later the CSM has gathered everyone bar the sentries outside the cookhouse. It is late afternoon and the sun is just starting to set.

Mark C-S steps forward and starts speaking. It is the most inspiring speech I have ever heard in my life. Thirty minutes later we are quivering, energised by his words. It is like the speech from *Braveheart*; we would follow this man into the gates of hell. It has such a galvanising effect on the company. If Mark C-S had ended the speech by running straight out into the green zone with no weapon we would all have followed him, screaming like banshees.

He doesn't though. He just walks over to me and asks if that was all right. I am almost speechless so I just politely let him know that it was spot on. I head over to Sam Kiley and ask him if he has recorded the speech. He hasn't and he is already kicking himself.

I take the brigadier into the ops room and we have a good chat. He is relaxed and easy to talk to and we discuss the tour so far. He is really keen to find out how things are going at company level and I am keen to find out how things are going for the brigade.

The cookhouse is still shut so I put a couple of boil-in-the-bag food pouches into the kettle. While we wait he tells me how well we have all done and how impressive the company is. He is so genuine and his comments mean a lot to me.

I introduce him to the signallers and he picks up on Private Cunliffe. Cunliffe was best mates with the fallen lads and has written a really nice eulogy. The brigadier has read all of the eulogies and remembers Cunliffe's. As Cunliffe starts to talk he begins to get upset. The brigadier gently leads him outside and sits there for an hour, talking to him.

I head round to the briefing area and have a chat with the two captains. They work in the brigade HQ and the brigadier thought it would be good for them to get out and see a FOB. They are nice guys.

'We are in awe of you and your company,' one of them suddenly says.

I am slightly taken aback, so I thank him.

'No really, we had no idea how bad things were in the FOB,' he replies.

It is good that they have come and seen it for themselves.

Before I head off to bed I have a chat with the brigadier. We decide that 4 Platoon will head back to Bastion for the 'ramp ceremony'. This is where the fallen are loaded on to the back of the aircraft for their flight back to the UK. I am pleased with that. It will be good for 4 Platoon to say goodbye to their friends. It also allows one of my platoons to recharge their batteries. Air conditioning, good food and showers will do them the world of good.

It does severely deplete my manpower, so we will have to throttle back while 4 Platoon are away. It is a small price to pay though and we could probably all do with a bit of a break.

WEDNESDAY 11 JUNE

I wake up feeling terrible, dehydrated and wrung out. I know that I am taking too much out of myself at the moment. I am driving myself on emotional energy and coffee. I have got to be the one that holds it together though – that is my responsibility as the company commander. Everyone under my command is more important than I am, so I have got to push myself on.

The brigadier has another walk around, chatting to as many people as possible. His visit has really helped.

Mid-morning we are told that helicopters are on their way, so the brigadier and 4 Platoon head down to the HLS. I walk down with Mark C-S to wave him off.

As I am standing there talking to him I start to feel really ill. I am pouring with sweat and my legs go weak. My vision starts to close in and I feel like I am going to collapse.

I can't collapse in front of the brigade commander so I make my excuses about needing to be in the command sangar as the helicopters approach and head back up the FOB.

By the time I get back to the briefing area I can hardly see. I find my camp cot by feel and collapse into it, sweat pouring off me. I feel terrible. I lie there gulping air and drinking water.

I hear the helicopters come and go and then the CSM comes to find me. He grabs Lance Corporal Horton, one of the medics, and they check me out. Heat injury seems to be the verdict. Relax in the shade and drink plenty of water is the remedy.

The CSM lets me know that there was a tonne of mail and goodies on the helicopter. There are a lot of fresh rations and other pieces of equipment we had indented for months ago. After the CO's and the brigade commander's visit, things are finally starting to happen.

The quartermaster has also sent a 'crash team'. Warrant Officer Zack Leong and a small crew have come to help the CSM sort out the sanitary conditions in the FOB. HQ have finally realised that there is only so much we can do with our limited resources.

I spend the rest of the day lying on my camp cot reading a book. The next few days are going to be all about rest and recuperation. I think we all need to recharge our batteries.

THURSDAY 12 JUNE

I wake up feeling like I have been run over. Headache, loose stomach and no energy. I take it easy all day. I either lie in bed reading or sit in the briefing area. I pop into the ops room but Brett has everything under control so I leave him to it.

The FOB is quiet. I think people are doing the same as I am; taking the time to relax and reflect.

I decide to start sleeping outside at night. A lot of people have dragged their camp cots outside. The temperature is hitting 48C by day and drops to about 25C at night, so the heat is relentless. The buildings retain the heat so it is nicer to get outside and get some fresh air. The downside is the sand and dust you ingest, especially if there is a breeze.

I position my camp cot outside and once it is dark I lie there staring at the stars. Afghanistan really does have the most amazing night sky. I find myself thinking about my hero, Winston Churchill, and what he would have done. He would have done what we are going to do. KBO. Keep Buggering On.

FRIDAY 13 JUNE

I wake up feeling much better. I can feel my strength returning. My stomach isn't quite right but I have got a lot more energy.

I wake up at 0400, just as dawn is starting to break. I lie in the relatively cool morning air taking time to think. I have a series of NLP mental exercises that I do, so I take my time to go through all of them. They involve anchoring and modelling excellence and I find it helps. I model excellence by mentally examining people that I find inspiring or who are experts in a particular field. I examine them in micro-detail, trying to ascertain the differences that make the difference. Once I have identified these subtle nuances I imagine myself 'in their shoes'. I imagine myself doing what they do, at the level they do it. My 'models' aren't anyone famous, they are a variety of people I have observed over time and have been impressed at the way they do something particular, such as how they communicate or project confidence.

I use anchoring for 'state management'. I mentally imagine a time where I am behaving in a certain way. A time where I made all the right decisions or a time I felt really calm and in control. I try to feel all aspects of that time – what I could see, hear, taste and feel. I then 'anchor' that emotion with a word or phrase and a unique physical gesture. The idea is that you 'fire' the anchor when you need it.

'Cool on da net' is a great example. I say this phrase and I instantly feel myself calming down.

I am convinced that my calm reactions on the ground the other day are due to the fact that I had mentally gone through 'crisis situations' and had already decided and rehearsed how I wanted to act.

At 0600 one of the signallers comes to find me with terrible news. Yesterday, C Company, 2 PARA, was ambushed while on foot patrol. It sounds like a close-in, well coordinated ambush involving small arms. Two soldiers were killed and their CSM was shot while courageously trying to get forward to CASEVAC the injured.

I just sit on my camp cot in shock. Another devastating blow for 2 PARA.

I go into the ops room to read the SITREP but there is no more detail than I have been told. Another incident within the brigade AO catches my eye. The CO of 5 Scots, Lieutenant Colonel David Richmond, has been shot in the leg during an operation in Musa Qala. I have worked with David Richmond in Northern Ireland and he is a fantastic guy. What a week 16 Air Assault Brigade is having. The poor brigade commander is spending the whole time flying around consoling units.

Further into the SITREP there is a glimmer of good news. An Afghan Police patrol in Lashkar Gah stopped a local when they noticed he had wires around his neck. When challenged, he tried to run off so he was shot. The police recovered an eight-kilo bomb belt comprising explosive and four kilos of steel ball bearings. Our incident, and the subsequent information from the brutal debrief we conducted, has meant that everyone in theatre has been made aware of the suicide bomber threat and their tactics. Our information is already saving lives. Another small consolation.

The cookhouse opens again after a very deep clean. I have porridge for breakfast and then soup and fresh bread for lunch. The fresh bread is amazing. I haven't tasted anything this good in weeks.

In the afternoon I receive a lovely long email from Jacko, the battalion 2IC. It really cheers me up and he has gone to a lot of effort to write such a long email. He talks of the company, leadership and decision-making and some nice viewpoints from the battalion HQ perspective. It is much appreciated.

SATURDAY 14 JUNE

I wake early after a pleasant sleep and go through my mental NLP programme.

I feel better enough to go to the gym. I know that I should probably take it easy but it is another way of clearing my mind. I head down to the gym and do some weights.

After a pleasant solar shower I go over to the cookhouse to have some breakfast. The food has drastically improved. We have a new head chef and, combined with the deep clean, things really are better. I have pancakes and some cereal which don't appear to have any adverse affect on my stomach.

I head to the ops room and write some reports. There is always some form of staff work to be done but I don't find that it is taking up too much time.

I spend the bulk of the afternoon reading and relaxing. I can feel my strength returning. I think the physical degradation has just ground me down. This is not the place to be unwell. You find yourself becoming hypersensitive to everything – especially the toilets! The place is unhygienic; there isn't much of a way round it, but it is improving. The toilets have been disinfected and coated with a new fly-killing paint which has really made a difference. You can't dress it up though, it is still a trench in the ground with a shed on top that 150 people use as a toilet every day. It would be more than 200 if the artillery and engineers didn't have their own.

I realise that we need to keep some form of patrol activity up, despite the lack of manpower. I have a chat with Sergeant Major Mitchell and Corporal Berenger and decide that we will send out a mobility patrol tomorrow. The plan will be to use the patrol to generate intelligence. Once we have enemy intelligence I will apply for a change in our rules of engagement that allows us to pre-engage (engage the enemy before he has engaged us) and then Corporal Berenger and the snipers will take over. If enemy are seen they will be taken out with .338 sniper rifles.

At 1820 hours everyone in the FOB, except those on sentry, gathers at the memorial. It is a very tasteful stone mound with a cross on top. On one side is a wooden panel with brass plaques on. Each plaque bears the name of each soldier who has been killed at FOB Inkerman.

We hold a small service to coincide with the ramp ceremony that is taking place back at Bastion. The service starts with the 105mm artillery guns firing illumination rounds. A short passage is read from the Bible, then I lead us in a prayer. We hold a two-minute silence before the guns fire again. It is incredibly sombre and, once finished, we all quietly drift off into the failing light. It was a small service but it felt appropriate.

Late in the evening we receive helicopters with more mail and fresh rations.

SUNDAY 15 JUNE

The mobility patrol heads off at 0400hrs. They head north up the desert for three kilometres then wait for first light. All of our intelligence assets are 'sniffing', waiting for the enemy to expose himself.

At first light the patrol spots the US Special Forces patrol just north of them so they sensibly pull back and relocate themselves near the power station. They find a good position of elevation and Corporal Berenger welds himself to his telescopic sight, willing an enemy to expose himself.

Typically, they don't. The patrol stays until 0700 but it generates very little intelligence, so I tell them to head back in.

We received sausages and bacon last night so breakfast is good. I then get handed a pile of mail that came in last night.

I head round to the briefing area and take my time with my mail, really savouring it. Mike Newman is having B Company T-shirts made for us and has sent me a prototype. They were devastated by our losses and wanted to send us all something, so they are having T-shirts made for all of us. It is very kind of them. He also sends me some very cool torches. There is a new one that is small enough to fit in your pocket. It has two settings, low and high. It is perfect for out here. You always need a torch on you because it is so dark at night.

Mike Malsz, a really good friend in the USA, has also sent me a parcel. He actually works for the torch company Surefire, so he has sent me another very cool torch and some magazines to read. I appreciate both Mikes looking out for me.

Early evening we have more helicopters to this location. Unfortunately we have to CASEVAC Private Beaumont. He is a new Tom who joined us out here and he is a cracking lad. He is six foot eight inches tall and a real grafter. He has struggled with the heat and collapsed with his second heat injury today. He is clearly in a bad way and I try to comfort him as he lies in the medical building shivering and pouring with sweat. Poor lad, he is really beating himself up about being sent back. There isn't much you can do about the heat though.

Beaumont is extracted and a second wave of helicopters arrive. They bring back 4 Platoon from Bastion and more mail and fresh rations. Captain Jon Little is also on board and has come for a visit. Jon is the mortar officer and currently works in battalion HQ. He is a really good guy. I have known him for years and consider him a friend, so it will be good to have him here for a while.

MONDAY 16 JUNE

I am up early. The FOB is continuing to return to normal, if there is a normal out here. I hang around the ops room just in case, as 5 Platoon is heading out on a local area clearance patrol.

I am in the briefing area reading a book when there is a big burst of fire from the front sangar and then an explosion. I grab my radio, stick my head round the door of the ops room and then head up to the front sangar.

Sergeant Major Mitchell is in the sangar and he gives me a quick update. As 5 Platoon is on the ground, the sangar has been on double manning. That means that each weapon system is manned and there are extra soldiers to observe the ground through binoculars. Mitch was looking through the binoculars at an area just outside Jusulay when he spotted three enemy arriving. They were only 150 metres from 5 Platoon. Mitch watched a heavy-set man in a light blue dishdash casually unfold the bipods on a PKM, lay out a belt of ammunition and set up to fire. Mitch put a burst of fire from the 40mm belt-fed grenade launcher straight on to him and Corporal Scott fired at the others with a GPMG. The heavy-set man was hit but as the others dropped down behind a wall. One of them fired an RPG at the FOB. The explosion was the RPG hitting the wall at the front of the FOB.

As I look through the 'ship's binos' I can see a head keeps popping up from behind a wall. Mitch tells me that the head belongs to the person with the RPG. We need to 'reach behind' the wall, so I call in 105mm artillery and 81mm mortar. After an initial adjustment we are right on it so I 'stonk' the area. This feels good, like punching back at the enemy and as I look back into the FOB from the sangar I can see a lot of Toms smiling as the guns and mortars fire.

Under cover of the artillery and mortars, 5 Platoon heads back in and they are all fine, which is a huge relief.

Mid-afternoon we have a UAV on station and Corporal Hickman sits outside in an old beach chair controlling. We identify six Taliban about four kilometres away. We can see their weapons, so I immediately call for permission to engage. We then go through an incredibly frustrating period which ends up with permission being denied. An hour later an Apache arrives but the enemy are long gone.

The CO rings and we have a good chat. He seems happier now and is pleased that the incident this morning went well.

Late afternoon the CSM comes to find me with a serious problem. The water pump is broken. We get all of our water from the well and the pump is essential. The engineers have tried to fix it but can't, so it will have to be sent back to Bastion. We have a small emergency pump that can cover us in the interim, but this will need to be resolved quickly.

Battalion HQ organise an emergency helicopter flight and the pump is sent back just after last light.

At 2230 I am woken up by a scream and a huge commotion. Mitch is rolling around shouting in his mozzie net. The CSM and I jump out of bed and try to help. Mitch is on the floor with his camp cot on top of him and all wrapped up in his mozzie net. We are desperately asking him what's wrong.

He tells us what happened. He had fallen asleep on his arm, which had gone dead. When he rolled over he smacked himself in the face with his dead arm. In his half sleep/dream he thought it was a rat on his face, so he grabbed 'the rat' – his dead hand – and threw it off as aggressively as he could. Thus launching himself out of bed, rolling his camp cot over and collapsing the mozzie net on top of himself.

The CSM and I are in hysterics. We are trying to help but we can't stop laughing. Eventually we free him. After that it takes me ages to get back to sleep.

TUESDAY 17 JUNE

It's great having Jon here. He is a good guy and it is great to catch up on all of the gossip. We are in such a bubble that I have no idea what everyone else is up to.

Jon attended a brigade conference before coming here and passes on that the brigade commander was singing B Company's praises. After his visit he told the whole conference what a great job B Company is doing considering the conditions we are living and operating in. I will make sure that this is passed on to the lads.

Today's challenge is the water pump. The main pump we sent back on last night's flight has, amazingly, now been lost. The small emergency pump can provide 5000 litres a day, which is only enough for drinking. When the cookhouse is open and there is no restriction on water usage, the FOB consumes on average twice that – 10000 litres a day.

The consequences are severe and if the emergency pump goes down they will have to fly water in every day. This is so serious that I am sure that it will all get sorted out quickly.

At 1900hrs Sergeant Radcliffe comes to see me. We have a local 'informant' who has been coming to the FOB at night over the past couple of weeks. 'Faisal' lives near the FOB. I have been introduced to him and he strikes me as one of life's great survivors. He helped the Soviets, he helped the Taliban and now he is helping us. He refuses to accept payment and never fully explains what his motivations are.

'Faisal' has told Sergeant Radcliffe that yesterday's contact killed two and injured two. They were all Taliban. This is good news. He then said that he had seen the suicide bomber in Star Wars village the week before. No one recognised him – meaning he was not from this area – and no one knew what he was up to. This is all useful intelligence that Sergeant Radcliffe sends on to our HQ.

I then have a final chat with Sergeant Robertson and Corporal Berenger. We are sending out a night patrol: 6

Platoon will escort the snipers out and then provide protection. The snipers will observe enemy transit routes and if the opportunity arises 'neutralise' any enemy. Sergeant Robertson is taking the patrol as Dave, the platoon commander, is down with D&V.

They are both happy and we run through some scenarios just to make sure that we have covered likely courses of action. I then watch them head off. I go into the ops room and stay there for two hours, listening to their sitreps. It is a professionally run patrol and once I am happy, I decide to leave them to it.

WEDNESDAY 18 JUNE

I have an amazing experience this morning ... I wake in the small hours feeling cold. It was wonderful; I haven't felt cold since I left the UK. I have to wrap myself in my sleeping bag but I don't really get back off to sleep. In the end I get up. I tuck myself in the company office with a cup of coffee and write a set of orders for a patrol that I am planning for tomorrow.

It will be big – two platoons, FSG, mobile FSG and the Vikings. The battle group is now switching its focus north to put pressure on the enemy grouping near Putay. Intelligence has found that the Taliban pretty much live in Putay and come down here to conduct operations. We want to put them under pressure, to remove their freedom of manoeuvre. This will be the biggest foot patrol we have done into a known enemy area. It is also a chance to really start taking the fight to the enemy.

Sergeant Robertson comes round after breakfast and

back-briefs me on last night's patrol. It was well run but nothing came of it. There was virtually no movement in the small hours so they headed back in. It was a good patrol and a good concept but we will need to refine this in the future.

I deliver my orders at 1000. There is a real buzz and I think everyone picks up on the size of the patrol and where we are going. You can tell everyone is keen to get out there and show the enemy who is in charge round here.

Sad news filters in over the afternoon. Four service personnel have been killed. Their vehicle hit an IED. The deaths include the first British woman soldier killed in Afghanistan. More bad news for 16 Air Assault Brigade, during a very hard two weeks. The poor brigade commander, more consoling visits to make.

After this I decide to go to bed early to get as much sleep as possible.

THURSDAY 19 JUNE

I am up at 0020 hours, which is horrible. I was having a good sleep. We get ourselves sorted and things are running well. Everyone is good to go on time and we head out at 0100.

We depart out of the bottom gate and move north up the desert. The idea is to stay out of the green zone in order to make navigation easier. It is easy going and with the NVGs we can see for miles. We make really good time, far better than I thought we would, so after four kilometres I call a halt and we have a forty-minute rest.

At 0300 we push on, with 5 Platoon leading. We make a left hook into an area designated KB8. We are about five kilometres from Putay and pushing into an area that hasn't been cleared before. I leave the mobile FSG out in the desert on the high ground. The elevation is perfect and, if needs be, they can provide a fire support base for us to work back to.

We push two kilometres into the green zone and then go firm. It is eerie at night, even with NVGs and an assault rifle.

At first light both the foot and mobile elements get spotted but it takes the enemy a long time to work out that they are talking about two separate organisations. This works in our favour in the green zone and we continue to sweep forward, making it harder for them to attack us.

We then receive intelligence that the enemy have worked things out. They are going to attack the foot call-sign.

We are now moving in a sweep back towards the FOB but we are a long way from home, about five kilometres. We manage to bump into two locals and have a chat with them. They are fairly indifferent and not very chatty.

As we move into the next sector the atmospherics changes immediately. The locals are sprinting out of the area in a sense of panic. The enemy are obviously out there and the locals don't want to get caught in the middle.

Reacting to this change in behaviour, 5 Platoon alters its posture, going firm and moving into cover.

This turns out to be fortuitous as, seconds later, the world in front of us erupts in small-arms fire. The weight of fire that comes at us is massive. The enemy have managed to put in an L-shaped ambush, meaning that we are taking fire from the front and the right flank. But 5 Platoon is a seasoned crew and they put down a huge weight of return fire. The point section is pinned down with PKM fire and our right flank is being hammered by PKM and AK-47. We are all under fire and the lead section is in a particularly precarious situation.

I start to move forward to get a better understanding of what is going on. I want to use artillery and mortars but the enemy are close – no more than 120 metres away, so I need to know where everyone is.

I come to the back of 5 Platoon and get directed forward to a tree-line. The lads are in a line behind a bank hammering away with rifles and machine guns. I find Wes and we quickly come up with a plan. Mortars on the enemy to the front and artillery on the flank.

The mortars go in first and this allows the lead section to break contact and get back to the rest of us.

We put a massive volley of artillery off to the right flank and I am in a perfect position to watch the 105mm high-explosive shells slam into the enemy position.

'That should do it,' I think to myself. As the fire mission finishes we all watch the dust settle to our front. There is no way anyone could have survived that.

Suddenly all the fire starts again. PKM rounds slam into the tree that myself and Lance Corporal Barker are sheltering behind. We collapse like dropped wetsuits. Wes starts rapidly checking himself for any hits, it is that close. I am in the process of telling the FOO to repeat the fire mission when the shout 'Man down' goes off in front of me. Someone has been hit.

Corporal Philip, a sniper, had knelt up to fire. He had just squeezed off a shot with the sniper rifle, taking a Taliban's head off with the .338 round, when he was shot in the shin.

I am just starting to work out a plan when Sergeant Marshall, the 5 Platoon sergeant, steps in. He has a great physical presence; he just walks forward and calls for rapid fire. Everyone starts putting a heavy weight down at the enemy. Two Toms then drag Corporal Philip back to Sergeant Marshall, who is now organising the CASEVC.

This is a nightmare. In the good old days someone would run forward, throw the casualty over their shoulder and run off with them. Now that we are all wearing 40kgs of kit no one is running anywhere. To carry one soldier out takes eight other soldiers. We need to take the casualty and all of his kit.

I pull back and talk to the CSM. His job is to organise the CASEVAC, my job is to make sure there is the security for it.

The casualty is taken by 4 Platoon, who also provide their own security. Now that we have a casualty I ramp up the mortars and artillery – I don't want anyone following us. I then leapfrog 5 Platoon back under the cover of a smoke-screen from the mortars.

The CASEVAC is brutal on the guys having to do the carrying. Four men carry the stretcher, four men are on standby to take over.

Fortunately the enemy doesn't seem to be trying to follow us and it all goes quiet. I call for James and the Viking troop to meet us at the power station – it is the closest easy-to-identify building.

An F-16 fighter jet arrives and offers assistance and after a few circuits he can't see any enemy. I am hoping that the presence of the fighter jet will dissuade the enemy from following up.

The mobile FSG are still on the high ground and they see two Taliban wheeling their own casualties away in wheelbarrows. The CSM and I think this is a great idea – much better than a stretcher.

We meet up with the Vikings and we all clamber on board. We have to race back as the MERT (Medical Emergency Response Team) Chinook is on its way.

We screech to a halt on the HLS and get Corporal Philip out. We are just in time, as the Chinook is approaching.

I quickly speak to Corporal Philip. He is high as a kite on morphine but really pleased with his confirmed kills – he got two today.

The Chinook lifts off and we all head in. I look at my watch and realise it isn't even lunchtime yet. What a morning.

The company is in good spirits despite the casualty. It was hairy out there today. We were firmly in an ambush, which is not a good place to be.

We get two pieces of good news in the evening. Corporal Philip is fine. The bullet passed through his shin and hasn't done too much damage. 'Faisal', the local informant, arrives and tells us that we killed three enemy and injured two. The enemy wounded tallies with the enemy in wheelbarrows the FSG saw. We are pretty pleased with this. It is an interesting area with a lot of enemy in it. Despite Corporal Philip getting injured, the lads feel it was a good patrol today. I have to agree.

FRIDAY 20 JUNE

The D&V is on the increase again which is hugely frustrating. We are doing all we can but we just can't get it under control. The FOB is just dirty and unhygienic.

Late afternoon I get a message to ring Jacko, the BG 2IC. He is quite upbeat. There is a whole troop of Royal Engineers earmarked to come to the FOB to make infrastructure improvements. He is sympathetic about the situation and tells me to just concentrate on my mission, don't worry about 'the other stuff'. This cheers me up.

Just before bed I am sitting with the two sergeant majors having a good chat. The CSM is shattered; he spends every waking hour trying to sort out the D&V problem. A few patrols in the green zone, wading through drainage ditches that the locals use as toilets is enough to challenge anyone's immune system.

At 2200 a flight arrives bringing more fresh food and lads who have just returned from R&R. They look relaxed and raring to go. Even better news for the rest of us, a replacement water pump is on board.

SATURDAY 21 JUNE

A local clearance patrol is mounted by 5 Platoon, which passes off without incident.

Morale in the FOB seems sky high at the moment. As I wander around I keep spotting random outbreaks of happiness. I am pleased that the pressure from HQ is not filtering past me and the CSM.

I wander to the toilets and I hear a cheer go up from 7 RHA's area. They are playing cricket and all enjoying themselves.

I can see clusters of Toms dotted all over the place and they are chatting and smiling. This all cheers me up. B Company is a fantastic company with an impressive heritage. And the engineers have the water pump working, so I can now stop worrying about water rationing.

*

We hit a low two weeks ago, physically, mentally and emotionally. That all seems like a long time ago. Two weeks is a long time round these parts. We have all had to compartmentalise and I think we realise that we owe it to the fallen to do our job and do it to the best of our ability. We have got to carry on and save our grieving until we get home.

Fresh food, health and hygiene improvements and a relaxed atmosphere has sorted us all out. I realise more and more that you can't look up for inspiration and motivation; you have to look down. The smile on a Tom's face when you stop and chat to him is all I need to cheer myself up. I feel that all of these experiences are making me stronger. My ability to problem solve and get to the nub of an issue is getting better with each day that goes by. There will be further challenges but we all know there is no way they will break us.

I spend the bulk of the afternoon in the ops room. We have just received orders for another big battle group operation in the vicinity of Putay. Op Ghartse Talander (Op GT) is due to take place in a couple of days' time and sees us returning up to KB1– where Corporal Philip was shot. Odds are this will involve some serious contacts, as there are a lot of enemy up there.

I back-brief the CO on my initial plan before carrying on with other staff work. There is a new tool for measuring effect. Each patrol now has to generate a convergence model that measures security, governance, narcotics, Afghan Security forces, local nationals and influence, for any area it visits and overlay this information on an electronic map. I then write an assessment for my whole AO. This is a pretty good tool and I am impressed with the thought that has gone into it.

SUNDAY 22 JUNE

An 'equipment care' day. The term 'rest day' was getting pounced on when I produced a patrol programme so now we call them 'equipment care' days. It allows us to carry out 'essential maintenance'.

I spend most of the day working on my plan and orders for Op GT. Having recently been up to this area I can anticipate the scale of contact we are going to get into and I want to make sure my plan is as swept up as I can make it.

In the evening I borrow Lance Corporal Barker's laptop and start watching *Deadwood*. I haven't been watching many films and I like the idea of getting into a series. *Deadwood* seems perfect for my viewing tastes at the moment. It's an easy series to get into and paints a tough, gritty picture of frontier life. Hard men, doing a tough job, in challenging conditions. Sounds familiar.

MONDAY 23 JUNE

I get up early with good gym intentions. I head down to the gym and do a set of pull-ups. My right bicep is on fire and I think I might be overdoing it, so I head up to the ops room and make myself a cup of coffee instead.

This turns out to be fortuitous as 6 Platoon is out conducting a local area security patrol. I am just having a chat with one of the signallers when the quiet is shattered by a large exchange of gunfire; only 700m from the FOB, they have been ambushed. They were ready for it, though. They had seen people that just didn't look like local farmers.

They saw a man in brown clothing, short beard and a black turban – the preferred dress of the Taliban.

The enemy has set up on the far belt of compounds and is firing at 6 Platoon, which is among the parallel belt of compounds a hundred metres away from them.

The platoon reacts quickly to the contact and by the time I am in the front sangar they have identified the firing point. I organise artillery on to the enemy and use the mortars to lay down a smokescreen to allow 6 Platoon to start extracting. The platoons are under instruction to pull back from these contacts in case it is a 'come on' into something bigger. When the company is on the ground we always follow up as we have the manpower and assets to take on a much larger enemy force.

Yet again the enemy try to flank the withdrawing platoon and walk straight into the arcs of 6 Platoon's highly successful gun group. Two enemy are cut down by GPMG fire.

The platoon all make it back in unscathed. They are all sweating and breathing hard but smiling.

I am chatting to some corporals from 6 Platoon when multiple bursts of PKM fire start sailing over the FOB. We haven't had them fire machine guns at the FOB before and it all seems a bit random. We are well protected behind the blast walls and the fire is just passing harmlessly overhead. Even the enemy are confused by this. We quickly pick up intelligence that they have no idea who is doing what to whom. Probably a young fighter firing off his ammunition so he can return to his commander and tell him how many infidels he has killed today. We leave him to it.

In the afternoon a helicopter arrives with the regimental sergeant major (RSM) and a work party. RSM Hobbins is the most senior NCO in the battalion and he is a legend. Humble, polite, hard working and intelligent, he is a perfect RSM. He is going to help us start the improvements to the FOB prior to the engineer troop arriving.

In the afternoon I deliver my orders for tomorrow's patrol, which will be our contribution to Op GT. We will conduct a large patrol up into KB1, just south of Putay. C Company and battle group HQ will be inserted by helicopter in the desert to the east of Putay then push into the village itself. This combined activity will squeeze the enemy and let him know that we aren't afraid to go into his 'backyard'. C Company will also target some of the narcotics facilities that are known to exist in Putay.

The RSM listens to my orders then approaches me afterwards. He politely asks if he can join the patrol tomorrow.

'Please do' is my obvious answer. It will be good to have him out with us. I let him know he can go with whoever he likes. He decides to go with the CSM, as they are mates.

TUESDAY 24 JUNE

I am up at 0220hrs after a decent sleep. I drink a bottle of warm chlorinated water, eat a three-pack of biscuits then get all of my gear on. Before I know it, it is 0300 and time to leave.

We depart out of the back gate with 5 Platoon leading, followed by TAC then a significantly beefed-up FSG commanded by Sergeant Major Mitchell. The CSM's group brings up the rear with the RSM and his work party tagging along. This gives me 80 people on the ground. There are nine GPMGs in the FSG giving me a significant amount of firepower.

I deploy a mobile element as well. Four Land Rovers will stay on the high ground in the desert and provide fire support and assistance with communications.

We move straight up the desert and again make good time. At the second large wadi, four kilometres north of the FOB, we hook left and follow it straight into the green zone. Wes has done a great job leading us out and by 0415 we are deep into the green zone. I call a halt and give everyone a half-hour break. This allows us time to remove our night sights and have a snack. In my case, more biscuits.

We push on into KB1. It seems even more eerie than last time as there are hardly any locals. Wes sees the odd one fleeing and lets me know but apart from that it is like a ghost town. I am struck again by how affluent it appears – nice compounds and very well-kept gardens.

The mobile call-sign starts to feed us intelligence they have been receiving. The enemy know we are here and are pulling together an attack. So far they have 20 fighters and they plan to break down into pairs and attack us on multiple fronts.

We continue conducting our sweep but slow it down so that we can be more methodical.

The constant trickle of intelligence starts to become frustrating. I hit a point where I want the enemy to just get on with it. I call a five-minute halt to have a breather. We have achieved the first part of our mission – clear KB1. The next part is to sweep back through the green zone, paralleling the river Helmand, targeting known enemy transit routes that are in the area.

After a break we push on with 5 Platoon still leading and the company now spread out over 600m, weaving its way around compounds. The ground is starting to become more open and interspersed, so we have to be careful not to become too bunched up.

I let the gap between 5 Platoon and my group open up as they are now in a low wheat field. I have just crossed a drainage ditch when I get a message saying that the enemy attack is imminent. The FSG is in an L-shape behind me, due to the nature of the compounds.

The contact starts from the rear: a small group of enemy fire PKM and AK-47 at the FSG. They get a huge weight of return fire sent back at them from the GPMGs, which shocks them.

I start to head back to get a better feel for what is going on behind me, when a huge exchange of gunfire starts in front of me – 5 Platoon is now in contact.

I am getting bombarded with information on my radio from 5 Platoon and the FSG as to what they have got going on. I am furiously multitasking. I have the information coming over the radio, I have my map out and I am trying to work out the best place for my group.

Suddenly, an RPG and PKM fires at TAC from our left flank. The enemy are 75m away and we can see them bobbing up and down behind a broken-down wall. We all drop into a tiny drainage ditch and try to hug the ground. I am so low that I have my cheek on the ground as I try to read my map. Decision made though – we will stay here.

TAC is 15-strong so everyone starts firing to suppress the immediate threat to our left. I now have contacts on three fronts and the amount of fire being exchanged in all directions is huge. It is so noisy we all have to shout. Lance Corporal Barker keeps monitoring the company net and providing me protection while the FOO, MFC and I start to coordinate the heavier assets. I can just see Sergeant Major Mitchell and he seems to be getting on all right. I call artillery on to his enemy and mortars on to the enemy in front of 5 Platoon. The enemy off to my left seem to be losing interest so I am happy that they are suppressed with rifles and 40mm grenades.

After the initial crump of artillery goes in Mitch tells me it is spot on. We repeat the fire mission and then receive intelligence that it has worked – the fire has landed straight on top of that enemy.

We seem to be getting the upper hand and I am keen to follow up this attack. I bring the FSG forward and get them to quickly relieve 5 Platoon. The FSG will continue to suppress the enemy while 5 Platoon put in a left flanking attack.

Once 5 Platoon are relieved I brief up Wes, then we all move off – 5 Platoon leading and TAC just behind. Flanking left allows us to hug a tree-line that runs in an oblique angle to our front that leads up to the set of three compounds that the enemy are occupying.

We move off and it all goes quiet. Wes asks me if he can clear the compounds in 'condition red'. This means that they will throw hand grenades in and follow up with bursts of fire as they enter.

I give him permission and they quickly sweep through the first two compounds.

I stay back in a ditch a hundred metres away watching the clearance, chatting to Lance Corporal Barker. Wes tells me that the first two compounds are empty. I can't see the point of doing 'condition red' any more, so I tell him to enter the third compound normally. What a decision that turns out to be.

As 5 Platoon enters the third compound they find three women and ten children all clustered together. 'Condition red' would have been a disaster.

Lance Corporal Barker and I just look at each other. I have no idea where that decision came from, but thank the Lord I made it. Wes was sound to want to enter in 'red'; I just thought it was a waste of hand grenades.

It has all gone quiet, so I think it is time to head off. I am just pulling my group back when a shout goes up. One of the interpreters has overheard the women talking about an enemy body. They are vague but tell us that the enemy are in two compounds to our north-west, on the banks of the Helmand river. We have swept by these compounds but not cleared them.

In all honesty it is going well today. Everyone is performing, so I think to myself 'what the hell'. Let's go and get them.

The FSG can still cover this move so I leave them where they are and push 5 Platoon on.

The platoon enters the first compound and sets up fire support to clear the second compound. My group is now 200 metres back with nothing but open ground between us.

I decide to move TAC forward and we start jogging over the open ground. I say jogging, but with all our kit on I doubt it is as fast as that.

The quiet is shattered as it all opens up again with gunfire.

This time the enemy have got it together. There are at least five firing points in a 180-degree arc to our front and fire is coming at 5 Platoon and my group from all directions.

TAC is committed, so I just speed up and start running for my life. Another two firing points open up at us and I can feel the rounds whizzing by me and hear them zip as they pass by my head. Bullets are impacting all around us.

This is hard work. Running with all of the kit on is a nightmare and I can feel how slowly I am going. Rounds are cracking over head and my mind starts to wonder what it is going to feel like being shot. I can sense my entire body and I am waiting for a nerve ending to register a small lump of lead travelling at supersonic speed slamming into me.

I see a drainage ditch to my front and keep heading for that. Suddenly I am there and I jump in up to my waist in murky, muddy water. The ever-present Lance Corporal Barker crashes in behind me and we both start firing at one of the enemy firing points, desperately trying to help the remaining 14 people that have followed me. One by one they dive in to the ditch. Thorburn – a hilarious Scottish signaller – does a full-on dive into the ditch and completely disappears under water.

He bursts back on to the surface chanting, 'Fuck me, fuck me, fuck me' – he is clearly not impressed.

Miraculously we all make it. I can't believe no one got hit.

I push on to the compound that 5 Platoon are in and we find the enemy body. There is blood everywhere. Wes points out the arc of firing points to his front and I realise that enough is enough for today. I am also struck by how stunning and inviting the river Helmand looks. We haven't been this close before – it is only a couple of hundred metres away. I would love to strip off and go for a swim.

I call the FOO and MFC up and they start a massive barrage to our front. They mix smoke in to cover our extraction and the whole scene starts to look like something from the Second World War. It is a very large barrage and as the rounds whistle overhead we pull back to the FSG. The barrage is obviously working, as we manage to pull back without any fire coming at us.

Once we link up with the FSG we head back to the FOB.

We are in by 0945. A six-hour forty-five-minute patrol with a two-hour contact. We are all shattered but elated. Morale is sky high. This was a huge contact with multiple firing points, AK-47, PKM, RPG fire in all directions. Contact on three fronts, rounds cracking overhead, mad dashes over open ground, heavy artillery barrages. This was a traditional 'infantry' battle and everyone has done a fantastic job.

I am relaxing in the briefing area with the sergeant majors after my solar shower when I am summoned to the ops room. HQ rings with bad news. C Company is still in a huge contact up near Putay. During the initial insertion a sergeant major was killed while trying to get forward and take the fight to the enemy. He was Mitch's best friend. They have let me know so that I can tell him.

I compose myself and head back to the briefing area. Mitch is chatting with the CSM. I realise that the only way to do this is just to tell him.

'Mitch, I'm so sorry to have to tell you this but I am afraid that your best friend was killed this morning on C Company's assault,' I say to him.

He just looks at me with a blank look on his face. They have been best friends for years.

I repeat what I have said.

He just looks back at me and says, 'Thanks for letting me know'. He grabs his cigarettes and starts to walk off.

'Are you going to be all right?' I ask him.

'I'll be fine,' he says and heads off.

I find the RSM and let him know what has happened. He is devastated; the sergeant major was one of his mess members and a friend.

We all agree to give Mitch a little space – not that it is easy to find personal space within the FOB.

Mitch spends most of the day smoking and getting his head round what has happened.

That night, just before bed, I have another chat with him. He is dealing with this incredibly well. The only thing he can't get his head around is the fact that he will never see his best friend again. I try to help but what do you say to a man who has lost his best friend? Another terrible blow for 2 PARA.

We are expecting Op Loam tonight so I deploy 6 Platoon to secure the Jusulay track junction. They head out just before last light and go through what is now a set routine. They secure the junction and stop all of the traffic. The light is just starting to fade as the 9 Squadron lads clear the junction, looking for mines. The traffic backs up in all directions as the 611 is quite busy at this time of night.

For some unknown reason a white pickup truck pulls round the stationary traffic and drives straight at the vehicle checkpoint. The section conducting the block starts shouting and gesticulating widely. The truck speeds up and puts on its high beams. Warning shots are fired but still it keeps coming. The lads have no other option. We have received intelligence that the enemy are going to target the patrol and this looks exactly like a vehicle-borne IED.

The section commander screams out the command and the gun group opens fire, as do the lads on the road. The vehicle is raked with fire from the GPMG and rifles and crunches to a halt 30m in front of them. Two Toms cautiously approach, expecting the vehicle to explode at any minute. As they look into the cab the horrible reality sinks in. The vehicle is full of civilians – one old man, two men and a child. All four are hit.

Immediately the shout for the medic goes up and Sergeant Robertson sends a sitrep to the ops room. Brett and I make some quick decisions. We deploy the FSG in the vehicles to collect the casualties, call for the MERT and send all of the medics and the doctor down to the back gate to receive the casualties. Once all of this is in motion I head down to the back gate to see how bad things are.

Things aren't as bad as they could be. All four locals are hit but they are stable and their injuries aren't life-threatening. Within twenty minutes the Chinook arrives and the casualties are whisked off to the hospital.

TUESDAY 24 JUNE

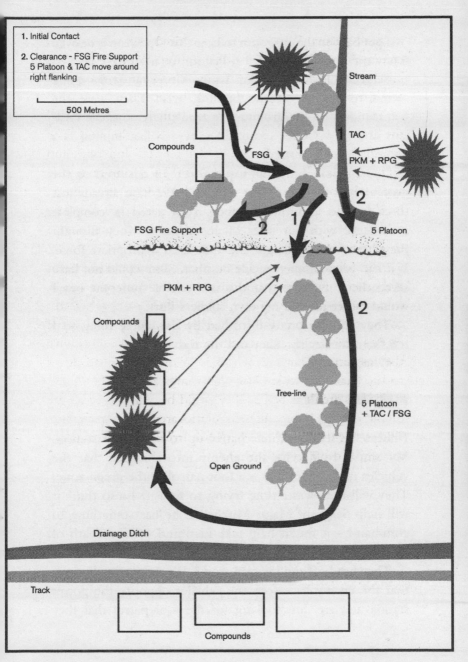

I get back to the ops room to hear that Op Loam is delayed for twenty-four hours. I tell 6 Platoon to head back in.

Sergeant Robertson and Lance Corporal Jenks come round to see me at the briefing area. They were the commanders on the ground. We aren't here to shoot civilians and in a COIN campaign every civilian injured is a potential enemy created.

It is a shame, but I can't question their decisions on the ground, and they made the right call. We have already lost three lads to a suicide bomber. They acted in complete accordance with our rules of engagement. They thought their lives were in danger and they used appropriate force. If it had been another suicide bomber, 30m would not have saved them. I realise that this is a terrible outcome but I would rather not see my own soldiers hurt.

They are also pretty disturbed by the whole thing so I tell them the reality. They did the right thing.

What a day.

WEDNESDAY 25 JUNE

I decide to send a mobile patrol up to the power station. My aim is to deceive the enemy into thinking that the vehicles mean that there is a foot patrol in the green zone. They will then waste time trying to find it. I also think it will help Sergeant Major Mitchell if he has something to command – it might help take his mind off the death of his best friend.

They head off and my plan works. We receive intelligence that the enemy have seen the vehicles opposite the power station and are now looking for the foot patrol that they 'know' is there. I am really pleased with this – it's only little but it's nice to come up with good ideas that work. Mitch seems to appreciate the distraction as well.

The rest of the day is taken up with FOB improvement. The delay in Op Loam has given us some time to play with and the CSM gets everyone going on tasks.

There is a lot of legacy detritus round the FOB – old sandbags, transit cases, rubbish etc. The FOB will always be dirty, due to the dust and sand, but it is amazing the difference a concentrated effort makes. Rubbish is burned, the briefing area is rebuilt, the cookhouse is deep cleaned, the toilets and the burn pit are moved.

This is all down to resources. If you have more resources – be it manpower or equipment – you can do more. The new fly-killer paint has made a huge difference. There are now lots of washbowls so people can clean their kit. We are also getting more fresh food, so at least people can build themselves up. They are only small things but they all help.

'Faisal' arrives once it is dark with a present for the 'commander'. I am summoned by Sergeant Radcliffe and presented with a live goat. This is a huge honour and I am grateful for the present although not really sure what I am going to do with it. Word spreads quickly and Private Biddulph from the mortar platoon comes to find me to ask if he can look after it. As he is a mortar man, I have all sorts of concerns about what he wants to do with it, but he assures me he likes animals. We decide to keep the goat in the deserted ANA compound and fatten him up for a barbecue.

THURSDAY 26 JUNE

The FOB is still a hive of activity. The CSM has got every spare person working. I spend the bulk of the morning in the ops room as I have my weekly assessment to write.

Op Loam is due to arrive tonight and I am going to use 5 Platoon to secure the track junction. I have a good chat with Wes. After the last incident I want to make sure that he is happy. He is, and they depart at 1830.

It would appear that there are more enemy in the area and, at 1850, 5 Platoon come under fire. It is only an AK-47 but the fire is quite accurate.

I head up to the front sangar and the enemy firing point is quickly identified through the 'ship's binos'. We need to deal with this quickly as the Loam convoy is on its way.

The lads start engaging with 40mm grenade launcher, .50cal and GPMG. I can clearly see the firing point so I order a small burst of artillery fire straight on to it. This does the job and we also notice a secondary explosion – this would indicate that the enemy had something else with them that has now exploded. I make a mental note of this and decide that we will go and check this out on our next patrol.

The securing of the track junction continues and there are no further incidents.

The Op Loam convoy rolls into the FOB at 2300. A bit later than planned, but fair one. I would not want to do their job. It's crazy – soldiers have to risk their lives driving plastic washing bowls and ration packs around this country because we don't have enough helicopters.

Op Loam quickly drops off seven full shipping containers, picks up our empty ones and heads straight off. They want to get out into the desert while it is still dark. By midnight, 5 Platoon is back in.

FRIDAY 27 JUNE

Due to the influx of stores from Op Loam everyone is busy again. There is a lot to be sorted out. There are a lot of construction stores that will be utilised by the engineer construction troop – their first task is to build a new kitchen and cookhouse. There are a lot of rations to be organised. They need to be rotated so that we use the oldest ones first. This entails the CSM and a work party getting 200 or so boxes of ten-man rations laid out on the floor and restacked in order. This takes most of the day.

The day remains quiet. It is the repatriation of the sergeant major today so a lot of the key personnel from HQ will be back at Bastion organising it. Poor Mitch – he doesn't look well at all, he is skinny and run down. What an awful day he must be having.

SATURDAY 28 JUNE

A Chinook flight arrives early morning. It drops off lads who have just returned from R&R and a lot of mail. It also brings in a military policeman from Special Investigations Branch (SIB) who is here to gather all the facts about the loss of the three lads. No one is looking forward to their interview but it has to be done for the coroner.

We also send out another group of people who are off on their R&R. Brett departs for his ten days off and David from 4 Platoon will stand in for him, leaving Sergeant Sykes to command the platoon. R&R puts a serious strain on available manpower but I think everyone needs a break from this. Brett's departure is one of my mental 'waypoints'. His R&R is before mine. His departure means that my R&R isn't that far away.

At 1400 I have my interview with SIB. It is horrible. I have compartmentalised this and I find it really uncomfortable going through it all again in fine detail. I can picture the whole scene in such clarity that I know why I don't want to go back there. It is a grim couple of hours. I understand the necessity but it leaves me feeling terrible.

I use this week's minutes on the sat phone and ring Andrea. This really cheers me up. It is just wonderful to hear her voice. She has been to Gamble's funeral and passed on a personal message to his parents from me. Andrea reassures me that they really feel part of the regiment and they are being well looked after. I find this comforting.

SUNDAY 29 JUNE

I send out 6 Platoon on a local clearance patrol. They do a sweep in front of the FOB, working their way through the unoccupied compounds 700m in front of the FOB before pushing back through Star Wars village. They generate some intelligence, but nothing happens.

I deliver a set of orders for a company-level patrol tomorrow. I haven't been out for a while due to the platoon-level activity and Op Loam.

Faisal came in last night and told us that the Taliban have taken over some compounds in an area we designate JA3. This area is right on the bank of the river Helmand and is one of the known enemy transit routes. It is 5km north-east of the FOB at the extent of the green zone. The Taliban are now living in these compounds and using them as a base from which to mount attacks on us. I have wanted to go up there for a while and this now seems a good time to go and have a look.

Late afternoon I am in the briefing area and Frank – the Dutch exchange officer – is throwing a small tantrum. Some of his socks have gone missing and he is cursing away to himself and trying to convince the CSM to do something.

I am trying to tune this out when Biddulph, the 'goat orderly', comes to see me. The goat is gone. He has no idea how but the goat has got out from the compound he was locked in. He isn't in the FOB so he must have got over an external wall. The CSM and I start having some fun with Frank. Maybe the goat stole his socks? The goat was clearly a Taliban sympathiser as he stole the socks and ran off. This gets Frank even more wound up.

I decide to include the sock/goat saga in my evening sitrep to HQ. I write that everyone should keep their eyes peeled for a goat wearing Dutch Army-issue socks as he is a potential Taliban sympathiser. HQ loves the story as well. Frank is even more unimpressed and goes off to sulk in a corner.

MONDAY 30 JUNE

I am up at 0445 and sort myself out. Normal routine – a cup of tea and a three-pack of biscuits. I never fancy eating too much before we go out. I'm not sure if it is nerves or just the fact that I don't like eating this early.

We depart at 0530, 5 Platoon followed by my group heading straight out of the front gate, over the 611 and into the green zone while 4 Platoon leave via 7 RHA gate, work through the Star Wars village and then cross into the green zone 300m west of us. I am trying to create a confusing picture for the enemy so they can't work out how many of us there are and – more importantly – where we are. I am hoping that the enemy haven't spotted all of us and walk into one of the other call-signs.

We advance 'two up'. This is both platoons advancing in parallel, about 300m apart. This creates quite a lot of mass in a small space.

We start to receive intelligence that the enemy is confused. He has seen us but can't work out how many of us there are. The intelligence feed continues to build and it is obvious there are a lot of enemy out there and they are close. It is quiet; there are no locals around, which is always a strong indicator that the enemy are here.

We are making good progress, covering a lot of ground in the early-morning light. We are four kilometres away from the FOB and nearly at our objective. I switch back to 'one up' by bringing 4 Platoon back behind my group. The 'two up' has achieved its aim – the enemy think that there are two separate patrols out.

As 5 Platoon continues its advance the silence is shattered by a massive weight of enemy fire. There are numerous PKMs firing and I count five RPG explosions almost straight away.

Wes sends a quick situation report. His lead section had just started to cross a piece of open ground when it came under a massive weight of fire. They are now stuck out in the open ground, pinned down by enemy fire. The second section have responded well, taking immediate cover in a canal and returning fire. Corporal Berenger is with 5 Platoon and he is doing a great job coordinating the return fire.

The problem is that the lead section is stuck out in the open with a massive gunfight taking place above them. They are all laid on the ground – they can't even lift their heads up for fear of being hit. The enemy knows that they are there and are pouring fire down on them.

I need to get forward as quickly as possible as the situation is so confusing. I lead off and TAC follows. I come to a compound that is between us and the contact and find a rat run – a small hole leading out of the back of the compound. At this stage I am just following the sound of the guns so I stick my head through and I find myself directly behind the second section in the canal. I clamber through and jump into the canal, TAC following on. Fortunately Corporal Berenger is there and he gives me a quick and accurate update.

I tell Wes to start pushing left, ready to put in a flanking attack while getting the CSM to bring up the FSG and snipers off to the right flank. They will provide fire support. Concurrently I get the artillery and mortars to start firing on the enemy positions.

As is often the case, the enemy have the upper hand until we can get all of our assets into place. Within minutes I have the FSG hammering away at them and two minutes later artillery and mortars start crashing in.

The lead section commander makes a bold call and starts his extraction as soon as all of the fire is going in.

The lads suddenly burst into view, sprinting towards us and crash into the canal just to the right. They look in shock and they can't believe no one is hit. I give them a minute to sort themselves out while telling Wes to start pushing left and start his attack – I want to cut the enemy off.

As soon as 5 Platoon moves round, the enemy is on the run. The lads keep them under pressure and can see them fleeing.

I decide to push on, switching 4 Platoon up front. I want to keep the pressure on the enemy.

Poor old 5 Platoon. We have been moving for ten minutes when we get a contact at the rear, once again on 5 Platoon. An RPG comes sailing overhead and then a big burst of PKM fire. It is all fairly wild and I assume that the enemy are trying to bait us into giving away our positions. Only one GPMG responds, which I think shows good fire discipline.

I realise that the enemy are trying to set up ambushes in front of us depending on our direction of travel, so I keep pushing us north-east before suddenly doing a 90-degree right turn and heading back to the FOB. It is 0930 and I think enough it is enough for one day. We are back in by 1000 hours.

This patrol certainly confirms that there are enemy present in the JA3 area. In fact it is obvious from the recent patrols that the closer you are to the river Helmand – and the further away from the FOB – the stronger the enemy grouping.

The new cookhouse opens for evening meal and the engineers have done a fantastic job. It is about 30m long, by 20m wide. It is made from wood and blast wall and has plenty of seating area so that now people can eat at a table rather than sit on the floor. The food preparation area also looks like it will be easier to keep clean. I have a really good meal which makes a change after four days on individual ration packs.

JULY

We are heavily into the tour now. I think it is now progressing as we thought it would. 'Fighting season' is in full swing and we are facing a determined, adaptive, credible enemy.

Many companies have suffered terrible losses and injuries. 2 PARA have had a particularly tough time and most of us have now been forced to face the realities of war. As the QM – a wise Falklands veteran – said to me before we deployed, 'If you pray for rain, you can't be disappointed with mud'. We all wanted to go into combat; we all wanted to 'fire our weapons in anger'. We have had to accept the 'mud'.

I am incredibly proud of the lads. They have taken everything that has been thrown at them – loss of life, injury, D&V, punishing workload – in incredibly good spirits. They bounce back very quickly and prove themselves to be a tough warrior breed.

For all the commanders, our jobs become more challenging each day. We have to keep getting out there and taking the fight to the enemy.

The company now has a good tempo. The challenge will be to maintain this to the finish.

TUESDAY 1 JULY

I plan another company-level patrol. We will push back up to where we were yesterday but concentrate on the area to the left of it, closer to Sangin. I really plan this in detail. I decide that we need to start locking the enemy down. We need to advance to contact, fix him, then destroy him. If we don't kill him today we are going to have to do it tomorrow. I decide that we will advance 'two up' again. Odds are only one of the platoons will become engaged and I can swing the other one round quickly and attack the enemy in a pincer movement. The theory is sound.

I deliver orders at 1000 hours and really try to add some zeal to them. It is all well and good me deciding that I want to lock down and kill the enemy, but I can't do it on my own. It is the lads that are going to have to carry it out. I try to add some energy and passion. I want them to buy my plan. It appears to work. The commanders walk away from the orders with a spring in their step. We shall see tomorrow.

WEDNESDAY 2 JULY

Up at 0250; this seems a real shame, as I was having a good sleep. We depart at 0340 out of 7 RHA gate. My aim is to get us as deep into JA3 as possible before first light but this quickly starts to unravel. The going is hideous. We cross ploughed fields that are slick with gooey mud. Each step cakes another heavy layer of wet mud to our feet. There is no moon so we can barely see 20m in front of us on NVGs. Despite it being quite cool at this time in the morning, I am pouring with sweat. I am glad of the ten-minute halt that I put in just before first light. I always find this first break sorts me out. I have a snack and my shoulders seem to relax. The load seems to sit better after this initial halt.

We are advancing 'one up' as it is easier on the command and control front. When in 'two up' it is time-consuming working out where everyone is. The lead is taken by 5 Platoon, followed by 4 Platoon. Sergeant Train is commanding 4 Platoon as David is manning the ops room.

We are approaching JA3, 700m from the river Helmand. I give the command to go into 'two up', with 4 Platoon pushing forward and becoming the right-hand platoon; I will stay behind 5 Platoon.

The enemy in front of 5 Platoon must be able to see 4 Platoon moving forward and realise that they are being outflanked. They open fire at a far greater range than we have seen before, 600 to 800m.

The initial burst of fire is huge, multiple PKMs and RPGs. The enemy must be about 800m away as the RPGs are air bursting around us.

I immediately run forward just as both sides of the fire

fight are getting going. I can see 4 Platoon on my right and 5 Platoon on my left. By following a small wall I get myself into a good vantage point and I can see the enemy as well. He is occupying a compound 400m away. RPGs are being fired at us from further away, from between gaps in the compounds. I come up with a hasty plan. I tell 4 Platoon to go firm and provide fire support and tell 5 Platoon to immediately start left flanking. Speed is of the essence – we have to cut off the enemy. Concurrently, I get the artillery to start firing on the enemy compound.

As 5 Platoon move off, I decide to follow them and my group has another dicey run over 300m with rounds landing around us to join them. I can feel the whole company is revved up today – we want to get the enemy.

The enemy starts pulling back as 5 Platoon rapidly approaches the enemy compound and clears it.

This left-flanking manoeuvre has automatically put the company in 'two up' so I swing the direction of approach half right and we all move off, 4 Platoon moving parallel to us. Our blood is up today and the company is moving really well.

The enemy open up again and an RPG sails straight down the middle of the column, passing over my group and airbursting near the CSM. The lead sections of both platoons put down a good weight of fire and the enemy starts to withdraw again. I think he has realised that we are trying to trap him in a pincer movement and he is not prepared to hang around.

I call on my mobile reserve – the Viking troop. They are in the FOB, ready to go, so I give James the order and he immediately deploys. My plan is to push the Vikings behind the enemy and we will continue to sweep towards them – hopefully trapping the enemy between the two.

We continue to sweep north-east. We are being heavily 'dicked', heads keep popping up from behind tree-lines and our progress is being reported to the enemy. He is desperately trying to put something together. He quickly identifies the Vikings and splits his force in two – one for the 'tanks' and one for us.

My aim is to meet the Vikings at JA3 but I become worried by intelligence I am receiving. The enemy are really trying to target the vehicles and I decide it will put them under too much risk bringing them deep into the green zone. I change plan. We will meet in Jusulay. I swing the patrol south-east and we push on.

The Vikings secure our meeting point, forming a wide circle over 200m, guns pointing out.

I start moving the company in bounding overwatch as there are so many enemy around.

4 Platoon make it to the vehicles first and have just managed to get on board when the enemy arrives. A huge amount of fire is directed at the Vikings; PKM fire and RPGs striking them.

My group and 5 Platoon are now to the west of the enemy – we can see the enemy firing from a tree-line and compound so we push forward to try to trap them. The Vikings aggressively push forward as well; .50cal machine guns firing away as they advance.

The enemy is exposed on the tree-line and Sergeant Marshall immediately puts accurate 51mm mortar fire on to them. This allows three Vikings to manoeuvre forward and they start hammering the tree-line with .50cal. I get the FOO to call in artillery. The fire is really accurate and we watch with satisfaction as the rounds slam into the enemy firing point.

All of the fire puts the enemy under pressure and 5 Platoon and TAC push down a track into the outskirts of Jusulay and board the empty Vikings. We trundle back into the FOB for 1000hrs.

I am really tired and dehydrated – there was a lot of running today. I am also really pleased. It went well and I could feel the pressure we were putting on the enemy.

I clean my weapon, sort out my kit and have a solar shower.

I then go to the ops room and write my weekly commander's assessment before heading over to brunch. I have a huge plate of corned beef hash and baked beans, which really hits the spot.

The CO rings in the evening and I tell him about our day. He is pleased with the way things are going. Battle group HQ is now in Sangin and fully functioning. He had come up with some plans for larger operations but there aren't the helicopters to support them. He tells me to concentrate on my mission for now – disrupting the enemy. We both agree I have done that today.

THURSDAY 3 JULY

After all of the activity yesterday most of us are pretty shattered. I try to keep today as low-key as possible.

I send 4 Platoon up to the Jusulay track junction to meet up with the ANA platoon. This is one of the joint patrols that Commander Karim and I have been trying to instigate.

As 4 Platoon patrols down the 611 it arrives at a scene of carnage. A local has approached the ANA checkpoint on a motorbike and they have taken a dislike to him. One of the ANA soldiers decides to fire warning shots without telling anyone. The remainder of the ANA Platoon think that they are in contact and start firing wildly in all directions.

At this, the 4 Platoon guys dive off the 611 and take cover in a drainage ditch as the scene unfolds in front of them.

I move round to the front sangar and watch through the 'ship's binos'. The poor British Army mentor with the ANA is struggling to get control of them. Even the enemy are confused – we receive intelligence that they are asking each other what is going on.

Once the ANA stop firing the mentor regains some control. After a quick discussion the ANA move over to the local on the motorbike, drag him off and smash him in the face with a rifle butt. They have obviously decided that this was his fault. They then let him go.

The joint patrol then moves into the green zone to do a small sweep on the outskirts of Jusulay. Understandably, 4 Platoon doesn't want any part of this but they get on with it. Fortunately there are no further incidents and 4 Platoon arrives back in the FOB not long after. We need to work with the ANA; it is the only way forward. I am sure there is a happy medium so they that they feel supported and we feel safe.

Commander Karim has suggested that he puts some of his soldiers in my sections. Understandably, at this stage, 4 Platoon is not convinced by this idea.

FRIDAY 4 JULY

To celebrate American Independence Day I have decided that we will have an inter-platoon sports day. I came up with this idea a while back and the physical training instructors from

7 RHA have put together an entertaining plan. There is volley-ball, football, cricket and a 'strong man' competition.

The day progresses well and the FOB resonates to the sound of laughter. The patrols have been intense recently and I think the lads deserve a bit of a break.

Inevitably, there are a few injuries. The doctor is kept busy stitching people – the ground is rock solid and there are a lot of exuberant tackles in the football. The major injury is Corporal Hickman dislocating his shoulder playing volleyball. We have to send him back to Bastion, which leaves me without a FAC. This is not ideal but I stand by the decision to have a sports day – the lads have really enjoyed themselves.

In the evening the chefs pull off a spectacular 'themed' meal. The food is brilliant, all created from ten-man ration packs. There is lasagne, curry and Chinese. The lads are on top form and I present a trophy to the overall winning team. Inevitably it is 7 RHA – they are always good at sports.

The FOB has a good feel to it. People are working hard and my challenge is to create a break for them.

My mind drifts to my own R&R, which isn't that far away. I realise that a break will do me the world of good. I am running things on my own personal energy, which is tiring. I can't wait to see Andrea and Rufus. I find myself retreating to a mental 'safe place' at night. I dream of going to St Agnes in Cornwall, which is just a wonderful place. I see myself going to my favourite pub in the world – the 'Aggie', as it is known. I picture myself in the bar with Andrea and Rufus, drinking a pint of real ale. I imagine having dinner in the superb bistro/bar, The Taphouse, the friendly warm welcome from Tim the manager, and the great food. I pray that I will make it to my R&R.

The 'loneliness' of command is starting to hit me. There is only one OC and everything rests on my shoulders. It is hard at times and I can feel myself compartmentalising more and more emotion. I am an outgoing person but I find myself doing more and more solitary activities, like reading or watching a DVD on a laptop. I have to make decisions – both big and small – all of the time. The pressure is relentless and I know that a brief spell away from here will give me the energy to see this through. Not long until my R&R. For now, I will just have to mentally go to the pub each night.

SATURDAY 5 JULY

A local area clearance patrol conducted by 5 Platoon passes without incident. The weather is really hot now, hitting 48C in the day, which is making everyone tired and lethargic.

The new cookhouse provides a large, airy, sheltered area and more and more of the lads are starting to hang out in there, which is good. The more people talk to each other the better. I worry about Toms hiding away in their accommodation, bottling up too much emotion.

SUNDAY 6 JULY

A helicopter arrives early morning with the CO of 45 Royal Marine Commando on board. This is our replacement unit. It is surreal having the team who will replace us come to visit. They are midway through their pre-deployment training and are in the middle of their commanders' visits to theatre.

I am really pleased their CO made it here. Inkerman is

usually missed off the list as there is too strong a likelihood that people will get stuck. If the enemy attack the FOB, the RAF won't come in.

I give him the guided tour and he takes in everything. He is very impressed with our new cookhouse. We spend an hour in the front sangar with me orientating him to the ground and talking through various incidents and challenges. This will allow him to tailor their training back in the UK.

As is usual at Inkerman, the helicopters due to come back to pick up the Royal Marines are on and off all afternoon. Eventually one returns early evening and takes them to Sangin. It seemed a good visit and he went away pleased.

MONDAY 7 JULY

I spend most of the morning with Sergeant Radcliffe developing a pet theory that we have. We rarely, if ever, see enemy transiting through the area with weapons. It would appear that there are weapon caches within the AO and they come to them, gather weapons, attack us, and then return the weapons. My plan is to start trying to find these caches. At this stage it is no more scientific than telling the Toms to start being more curious, but we are pretty convinced that we are right.

In the afternoon 4 Platoon go into the Star Wars village and try to chat to some locals. Sergeant Radcliffe goes with them and is surreptitiously trying to develop our cache theory. Nothing conclusive yet, but we are convinced that we are right.

TUESDAY 8 JULY

I spend the morning in the ops room doing various pieces of work. With Brett away there is a bit more to do but David is doing a good job.

In the afternoon I deliver orders for tomorrow's patrol. I explain the cache theory and tell the commanders that we need to explore this. We need to do thorough searches of compounds and likely cache areas. We will head back up to JA3 and conduct a more detailed search of some of the compounds and surrounding areas.

After the orders I ring Andrea on the satellite phone and inevitably we start talking about R&R. I just need a bit of normality – to be with Andrea and Rufus, walk barefoot on carpet, use a toilet that flushes and enjoy a real shower. It is the little things that I really miss.

WEDNESDAY 9 JULY

I am up at 0330hrs and we depart at 0400. I have 6 and 5 Platoons plus the FSG and a full detachment of snipers out today. We know what the JA areas can be like so I have come out 'heavy'.

With 6 Platoon leading we make rapid progress through the green zone on NVGs. We avoid any ploughed fields after the other morning's workout.

We hit the top corner of JA3 and I decide that we will re-orientate two up and then head west. This will enable us to straddle the belt of compounds that run east to west through JA3. The platoons can search for caches as they see fit.

I decide to move 5 Platoon round to our north. While

they are moving round, the rest of us will take our NVGs off and have a break. I will then let 5 Platoon do the same.

I am with 6 Platoon and, realising that we will probably be here about thirty minutes before 5 Platoon are ready, I casually wave over to the closest compound and say to the platoon commander, 'Give that a search, might as well while we are here'.

Tom – the new platoon commander of 6 Platoon – details a section to go in and have a look.

Minutes later Lance Corporal D-P appears with a huge grin on his face. He has found two Soviet hand grenades. Looks like we may have something.

I detail the engineers to go in and conduct a thorough clearance – they are the experts at this kind of thing.

We hit the jackpot. The engineers find a sizeable cache just outside the back of the compound in the bank, next to a stream. A hole has been dug and lined with rubber. Inside is one RPG launcher, 13 RPG rockets, one AK-47 with six magazines, 700 rounds of AK ammunition, 300 rounds of PKM ammunition, 18 hand grenades and two mortar bombs. It just keeps coming and the engineers are relishing their work. They stack everything up against the compound wall.

Whilst this is going on I reorganise the company into all-round defence. We then start to receive intelligence that the enemy is aware that we have found one of their caches. Plus we start to see movement around us. It is obvious that the enemy are closing in. We then hear that this compound belongs to 'Saddam', the local enemy commander, and these are his weapons.

I spend a painful amount of trying to get permission to blow up the weapons. HQ want to send the bomb disposal team in by Chinook but it is obvious at this point that there are a lot of enemy closing in on us. There is no way that a Chinook would be able to land.

In the end HQ relent and we get permission. By this point we can literally 'feel' that the enemy is all around us and 'Saddam' is directing as many fighters as possible over to attack us.

Sergeant Dale stacks the cache against the compound wall and lays a couple of bar mines on top. We need all of this lot to disappear.

A huge explosion disposes of the weapons, and also knocks half the compound down. I'm not sure how 'Saddam' is going to take this.

I get the platoon commanders in and we have a quick chat. We know there are a lot of enemy out there and more are coming in by the minute. We cannot afford to get fixed. If we stop moving the enemy will surround us and pick us off. I decide we will move in a direct route back to the FOB and keep going. If we get contacted we will roll through it, smashing the enemy with artillery and mortars. Looking at the map, we have five kilometres to go. This is going to be a long morning.

We push off, 6 Platoon leading, my group, 5 Platoon slightly offset to the north and the CSM with the FSG to the rear. This puts us in a 'box' formation and more compact. This means we are harder to attack and we have more concentrated firepower.

We have been going all of ten minutes when it all explodes to our front. The lead section of 6 Platoon is in contact already.

The formation I have chosen works well. With 5 Platoon off on the right flank the enemy is in danger of being outflanked so he starts to pull back, straight into 5 Platoon.

As soon as the lads tell me where the enemy is I get the FOO to start hitting them with artillery. Very quickly this feels like a fight for survival.

We receive intelligence that 'Saddam' has found out that we have blown the cache and half his compound up. He is apoplectic and directing every fighter he has to attack us. This should be interesting.

I urge the platoons to keep rolling and they deal with things as quickly as they can. There is fire going in all directions but we are still pushing forward. We have to smash through them.

Within thirty minutes we are being attacked from all flanks. Both platoons, my group and the CSM's at the rear are all coming under fire from various enemy groupings. It is nuts, we have never seen anything like this. I have mortars and artillery firing on different targets and we are desperately trying to get anything else available to come and help us. We are hitting them with everything that we have got.

After three hours of rolling contact it starts to go quiet. The weight of enemy fire starts to tail off and it becomes sporadic, more like lone gunmen. We have managed to cover 3.5km, which is impressive considering what we have been fighting through.

We hit the outskirts of Jusulay and are only 1.5km from the FOB when we take a casualty. I am not entirely sure I am hearing the radio message correctly but 5 Platoon is telling me that someone has hurt their back.

I push forward to try to find out what is going on. I meet Sergeant Marshall and he confirms that one of the Toms has hurt his back. I tell him not to be so daft – has he any idea what is going on, tell the Tom to push on.

'It's Kinell,' he tells me.

That changes things. Kinell is a very tough Tom from 3 PARA that I have got to know quite well. There is no way this is minor if he is saying he can't move.

I go over and chat to him and he is in serious pain – his back is in spasm and he can't move.

After four hours of fighting most of us are out of water and I realise that a CASEVAC will be really dangerous. I call for the Vikings to come out to collect him.

Within twenty minutes, James and his troop arrive. Unfortunately this has given the enemy a chance to close in. Kinell has just been loaded on board when the tree-line erupts with fire directed at the Vikings. At the same time SPG-9 rockets and RPGs are fired at the FOB.

I can't believe the amount of fire being put down by the enemy. It is like a firepower demonstration. Fortunately he is focused on the vehicles and the FOB, so those of us on foot manage to head straight into the Star Wars village and in through 7 RHA gate without being spotted.

Everyone moves into the FOB and runs for cover. SPG-9 rockets are still sailing into the FOB and I can hear our front sangar hammering away.

I run straight up the FOB and into the ops room.

Brett just looks at me in amazement – we have never seen anything like it.

I move round to the front sangar and coordinate fire on to the SPG-9 firing points.

'Saddam' is still going mad and directing his fighters to fire everything at the FOB.

Another SPG-9 whistles in and suddenly the shout of 'Medic!' is heard.

One of the engineers from the FOB development troop has decided to go out and fill his water bottle up in the middle of all this. A fragment from the last SPG-9 has hit his upper left arm and shattered the bone. It is nasty and we will need the MERT.

I am still trying to get my head around why someone would walk out into the open during all of this when I realise that we can't call the helicopter on to the normal HLS – we are still under fire. We will have to switch to the alternate HLS, which is two kilometres out in the desert.

I head back to the ops room and brief Brett. James arrives and we come up with a plan. The Vikings will take the two casualties, head into the desert and secure the HLS. Once the helicopter has picked up the casualties they will head back in.

The first Vikings head out to clear the route and I walk round to the one with the casualties in it. Kinell and the sapper are in the back and they are both in pain. I have a quick chat with them and try to cheer them up. Suddenly there is an explosion. Someone shouts 'Mine'.

I clamber on to the roof of the Viking and look out the back of the FOB to see one of the vehicles in a dust cloud. It has hit a mine.

Quickly the occupants of the vehicle let us know that they are all right. The mine was small and has only blown off a track. The pressure release of knowing that they are all right causes most of us to start laughing.

I turn to Brett and ask, 'What next'?

The Chinook arrives and the pandemonium is explained to the pilot. He tells us not to worry about the alternate HLS – he will come straight in. I appreciate his bravery, as we are running out of options at this end.

All of the sangars to the front start suppressing enemy positions and the Chinook sweeps in. Within thirty seconds he is away, casualties on board. He wants to get away and we want to get back under cover.

I head in to the ops room, buzzing with adrenaline. Brett smiles at me and says, 'Coffee?'

I look at my watch. It is 1100. I just start laughing. What a morning.

As I take my first sip of very strong Starbucks coffee I realise that today has been an OPTAG day.

OPTAG (Operational Training and Advisory Group) conduct our pre-deployment training. They run us through 'scenarios' and inevitably they hit you with something new and more complex every hour to overload you.

Brett and I start chatting and we agree that if you had a weapons cache find and destruction, a four-hour contact, bad back casualty, contact on vehicles and FOB, another casualty in the FOB, a mine strike and a CASEVAC within the space of seven hours you would think it was a joke and completely unrealistic. We have just had an OPTAG day.

THURSDAY 10 JULY

I think most of us are still buzzing after yesterday's epic. It is even more amazing on reflection.

We are basking in our own sense of success when bad news arrives. The news is sketchy but C Company has had a serious incident – three serious casualties and five lightly injured. The message also says that it is one of our own Apaches that has caused the casualties.

This has an instant effect on morale. We all have friends in other companies so this hits us hard. It is even more distressing that it is one of our own Apaches that has caused it.

In the afternoon we have helicopters come in. More people out on R&R and refreshed-looking people arriving back. We also receive a search dog – Sasha – and her handler, Lance Corporal Rowe. I had requested a search dog based on my cache theory and after the sizeable find HQ now agrees. I should be able to put her to good use.

FRIDAY 11 JULY

I dispatch 5 Platoon down to the Jusulay track junction to meet up with the ANA platoon. The plan is to try a joint patrol again. Creating a standing 'western' Army from what are effectively tribes is a challenge. The Afghans are great warriors though. They are tough as granite and fearless fighters. It is harnessing this energy and focusing it that will take the time, but I am sure the results will be impressive.

This patrol starts better than the last. They manage to quickly get themselves sorted and 5 Platoon head off to the disused compounds in front of the FOB. This will only be a short patrol but we have got to start somewhere. Within an hour it all starts to unravel. The ANA soldiers start arguing with their platoon commander. Their British Army mentor sensibly decides to call it a day before discipline completely breaks down.

Interestingly, I am told that we will be getting an ANA platoon permanently at the FOB. This will bring its own set of challenges but it will be really useful. It will give me another manoeuvre group, gives me a large group of people who can deal with the locals and puts an Afghan face on what we do.

SATURDAY 12 JULY

I send 4 Platoon out on a local area clearance patrol. They head out into the desert, loop round into the green zone and then clear right to left in front of the FOB, working down the unoccupied compounds. I want these compounds cleared as much as possible because it would be easy for the enemy to fire a weapon quite accurately at the FOB or one of the sangars from here.

Once the platoon has cleared the belt of compounds they turn left and start heading towards Star Wars village. They will weave their way back in through there.

As they start heading into the village two enemy appear on the roof of one of the recently cleared compounds with a PKM. This is done in full view of the front sangars, so the pair of them get dispatched with a burst from the 40mm grenade launcher. These can't be very bright enemy on this assignment.

I decide that I will really clear this area in detail now that I have Sasha the search dog here.

As 4 Platoon works its way through the village one of the Toms glances through a window of a building and spots what looks like an IED. There is definitely a pressure plate and it is just sat propped up against a wall in the compound.

The platoon commander lets me know via radio and I start to coordinate the IED disposal team to come to this location.

Then the brother of the compound owner arrives, weaves

his way into the compound without the lads spotting and picks up the IED. The next thing the Toms know a very friendly local is stood holding the pressure plate. It is obvious that there are no explosives and the local agrees to bring the device to our unexploded ordnance pit at the back of the FOB. This all feels like another random day at Inkerman.

In the afternoon I receive an email from the CO, with more information about the direction the second half of the tour is likely to take. It looks like there will be a delivery of a third turbine to the Kajaki dam. The window is late August for this to happen and it will be a big operation. The 611 is in such a bad state of repair it will need improving as the plan is to drive everything up. I think that we should try to involve the locals and make sure that they know this will be for their greater good. It is not in the Taliban's interest to interfere with this anyway – they will be able to tax the electricity in the areas they hold further down the valley.

We are due another air drop tonight so Sergeant Train coordinates all of the activity. He does a great job sorting out 6 Platoon, drivers and vehicles and they all head off before last light.

I sit in the ops room and listen to his progress reports. There are quite strong winds but the drop is going ahead.

At 2200 hours a C-130 Hercules drops three pallets of equipment. Inevitably the kit either drifts off the drop zone – in one case by ten kilometres – or smashes into the ground. At 0130 Sergeant Trains calls for mortar illumination rounds as they still can't find some of the parachutes and kit.

SUNDAY 13 JULY

I wake up in the morning absolutely covered in sand, the disadvantage of sleeping outside when it is windy. I shudder to think how much I have ingested.

The drop zone party have returned after their epic night and Sergeant Train is still trying to sort out stores and para-chutes. He hasn't been to bed yet.

I make myself a cup of coffee and head round to the office. I want to plan tomorrow's patrol. I haven't been out for a few days and I am feeling a bit restless. I get this each time I sit down to write a plan: I feel quite energised. I visualise how I see things going and try to explore all of the different options. There is an element of amateur psychology to this. I try to imagine what the enemy will do, what he will think and how he will react to my actions. I try to work out how I can deceive him and try to spot what we haven't done before. I also try to be clear as to the exact effect I want to achieve.

This far into the tour, and with the experiences we have been having, I am learning a lot – about myself, about leadership and command. I have developed a sense of higher purpose. Leadership is about those below you, not those above. I am also fully aware that there is a huge difference between what I want to do and what I need to do. If I am going to take people into harm's way, it had better be for a good reason.

Tomorrow's patrol is my most creative yet. We are going to concentrate on the power station and 'Saddam'. We keep receiving intelligence that the power station is being used by the enemy as a place to form up and then come down and attack us from. 'Saddam' operates in this area. I have a lot of high-level intelligence assets at my disposal and my plan is to draw 'Saddam' in through a series of company rummages to make it look like we are looking for caches. Once he comes in we will triangulate him and the plan is then to use the snipers to 're-educate' him.

I really sell this plan in my orders. It is creative and it is really taking the fight to the enemy. The lads seem to go for it. Everyone wants the chance to kill 'Saddam'.

MONDAY 14 JULY

Up at 0245, cup of tea and a three-pack of Bourbons and I am ready to go at 0320. We depart via the rear gate at 0330, 6 Platoon leading, my group and then 4 Platoon.

As always, when travelling up the desert we make quick progress. The power station is only four kilometres away. It is nice and cool at this time in the morning. The only downside to the desert is the constant fear of IEDs. As I walk along I have to turn my mind off as I find myself wondering what it would feel like to step on one. Not helpful.

We arrive opposite the power station just before first light. I push 4 Platoon slightly north to act as a buffer. I place my group with the snipers on the higher ground that overlooks the power station and I send 6 Platoon in to clear it.

I am in a good position to overwatch all of the activity and also watch a fantastic dawn. The mountains off in the distance look incredible as the sun rises from behind them and the light spreads across the green zone.

6 Platoon has a really good look around and inside the power station. The security guard acts very suspiciously and

seems desperate to get to a large CB radio that is inside the main building. I tell 6 Platoon to make a note of the frequency. The platoon commander then pretends not to notice as the security guard moves over to the CB and turns the frequency dial. He obviously didn't want us knowing that one.

They also find a lot of medical supplies that the security guard can't explain. This all seems to confirm enemy activity in the area.

We are getting a lot of intelligence at this stage and the situation is starting to build. We can see locals streaming out of their compounds in the green zone and heading off into the desert. Concurrently we track three 'fighting age males' heading into a compound from the desert.

While it is still quiet I decide to push 4 Platoon across the open ground to their front. At least we will have a foot in the green zone and they can track the three men.

Once the search of the power station is complete I push my group over to join 4 Platoon. Crossing the open ground is quite nerve-wracking as we have now received intelligence that the enemy is set up and good to go. Once my group has crossed over I get 6 Platoon to move over as well. This gives me the whole company ready to move forward.

As 4 Platoon begins to sweep round, we are effectively starting to surround the compound that the three men disappeared into.

Then 4 Platoon, continuing to push forward, come under fire from the target compound. Four RPGs and rifle fire is directed at them. The enemy is obviously under pressure as the fire is fairly inaccurate but 4 Platoon's reaction is impressive. They put a heavy weight of fire down and start aggressively moving towards the compound. They suddenly see the three men pop out of the back and run off deeper into the green zone.

I decide we will follow this up, so I start to bound the platoons forward, with 6 Platoon providing overwatch. As 4 Platoon is moving we come under contact again. This time an RPG is fired at my group. I am with Lance Corporals Smith and Robert, two snipers, when an RPG flies one metre above our heads and detonates just behind us.

The three armed men are seen by 4 Platoon entering another compound 250 metres to their front, so we fire artillery straight into it. Only two of the men pop out of the back this time. Intelligence also hears the enemy asking if the 'Four enemy they have pushed into the area are there yet and can the two casualties walk?' We seem to be having an effect.

We push on, heading north and all the while getting deeper into the green zone and further from the FOB. My blood is up today. I want to chase these people down and get them. I am fed up with this cat and mouse – how dare they fire at my company?

We keep coming under rolling contacts – the enemy fires RPGs and rifles at us, then immediately pulls back. It is frustrating but it feels like we are putting him under pressure.

We approach a piece of open ground that is ringed by compounds. The enemy are firing at us from the other side. The frequency and number of enemy firing points is increasing but I am oblivious at this stage, I am too focused on working out how to trap the enemy and kill him.

I start to swing 6 Platoon round for a left flanking assault but the amount of fire we are under is slowing people down. I am pushing them hard to keep moving. The intelligence assets I have today are starting to feed me a lot of information. I am told that there are eight different enemy call-signs to my front, two to my left and four to my right. Each call-sign will be a minimum of two enemy fighters so the situation is really starting to build. There are probably 20 to 30 fighters out there.

At this stage I haven't noticed what is going on, I am too focused on trying to work out how we can push forward.

I pull out my map and as I stare at it I am hit by something. We haven't seen the enemy give ground so easily before. Why would he keep pulling back and suddenly stop in this area? As I stare at my map it hits me. This is a huge ambush and he is trying to draw me into it. As I look at the map I realise it is perfect for it. The compounds are in a large inverted tear shape. The enemy is setting himself up around the top and is drawing me into the middle.

I am also reminded of the question that I continually ask myself now. What do I *want* to do and what do I *need* to do? The two are radically different. I want to follow the enemy up and destroy him. What I need to do is disrupt the enemy and bring all of my guys in safely. We have stretched our luck enough.

I immediately loop the company around and we head off in the opposite direction – back towards the FOB. No point walking into a trap.

The company was moving really well, I am getting some good manoeuvre going and I feel that confident today that I *want* to follow the enemy up all the way back to Pakistan. That's not what I *need* to do though.

There is a bit of posturing from the enemy but nothing else happens and we clear our way down the edge of the green zone, next to the 611, into the FOB. We are back in by 1000hrs.

I go straight to the ops room and chat to Brett. He shows me the master map. He has put a mark on every identified enemy firing point. It is as I suspected. The enemy were surrounding us. Brett was getting concerned as I kept pushing forward and was about to point this out to me when I suddenly figured it out for myself and swung the company round.

I learnt a valuable lesson today. Keep your head. Keep reading the situation in front of you, not the one that you would like to see in front of you. Remember – this is a clever, thinking opponent. He will punish you for your mistakes.

We are all tired but happy. The enemy took casualties today and I think that my plan worked. No 'Saddam', but we proved the level of enemy activity around the power station.

TUESDAY 15 JULY

A quiet day today after yesterday's patrol. I send 5 Platoon out on a local area clearance patrol and fortunately it is quiet. The weather is really warm now and most people, if they aren't doing something constructive, just seek the solace of shade and a book.

WEDNESDAY 16 JULY

A plan is starting to take shape for a surge operation in my area of operations 20–28 July. At that period, 3 PARA has a company available and the plan at this stage is for them to come to the FOB and work out of here for a week. This has the advantage of increasing the numbers operating in the AO and also brings in another company commander to run things while I am away.

The company commander – Stuart – arrives by helicopter for a quick visit so that we can have a chat before I disappear on R&R. I have known Stuart for years so the briefings are easy. I am keen for him to continue the search for the elusive weapons caches. With more manpower available he will be able to saturate key areas and conduct really detailed searches, something we are struggling to do at the moment. Plus there is the search dog so potentially some real progress can be made.

Stuart is happy with all of this and we spend most of the day catching up, talking about our different tour experiences and all of the other regimental gossip that is going on. It sounds like 3 PARA is having a different tour to us. They aren't in a ground-holding role and are spending more time surging into areas for specific operations. It means that they are seeing far more of Helmand than my ten-kilometre square box. It sounds interesting but I am quite happy with my FOB and my mission. I feel I have more autonomy by being stuck at Inkerman.

THURSDAY 17 JULY

I spend the bulk of the day in the ops room working out the patrol programme for the next ten days. Having had a good chat with Stuart, I want to get all of this done so that he doesn't have to worry about it. It feels strange planning activity that I know I won't be involved in. I also know that I need a break. I am absolutely shattered and I know that some rest and decent food will do me the world of good.

In the afternoon I head down to the stores area for a brew with Sergeant Payne. Lance Corporal Rowe is in there with Sasha. I end up having a long chat with him – he seems a really nice guy. We talk about the capability of the search dog and then drift on to general dog chat. I realise how much I am missing Rufus, my cocker spaniel. I also think how nice it must be to be a dog handler – it looks like a great job.

FRIDAY 18 JULY

I wake up at 0300 with a serious 'Christmas morning' head on. I am due to fly out on R&R today. Although it will be a drawn-out process getting home, potentially I will be on my way soon.

I can't get back to sleep so I get up at 0445. I go into the ops room and have a chat with the duty signallers before making myself a fresh coffee and moving outside. I find myself a quiet spot and just sit there for the next hour and a half. I watch the most amazing sunrise and then watch the FOB come to life. The hustle and bustle starts around 0600 as people start to get up and by 0700 people are heading to breakfast.

Sitting, reflecting, is a nice experience. I consider myself a 'warrior' now. I have been in combat and experienced the highs and lows. We have had a lot of good days and one terrible day. I know that I have been learning a lot – about command, leadership, the company and myself. I feel far more introspective. I think that combat strips away the superfluous clutter in your life and makes you focus on what is really important. Without the clutter it is easier to be honest with yourself.

I also know that a break will do me good. I have to make decisions all of the time and I am under constant and significant pressure. It will be nice to have that pressure lifted. I know that I will come back from R&R refreshed and ready to push to the end.

Worryingly I have a touch of the 'lurgy' as well. It's not too bad. Every now and then I get hit with a wave of nausea and I am 'loose'. Just what I need.

I go through the day with constant conflicting messages – the helicopters are on, the helicopters are cancelled. In the end I just go and sit in the office and watch a DVD on a laptop. At 1520 one of the signallers bursts in and tells me that the helicopters are ten minutes' away.

In a flurry of activity I get all of my kit on and, with some help, get my bags down to the HLS. Due to the rush a wave of nausea has come on and I am pouring with sweat.

I just have the chance to say goodbye to the CSM and Brett when I hear the Chinook approach.

The helicopters touch down, sand blasting all of us who are waiting. A load of guys from 3 PARA run off and we are given the thumbs up – fifteen of us run on board. In minutes the Chinook has lifted off and is on its way.

The journey is terrible for me. I already feel sick and the flight doesn't help. Thirty minutes later we touch down at Bastion. Fortunately, the CQMS is there to meet us. He quickly whisks us through a de-kit process. Effectively everything is locked in a shipping container. I have left my pistol, hand grenades and most of my ammunition at the FOB so this doesn't take long.

I move into the accommodation, which is made up of long, 20-man air-conditioned tents, joined together by a central spine. It feels amazing to be somewhere so clean. I lie down and let myself cool down until the nausea passes. I then head for a shower. I treat myself to a flushing toilet break before having a nice, long, real shower. This is all sensory overload.

I am all alone in the tent when Ben sticks his head through the flap. Ben is a captain from 2 PARA and based at Bastion. He tells me not to be such a loser – hanging out on my own and moves me into his tent. As Ben is permanently based here, he is really well set up. He gets me a camp cot with a mattress and two pillows. He shows me where all of his food is, tells me to help myself, then disappears for a briefing.

I treat myself to another lie down and this strange feeling washes over me. I realise that I am not under any pressure. My system almost grinds to a halt. With the pressure gone I realise how deeply tired I am – I drift off to sleep.

I have been asleep for about two hours when I am woken by someone coming into the tent.

Through sleepy eyes I look up to see Nick. Nick is the adjutant of 2 PARA and a really good friend of mine. I am so pleased to see him. He is normally based at Sangin and I haven't seen him since we deployed. Nick is back for a short course that is being run out of Bastion.

This is just great. Nick and I head for evening meal and a proper catch up. The food at Bastion is incredible. Lots of choice, salad bar, ice cream, it blows my mind. This is all very different from those that are forward in the FOBs. After dinner Nick and I grab some Cokes and have a really long chat. He has all the HQ gossip and tells me how life is in Sangin. He is keen to hear how B Company is and what it is like out at the dreaded Inkerman. He says that in Sangin they all know when B Company is on patrol as they can hear the artillery firing! It is great to see him.

SATURDAY 19 JULY

I wake up on a mattress with two pillows in an air-conditioned tent having had the most incredible sleep. I must have slept for ten hours. I can feel my system grinding to a halt. I have been pushing myself so hard in the FOB. With the pressure off, I can feel how low on energy I really am. It is as if I have realised how empty I am and it leaves me feeling weak and hollow.

After breakfast I bump in to Colour Sergeant Jim Child. I have known him for most of my career and he is a really good guy. He grabs a Land Rover and drives me round to one of the coffee shops so that we can have a brew and a catch up. It all seems quite strange. I am sat in this very trendy café, in Bastion, drinking a latte planning the officers' mess Christmas ball. I am in charge of the mess committee and Jim helps me. He thinks that we should be booking entertainment now, to beat the other messes. All very surreal. After the function planning he manages to get me loaded on to a flight to Kandahar, which has even better facilities.

I fly at 2140 hours and, with my rather unsettled constitution at the moment, the flight is grim. I arrive at the transit accommodation feeling wrung out.

SUNDAY 20 JULY

I wake up after a terrible night's sleep. I have the sweats and I have to get up to go to the toilet a number of times. I should see a doctor but I am worried that he will stop me flying home. I am practically willing myself better as I don't want it to spoil my R&R. I am due to fly tonight, arriving at Brize Norton tomorrow morning.

MONDAY 21 JULY

I walk through the arrivals gate at Brize Norton and Andrea is there to meet me. I have a whole kaleidoscope of emotions rolling around in my head. I am overwhelmingly happy but I am also nervous. I can feel a degree of anxiety – almost skittishness. England seems such a contrast to my 'other life' at the moment.

As soon as I see Andrea's beautiful smiling face everything is instantly better. I am so pleased to hold her in my arms. Everything feels good.

We walk out to the car park and Rufus is there. I give him a huge hug and I am a little worried as he is slightly standoffish but he soon comes around.

As we drive out into the stunning Oxfordshire countryside I can't believe how far I am from my FOB, and my lads.

TUESDAY 22 JULY

I am enjoying padding around barefoot in our house in Colchester when the phone goes. It is Tam – the rear party duty officer from 2 PARA. He asks me how my leave is going and we have a chat before he tells me the reason he is ringing. He has bad news. There has been an 'incident' at Inkerman.

A company-level patrol got into a huge contact in one of the areas that I asked Stuart to clear. Lance Corporal Rowe and his dog Sasha were killed instantly by an RPG and six of my lads were injured. The casualties are all back at Bastion and stable. That's all he knows at this stage.

I put the phone down and I just don't know what to do. I feel so helpless and guilty for being away. I can picture the FOB and the lads and I know the impact this will have on them. Lance Corporal Rowe was such a nice guy. I am speechless. I have to go and sit in the garden and gather my thoughts. Andrea comes to find me and comforts me. I am beating myself up for being away. I never should have taken R&R. Deep down I know that I need to recharge my batteries but this is horrible, I feel so helpless and I can't stop thinking about my poor company.

WEDNESDAY 23 JULY

We head down to my favourite place in the UK, St Agnes in Cornwall. It is a fantastic village – my mental 'safe place'. My sister owns a house there and my whole family are down.

I sit in the 'Aggie' drinking a pint of St Austell ale and I feel incredibly grateful to be here. The welcoming atmosphere of this wonderful pub helps me to relax and it is nice to be here after spending so much time thinking about making it back. I am also mindful that the tour isn't over yet. I try not to dwell on this so I just relax and enjoy myself.

Deep in the green zone the lads use a canal for cover.

Maintaining communications on patrol.

The lads secure a bridge into the green zone just past the power station.

Opposite: Reverse denial: The engineers rebuild a gap in the wall that enabled the enemy to fire RPGs at the HLS.

Power station clear and heading into the green zone.

The weapons cache on OPTAG day.

Viking vehicles dcep in the desert.

Using all available cover: A GPMG gunner and his number two shelter behind an old wall.

Waiting for the enemy to arrive: Set up on a compound roof waiting for the imminent contact.

Dealing with mass civilian casualties after an airstrike north of the FOB.

Machine gunners from the Fire Support Group cover a Platoon moving across open ground.

Still grinning: The Padre took this picture and you can see the strike marks on the tree above my head.

Afghan National Army and a B Company mentor.

The memorial to the fallen in FOB Inkerman.

AUGUST

July was another hard month for B Company and 2 PARA.
More deaths and more casualties. The enemy seem to have really
found their stride now. The constant challenges combined with
the blast-furnace heat mean that there are no respites. The
company is taking the knocks and I know the attrition will
start to have an effect in the end.

My R&R has done me the world of good. As guilty as I
have felt being back at home while my lads are in Afghanistan,
I know that I needed the break. I needed to top up my energy
so that I can see this through to the finish.

I can't wait to get back to the company. I want to give this
everything I have got now. No need to pace myself; just go for
it. I feel the clock ticking down. I want to get back out to the
company because the sooner we get on with it, the sooner we
will be coming home. I am conscious though that my time as
a company commander in combat will also be coming to an
end and that actually makes me quite sad. What are the chances
I will ever do anything like this again in my military career?

MONDAY 4 AUGUST

I am sitting in the departure lounge at Brize Norton waiting to fly back. I am taking the time to gather my thoughts. Returning hasn't preyed on my mind until yesterday. The inevitability of saying goodbye to Andrea again sank in. Although we were both positive that I am over halfway and the next time we see each other I will be back for good, the reality of the danger is never far from our minds.

Andrea dropped me off at the barracks in Colchester at 0100 this morning. It was then that I realised that I wouldn't see her again for another two and a half months. She got really upset and, as I waved her off, I felt myself praying that I make it back safe and sound.

We arrive at Brize Norton to be told that there is a twenty-four-hour delay. They take us straight to a small RAF hotel called the Gateway House. I am so tired by the time that I get to my room I couldn't care less what happens next.

After a good sleep I realise I have a whole day to kill and

this gives me time to gather my thoughts. Now that I have said the painful goodbyes I am looking forward to getting back out there and getting the job done. I have brought some entertainment to take back with me; I had been a bit Spartan over the last few months. I am returning with an iPod and DVDs of Rick Stein, Ray Mears and River Cottage. These should keep me entertained.

I spend the afternoon in my room reading various books and magazines before having a nice long bath – might as well, before I am back on solar showers.

The delay has created a phased transition for me. Instead of heading straight back out I have time to refocus on what I know I have to do.

I have a really nice chat with Andrea on the phone. It dawned on me that we spent some quality time together on R&R but we didn't really talk about much. I suppose Andrea didn't want to bring anything up. So we use this opportunity to talk through how we feel. I go to sleep calm and relaxed.

TUESDAY 5 AUGUST

I am up at 0500 and down at the departure hall for 0545. The fun and games begin almost instantly. The aircraft is a different model to the one the RAF planned to use – this one is a converted freight aircraft so there are no overhead lockers. This means that we have to check our baggage into the hold, which annoys everyone.

We take off and after five minutes the captain announces that one of the flaps is stuck and we will have to turn back. I watch out of the window as we dump fuel over the Channel and I think to myself that this can't be good for our carbon footprint. We then land back at Brize Norton. I am just getting myself mentally prepared for another night at the Gateway House when they find another aircraft. An hour and a half later we are on our way again.

We fly to Cyprus and then have another wait before we are shuttled into Kandahar at midnight.

WEDNESDAY 6 AUGUST

After a short wait at Kandahar I manage to get on a C-130 to take me to Bastion at 0400 hours. I walk off the back ramp just as dawn is breaking and it is a great sight. It is also a good feeling. I am happy to be back. Although I am shattered from the travel, I am nearly back with my company and I can't wait.

I find Sergeant Train, who is doing an excellent job standing in for the CQMS, and have a brew. It gives me a chance to catch up with him. He starts trying to pull strings to get me back to Inkerman as quickly as possible.

Within thirty minutes he returns with a big grin on his face. He has got me on a flight.

At 1000hrs the Chinook takes off with eight of us on board and a large under-slung load. It is a very pleasant flight.

Before I know it I am running off the back ramp and I am back with B Company; where I should be.

I am tired and disorientated from all of the travel but delighted to be back. It really does feel great. I had no idea how much I was missing everyone. I get a nice reception, people seem pleased to see me and quite a few Toms come up and ask me how my R&R was.

I can feel myself 'revving up', drawing energy from the

lads and from being back here. I feel more professional now that I have had some time to process all of my experiences. I am determined to push myself hard until the end. The break has allowed me to think things through and to recharge my batteries. I realise that I have further opportunities to get the most professional satisfaction out of all of this and I am determined to take them. This opportunity isn't going to come again.

I spend some time catching up with Brett. The company has been working really hard over the last ten days and most people are shattered. There are surge operations being planned starting on 10 August, so I agree with Brett that we should have the next couple of days as rest. Once we have the plan sorted I excuse myself and go round to my little area to sort myself out. I am shattered.

THURSDAY 7 AUGUST

I spend the bulk of the day wandering around the FOB catching up with people. I am so pleased to see everyone and I want to find out how they are all faring after the loss of Lance Corporal Rowe and the casualties. I find most of the company are shattered but still positive. They are keen to get out there and take the fight to the enemy – after they have had a couple of rest days. Seems fair enough to me and I reassure them that we are not out until the 10 August.

FRIDAY 8 AUGUST

I had a terrible night's sleep last night. I just couldn't turn my mind off. The mornings are now getting cooler so I am able to go to the gym a bit later. During R&R I continued to train hard and I want to keep this up in the FOB. I try a thirty-minute run around the inside of the FOB. This works out at 12 laps and is just about tolerable before skull-crushing boredom sets in.

We are having an equipment care day today and the FOB seems quiet and relaxed; most of the Toms are taking the opportunity to catch up with some sleep. After my training session I have a solar shower, make a decent coffee and then spend most of the morning in the ops room conducting patrol planning.

It is quiet until mid-afternoon when the local enemy sniper opens up. This is a recent occurrence. Every day, mid-afternoon, a lone sniper fires three to four rounds at the FOB and then disappears. This is insulting my own snipers' professional pride and they are all set up, observing to the front in various elevated positions around the FOB, trying to spot him and ultimately remove him. No joy today, though.

We have a combat camera team here with us at the moment. I give an interview mid-afternoon but I have no idea if it will go anywhere. They seem a nice bunch and they are coming out on the patrol with us on 10 August.

SATURDAY 9 AUGUST

I have another disturbed night's sleep. I just can't turn my mind off and I lie there thinking things over and over until the small hours.

Despite the broken sleep I get up at the usual time and go to the gym. I realise that I have a lot on my mind at the moment: my first company patrol is tomorrow and I haven't been out for a while. The company needed to recharge its batteries after the ferocious couple of weeks it has had but I could do with getting back out there. To some extent I feel guilty for having been away. I need to get back out there and get back into the swing of it.

After my workout I sort myself out, get a coffee and write my orders. It is now much cooler early morning and the sun isn't strong enough to heat the water in the solar shower. I can't face a cold shower so I leave it to heat up and I will come back to it after I have planned the patrol.

Planning and writing my orders helps settle my mind. I can feel my rhythm returning; feel my 'edge' sharpening.

I deliver my orders and, as always, I throw myself into the delivery. I can feel the break has done me good, I have more energy and passion. The lads seem happy and after they have drifted off I spend the rest of the morning sorting out my kit.

In the afternoon 6 Platoon heads out on a local clearance patrol. We now have a platoon of Afghan National Army (ANA) living in the front compound of the FOB, so 6 Platoon go out with eight members of the ANA. The ANA are desperate to go out *en masse*, but with no mentors it is a challenge controlling them, so we keep their numbers low at this stage. We will have to build up to having the whole platoon out with us.

The patrol passes without incident and I head off to bed early, desperately hoping that I can get to sleep as we have an early start tomorrow.

SUNDAY 10 AUGUST

I have a terrible night's sleep again. I am still awake at 0100hrs and I have to get up at 0240. I get up at 0245 and don't feel too bad considering. It is probably the anticipation of my first patrol for quite a while.

We leave at 0330 from the back gate, 5 Platoon leading, TAC and then 4 Platoon. The CSM is on R&R at the moment so Mitch has taken over; he brings up the rear.

We cross the 611 and head straight into the green zone. The going is really hard and I can't believe the difference in the crop. The corn is now six to eight foot high and all the fields are full of mud that feels like it wants to pull your boots off. Each step adds another layer of heavy mud.

Despite the hard going we make good progress and at 0420 we stop and take off our NVGs. By 0530 we are in the target area, designated KA7 and five kilometres north of the FOB. It has a large canal running through the centre of it, which is a tributary of the river Helmand.

At 0600hrs we go firm, each group occupying a compound. I have had to adapt my plan to the crop. There is no way we can find the enemy in these cornfields. The plan is to use the compounds to get elevation then suck the enemy on to us, that way we can make best use of our weapons systems.

The plan appears to be working as by 0700 we are getting intelligence that the enemy are coming to attack us and we can see and hear suspicious activity to our fronts. Despite the build up of activity – voices and the sound of motorbikes – by 0800 nothing has happened. I am growing concerned that we will be out too long in the heat.

I attach my group to 4 Platoon and we start to clear some of the compounds to their front. This speeds things up. Sergeant Sykes has just positioned a section on the roof to provide overwatch when RPGs and PKM are fired at us and 5 Platoon has RPGs fired at the compound it is occupying.

The section on the roof is really switched on and they quickly identify the enemy firing points to the north and return fire; 5 Platoon are just as quick and are soon suppressing the enemy with machine guns.

I am just organising mortars on to the enemy when we get contacted from the west – more RPGs. I get the mortars to fire to the north. This has an immediate effect as, once the mortars have finished, we can hear men screaming. I get the artillery to fire to the west. The rooftop section see a motorbike depart with an injured man on the back. They let it leave.

We start to head off and the enemy quickly loses us. It is getting warm and humid in the crop fields; it really feels like being in the jungle. The rest of the patrol passes without incident and we are back in for 1130. Quite a long patrol but a success, as far as I am concerned.

It was very slick today and the concept of using the compounds as overwatch is a good one. The lads were very switched on and got the information that I needed to me quickly. It feels great to be back into the swing of it and back in action with the company. I realise that I needed it – to be back out there with them. I am not looking for trouble, but we have a mission and we are going to get out there and do it.

I feel really happy to be here. My R&R was great but I felt guilty. This is where I should be, out here, with B Company, commanding them. I really missed the lads and it was great to see them in action today. The rest days – or, rather, 'equipment care' – I managed to give them seems to have done them the world of good.

The afternoon is a challenge as I am so tired. I don't want to have a sleep because I need to get back into a routine but I keep drifting into 'zombie' mode. I am also 'loose' at the moment; to be expected with the travel, change of diet and back to ingesting handfuls of sand and dust each night. I am just worried that it will develop into D&V. As long as it stays as 'traveller's stomach' I am happy, although I again have the paranoia that I will get 'caught short' on patrol. No matter how you explained it to the lads they would have a field day – that you were so scared you soiled yourself. Not good.

MONDAY 11 AUGUST

Fortunately I have a decent night's sleep and I wake up at 0545hrs. I head to the gym and do a decent workout.

I decide to skip breakfast as I am not that hungry. I have coffee and biscuits instead; I just love biscuits. This turns out to be a bit foolish as it leaves me feeling hungry and dehydrated later in the morning.

There isn't much on today so I get on with some work. I complete my weekly area assessment and email it off to James Coates, the new battalion 2IC. Jacko has handed over and headed back to the UK. I intersperse the office work with reading a book, which is a nice way to spend the day.

James sends me quite a detailed response to some of my questions and he gives me a good feel for how the next couple of weeks are going to pan out.

The plan to deliver the turbine up to the Kajaki dam – Operation Oqab Tsuka (Op OT) – is well developed. A Company, 3 PARA will arrive at this location tomorrow and over the next few days we will put a new patrol base in about a kilometre from here, up the 611. I have already picked the location. It is a fairly large compound that overlooks the 611 and, crucially has a well, so they should have their own water source.

The aim of this patrol base is to create the impression that we are reinforcing along the 611 as that is the route we want the enemy to believe the turbine delivery convoy will take. It has now been decided that the convoy will take a desert route. Effectively, we are the deception plan. We will start increasing our activity and with the extra company at the patrol base I am pretty certain that the enemy will buy the plan. We want to create the effect without pushing him too hard; we don't want him to be pushed out of the area.

The plan looks good and all of this activity will make the time pass more quickly. I am keen to get the maximum out of all this and rack up more experiences, but none of us wants the time to drag. I think Op OT will keep us busy and the time will fly by; we will be handing over to the marines before we know it.

I give orders in the afternoon for tomorrow's company-level patrol. We need to keep the pressure on the enemy to create the space for A Company to insert into this location.

TUESDAY 12 AUGUST

I get up at 0315 after a pretty good sleep. It still amazes me that it is possible to have a decent sleep even though you know the odds are that when you head out you will be in a fight with someone absolutely determined to kill you. I would have thought it would prey on my mind and the anxiety would keep me awake. I suppose we have learnt to tune it out. I am more concerned about my stomach.

I have a cup of tea and some Bourbon biscuits. You can't beat a cup of tea and a handful of biscuits before a gunfight. We head out 7 RHA gate at 0400hrs – 4 Platoon, TAC then 6 Platoon.

We initially head to independent objectives in the green zone north-west of the FOB. I want to use the corn to our advantage and make it harder for the enemy to pinpoint our exact location. We are in secure locations by first light and remove our night sights, before continuing north-west, deeper into the fields.

Due to the corn I am using bounding overwatch all of the time. I move with 4 Platoon while 6 Platoon provide cover. Intelligence starts to build quickly and we are informed that the enemy has managed to generate an impressive number of fighters in a very short period of time.

We continue to push forward through a cornfield when a lone shot rings out, followed by another one. I am told on the radio what has happened.

A local suddenly appeared in the cornfield and headed straight towards the rear man of the FSG. The machine gunner shouted at him to stop, but he didn't. A warning shot was fired but the man kept coming. The second shot was the local being hit with one round to the stomach.

By the time I get to the rear of the patrol the medics are treating the local. He isn't a suicide bomber and we have no idea why he wouldn't stop. I call for the Quick Reaction Force (QRF) and get the FOB to prepare a CASEVAC for the local. We are fairly close to a track so we move him back and wait for our vehicles to arrive.

It is all very slick and within fifteen minutes the vehicles arrive and take him away. Unfortunately, ten minutes later I am told that he has died of his injury and the helicopter has been turned off. What a waste of a life; if only he had just followed the instructions.

We continue with the patrol and push into the area designated KA1. The pause to treat the local has allowed the enemy to get even more fighters into the area. The KA1 compounds are in good order and there are a lot of vegetables growing. It is also spookily quiet, there is not a single local around.

I decide that we will slow things down and take it steady. We will bound from compound to compound. The enemy have had plenty of time to get ready.

We take over a large compound and I push everyone inside; 6 Platoon will provide overwatch while 4 Platoon conducts the next bound.

I get intelligence that there are at least 18 separate enemy groupings trying to surround us and that they are ready to attack. I start to key up the mortars and the artillery so they are ready.

I push up to the north of the compound and climb up an inner wall so that I can look over the ten-foot high outer wall; 6 Platoon does the same and are looking over, ready to fire if necessary. I take a look at the area. There are compounds every hundred metres or so, all interspersed with corn or overgrown hedgerows. It is very close country.

Once I am happy that I can see the route they will take I tell 4 Platoon to push out.

They start to head out of the large compound gate and work round the wall before pushing north. The first and second sections are conducting their own bounding over-watch and they have gone fifty metres before it erupts all around us.

The fire is intense, really intense and it initially stuns us. The enemy have managed to close on three sides and we get attacked from all three directions at once. Multiple RPGs and PKM fire starts slamming into the compound and into the lead section that have – fortunately – just made it to a tree-line.

The lads realise that the lead section is dangerously exposed and start putting a massive weight of return fire down.

I am getting so much information shouted at me I have to start rapid multi-tasking. So far seven separate firing points have been pointed out to me. I am desperate to get the lead section back as they are really out on a limb.

I use a GMLRS (rocket) on to the enemy to the west, mortars to the east and artillery to the north. I am trying to surround us in a bubble of fire, to get the cut-off section back. We will then break out to the south.

Sergeant Sykes runs over and briefs me on his plan. He wants to push the remainder of 4 Platoon out to cover the extraction of the lead section. I give him the go ahead. I still can't believe how much fire we are under, it is deafening. I have got to get that section back.

TUESDAY 12 AUGUST

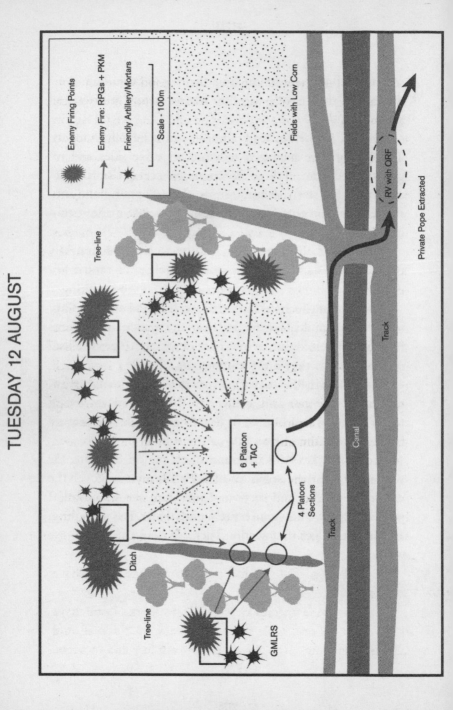

I climb back up the wall as it gives me a good vantage point. The mortars and artillery are smashing in now but we are still under a lot of fire. I look around and I can see 6 Platoon working like Trojans to keep the enemy away from the section of 4 Platoon. The lads are almost oblivious to the amount of fire they are under; they are so desperate to help their mates. I suddenly see a mass of bullet strikes all around Private Wilson. He falls back from the wall. It looks like he has been hit. He hasn't, but the belt on his light machine gun has been severed, the rounds have landed that close. He quickly sorts out his machine gun and, without the remotest hint of hesitation, climbs straight back up and continues firing.

I look round to see the last section from 4 Platoon heading out of the gate. I glance back over the wall trying to see the rest of the platoon's progress. An RPG passes really close over my head, forcing me to duck. As I duck I look back round and watch the last man from 4 Platoon leave out of the gate. Time then slows down, as I watch the rear man disappear in an explosion. The RPG has impacted on a tree directly above him and he is consumed in an instant brown cloud.

I just stare at the scene and think 'Oh my God'.

Mitch runs over and I see two Toms drag in a limp soldier by his arms. His kit is in tatters, he is blackened from the explosion and lifeless. It is like they are dragging an empty wetsuit.

I can't believe it. I can feel my innards churning. I have lost another soldier.

Mitch and the medics quickly get to work. I still have the contact to deal with so I climb back up the wall and start coordinating more targets for the artillery and mortars

I manage to get Mitch's attention across the compound – he is about 20 metres away but the gunfire and explosions are making communication challenging.

Mitch just looks at me, smiles and gives me a thumbs up.

I can't work this out. So I shout, 'Is he dead?'

Mitch just grins and gives me a thumbs up.

I am completely flummoxed so I shout again, 'Is he dead?'

'No, he's fine,' Mitch shouts back.

Lance Corporal Barker and I look at each other, both confused.

I jog over and speak to Mitch.

'Is he dead?' I ask again.

'No, he's fine,' Mitch tells me.

It is Private Pope. Looking at him you would have thought there is no way he could have survived. His kit is charred and in tatters, torn and lacerated. Amazingly he is only slightly injured – a piece of shrapnel has gone through his ankle. It's a miracle and I am so happy. He is concussed from the explosion and pretty shaken up by the experience, but at least he is alive.

This has really got my blood up. 'How dare they' I think to myself. I get back in position looking over the wall and get everyone to up the rate of fire. It's time to teach the enemy a lesson.

By now 4 Platoon have fought forward to the next compound. Using section fire and manoeuvre they have bounded forwarded, picked up the stranded section and pushed on.

The contact has already lasted an hour. I really want to get things moving and smash the enemy. I am incensed by Pope being injured and really want to get these people.

Their fire is starting to tail off so I see this as our opportunity.

I go and see Pope. I tell him that I want to keep pushing forward so he will need to hang in there for a while longer. He is really shaken by the whole thing. He tells me that he actually saw the RPG heading straight for him and in that split second he thought he was dead.

I start to get things moving. I am just desperate to push into the enemy. In reality, I'm not thinking clearly.

Mitch and Sergeant Vellor – the medic – come and see me. Although Pope is stable they think it is best if we get him back to the FOB; there might be more damage than we realise.

Again, I am reminded of the fundamental difference between what I *want* to do and what I *need* to do. I *want* to chase the enemy down and make him pay. I *need* to get Pope back to the FOB.

I change the plan. We will head back in.

I quickly pull back 4 Platoon and they move to our south. Once they are firm the rest of us pull back through them. Pope is carried in the middle by the FSG.

We move in to Jusulay and meet up with the QRF vehicles. They take Pope while the remainder of us walk back in.

It is quite surreal. There are locals in Jusulay, just 500 metres from the contact, just going about their everyday business. They watch us with a look of indifference.

By the time we get back in Pope has been extracted by Chinook. The medics seem to think that the wound isn't too bad. I am so pleased. He is such a nice lad and I honestly thought he was dead.

Despite Pope being injured I think today has gone well. The snipers got three confirmed kills but I am sure there will be a lot more once we get some intelligence feedback.

It was intense. It was a solid gunfight for over an hour. I would estimate that there were at least 40 enemy fighters out there and you could almost sense their determination to surround us. It was a hard fight.

I don't have much time to gather my thoughts as at 1400hrs A Company 3 PARA start to arrive by Chinook. This will put some strain on my poor old FOB. There will be more than 400 of us here. Nice to have visitors, though.

WEDNESDAY 13 AUGUST

It is a busy time and the FOB is groaning with so many people in it. All of the breakfast cereal is gone, which is hugely depressing. We are extending every hospitality and they seem appreciative. We should have hidden the cereal, though.

I spend the morning briefing Matt Cansdale (A Company, 3 PARA company commander) and his team. It is nice having Matt here. We have spent a long time just chatting and this really keeps the spirits up. It is just good having someone at the same level to talk to. I think talking about what we have been up to has also made me more introspective. Airing the experiences takes me back to them and I find myself going over certain aspects, all the while looking for the 'key takeaways'. What have I learnt? What do I want to anchor? My obsession with 'warrior improvement' is making me both a participant and an observer. I constantly review my assumptions, ones that I have formed through my study, to see if they are valid.

Since R&R this whole experience now seems much more time limited and I am determined to get the most out of it. This will all be over in six weeks' time. It is such an amazing honour and privilege to command men such as these. The experiences I am having will shape me for the rest of my life and we are now, all, firmly part of the regiment's history. On a personal level, it has given me the opportunity to experience something I have thought about and studied for so long. I have been to war. The overall campaign might be counter-insurgency but, at this level, it is war.

In the afternoon I take Matt and his commanders out on patrol so they can see the compound they will occupy and also allow them to see the power station and the green zone. We stick to the desert and don't get too close to the compound so as not to give the game away.

Matt is concerned that the compound is too small but it is the only option. It is the most dominant one in the area

We spend the rest of the afternoon refining the plan for his insertion. I think the enemy will see we are trying to secure more ground and will attempt to prevent us from getting established.

In the evening Matt and I have to back-brief the CO by radio on our respective plans. Matt hasn't worked for the CO before so it takes a while and a lot of questions before the CO is happy. Matt decides that the patrol base will be called Emerald.

THURSDAY 14 AUGUST

A Company inserts in the small hours, while it is still dark. They surround the compound, knock on the door and politely ask the occupants to leave. They are handed some cash and told to report to the FOB, where we will start paying them rent for the use of their compound.

At first light one of our large trucks races down the 611 and delivers a shipping container full of stores. He manages one more run before the enemy show up. It doesn't take the enemy long to work out that we are trying to establish another base. Fortunately, A Company has had enough time to fortify the compound.

They start getting hit with SPG-9 rockets and Matt responds with everything at his disposal. We have 12.7mm machine gun fired at us in the FOB.

It is safe to assume that the enemy think that it is 'us' putting in the new PB, not another company. This should work really well when both companies head out on the ground: the enemy won't have seen numbers like that in a long time.

In the afternoon I send a platoon-level clearance patrol out on the ground. I want to keep the patrol sizes down until both companies head out, so as to retain the element of surprise.

FRIDAY 15 AUGUST

A Company is getting on well and they finished their fortifications late last night. Matt has been sending me regular updates by radio. They are cramped in there but it is working.

The only drama we have had so far is that the well is dry, but they have enough bottled water for now.

Matt deploys a platoon-level patrol in his immediate vicinity. Once they are back in I send out one of mine. No need to let the enemy know how many of us are here just yet.

In the afternoon I give orders for a company-level patrol into an area called Mian Rud. We have previously only got to the outskirts of this area, which is on the banks of the river Helmand, five kilometres north of here. Battle group HQ wants me to clear a small island created on a split in the river. It has about ten compounds on it and is being used as an enemy staging post. Or so they think. Our local intelligence sources are adamant that it isn't used by the enemy. HQ won't budge though; they want me to clear it. While we are on the ground Matt will patrol at the same time. It will be interesting to see how the enemy react to so many people on the ground.

SATURDAY 16 AUGUST

We leave at 0330hrs and head straight towards Jusulay. We pick up the Jusulay track and use this to head north as quickly as possible. I have 4 Platoon leading and 5 Platoon are following my group. We make really good progress by using the track. It enables us to cover three kilometres in an hour. For the first time on patrol out here I am chilly when we do our halts.

Despite Mian Rud being five kilometres away, we are there before first light. As always, the ground is constantly changing. Battered compounds to affluent compounds; cornfields to vegetable patches to marijuana crops. It is all different. It is actually good to be going somewhere different. Getting all the way up to the banks of the river has become a bit of a personal goal. I am not aware of anyone else making it up here on foot; of course, we have got to get back as well.

Just before first light we go firm, have a snack and remove our NVGs. As dawn breaks I can see that we are just short of the river bank and about 150m from the small island that HQ wants me to clear. We have to cross 300m of scrub and shale beach to get to the island.

We cross at the shallowest point we can find, the water still coming up to our waists. The water is freezing but refreshing. It is nice to be in something so fresh, as opposed to the drainage ditches in the green zone that are full of human excrement.

The island is only 500 metres long and 300 metres wide. I bring both of the platoons up next to each other and start the clearance, with us stretching across the whole width of the island. The first compound is occupied and the inhabitants are happy to talk to us. They are adamant that the enemy doesn't come here.

As we continue our sweep a growing sense of dread starts to creep into my mind. The more I study my map, the more I realise how exposed we are. We are on a small island out on the river Helmand. Whatever happens, we are going to have to cross back over 300 metres of open ground to reach the 'home' bank: a home bank that could by now be occupied by the enemy.

What isn't helping my growing concern is that Brett is on the radio saying that they are receiving a lot of intelligence reports. There are now 17 separate enemy groupings converging on our area, plus an enemy commander.

We sweep to the end of the island and by 0800 even we

are aware of the amount of activity off in the tree-line. We can hear mopeds (a quick enemy-delivery method) and men's voices shouting.

I now have a small unmanned aerial vehicle (UAV) in the FOB. Brett clears it for launch and before long it is slowly circling above us, monitoring the situation.

The intelligence is very clear. The enemy are converging on a particular compound to receive orders from their commander.

I pull out my map and stare at the ground. It is a nightmare. This actually looks like one of our training ranges that we use in Kent, although this time we are down at the target end, not at the firing point.

I am cursing myself for being so stupid. I should not have allowed us to get into this situation. We are dangerously exposed and I have created the perfect conditions for an enemy ambush.

Mitch walks over to me. I am honest with him about how I see the situation. He agrees with my assessment but is pretty nonplussed by the whole thing.

'Oh well, what else can we do?' he says.

Fair one. I can stare at my map as much as I want; it isn't going to change anything. I also realise that, for the first time out here, I feel properly scared. If the situation was reversed, if we were set up, in cover along a bank, while 90 people crossed a large pebble beach towards us, none of them would walk away.

I tell 5 Platoon to start crossing while 4 Platoon remains in a position to cover them. I follow on.

It is eerie. We can hear voices in the tree-line and I am still receiving intelligence reports.

We get 100 metres and nothing has happened. I decide to keep pushing 5 Platoon on rather than stopping out in the open. I stay with them, as I feel it is only right and proper.

I am amazed that the enemy haven't opened up yet. Then someone in 5 Platoon spots someone armed on the compound where the enemy have been gathering. The UAV is in the air so I get Brett to see if there are any locals in the area. He can't see any.

I decide to go for GMLRS. This is a pinpoint accurate rocket with a large explosive warhead on it. Launched from 20km away, it will still land within a metre of its intended target. I hope to limit the damage with one of these and I would assume that the locals have fled anyway; they don't usually hang about.

It takes a while but I get clearance to use the GMLRS and I ask for three to converge on the centre of the compound.

The effect is incredible. The GMLRS doesn't make any noise, it is travelling so fast, it just slams in. Three huge explosions, all in exactly the right place. At the same time that the rockets explode a burst of enemy PKM fire is let loose at us but that is it. It then all goes quiet.

The effect on the enemy is instantaneous. All of the intelligence messages switch from plans to attack us to plans to evacuate their wounded.

We can hear a lot of motorbikes speeding away. We use the confusion to our advantage and cross the open ground as quickly as possible. We arrive at the scene and the compound is obliterated. Unfortunately, it hasn't been as clean as I had hoped. There have been civilian casualties. They weren't in the compound, but were hit by a piece of flying masonry from the target compound.

I am devastated but realise I have to keep on top of the situation. I get security out immediately, as there are a lot of enemy out there. The medics see to the injured. They don't think they are too bad.

Out of the corner of my eye I can see a local elder having a blazing argument with a young man; a 'fighting age male'. The elder keeps waving him off, as if he is telling him to leave. Eventually he does, on a moped, glowering at us as he passes by. Looks to me like the locals have just told the Taliban to go away.

I speak to the elder and offer to evacuate his wounded. He is adamant that they want to do it themselves. Once the medics are happy that the casualties are stable they are loaded into a local minibus and driven off.

I apologise to the elder but firmly inform him that we know that there were enemy in the area. He is non-committal, but not disputing it.

We head back to the FOB. The remainder of the patrol is quiet, which I have not seen before. I have also not before seen that number of enemy converge on an area, get themselves set up and then just back off.

Once back in the FOB the intelligence is good. We hit a substantial enemy grouping. Initial indications are that five were killed and 20 injured. The best enemy message I am shown is 'No, don't fight; we have taken too many casualties as it is, just hide'.

The aftertaste is unpleasant though. None of us wants to hurt the locals. I am really beating myself up over it. Predominantly I blame the enemy, though, for setting up in an area and not getting the locals to leave.

Fortunately Mitch comes round for a chat. After a good

honest chat with him I realise that I had very little option. As unpalatable as it was, I still managed to bring all of my soldiers back in. Any patrol from which I bring back all of my soldiers without a scratch is a success as far as I am concerned. Unfortunately, I am going to have to chalk this one up to experience.

SUNDAY 17 AUGUST

There is inevitable fallout from the injury of locals and I have to send a lot of reports off to HQ. James, the battalion 2IC, is brilliant and couldn't be more helpful. He gets a full report from me on the secure phone and then completes most of the paperwork on my behalf. His approach is to back the man on the ground and he goes a long way to putting my mind at rest.

I spend the afternoon reading. I am trying to get some rest. This is going to be a busy period and I am taking the company out every other day. It is tiring for me but even worse for the lads. They often end up doing back-to-back patrols due to the shortage of manpower. Even when they aren't on patrol they still have to do guard duty in one of the sangars. It is a relentless grind for the Toms and it is amazing how well they take it. They seem to suck up all of the trivia as penance for being allowed to get out there and fight the enemy. They really are amazing.

Up at PB Emerald, A Company are constantly occupied. They are sending out patrols and when they don't the enemy creeps in and fires rockets and RPGs at them. I spend most of the afternoon reading a book and listening to our mortars firing in response to a call from Matt.

I give orders for tomorrow's patrol and then have an early night.

MONDAY 18 AUGUST

We depart at 0330hrs and head north-east from the FOB to an area designated KA7. I am always fascinated coming up here. The locals always leave so quickly it leaves a ghost-like shadow of their presence – a kettle still on the fire, food still on the table. I want to tell them that we are here to help but I never get the chance.

A good route has been picked by 5 Platoon; they are really adept at night movement now. They are a very slick team and Wes always understands my intent. I can rely on him to get me on target, on time, at night. This is no mean feat, as patrolling and navigating through corn at night is incredibly challenging. We are all helped by a clear morning and good moonlight. At first light we remove NVGs and continue sweeping round KA7 and KB1. This area is two kilometres west of Mian Rud and close to the river. Unsurprisingly, there are no locals but what is strange is that we are generating very little intelligence.

It gets to 0800 and the enemy still aren't planning anything hostile against us. Maybe having two companies in the area is putting them under too much pressure.

We continue pushing forward and then the atmospherics quickly start to build. Brett is relaying intelligence to me; the enemy are getting it together and preparing to attack.

They wait until we are slightly exposed, in one of the more open areas next to a canal, a small offshoot of the main river.

A heavy weight of RPGs and PKM fire is directed at both the lead platoon and my group. I start to run for cover and I can hear and feel the weight of fire increase, rounds cracking over head. This is always off-putting. The increase in fire means that they are shooting at you, not just towards you!

Wes identifies the enemy firing points and quickly gets the information to me. I hit them with 105mm artillery and mortars. The enemy have engaged the lead section of 5 Platoon at very close range so to break their attack I call the mortars in danger-close. The lead section is sheltering in a bend in a stream and this allows us to bring the mortars in 50 metres to their front. The contact lasts for about twenty minutes and then the enemy fire starts to tail off.

Wes has identified a small canal to his front so we start aggressively pushing forward, using the canal as cover. This seems to overwhelm the enemy and it soon goes quiet. The use of the canal also allows us to flank around the compound that the enemy were using and catch a man before he has time to escape. The RMP corporal has a kit that tests for explosives and the man comes up positive – he was just firing a weapon. We take him with us and I organise for the ANA Platoon to patrol out and take custody of him.

We start to head back in, linking up with the ANA in KA4. They take the prisoner from us but seem unconvinced by our magic dye that says he was firing a weapon. They prefer to see a weapon.

We arrive back in the FOB at 1100. I go through my familiar routine. I still relish the experience of stripping off all of my hot sweaty patrol kit and having a solar shower out in the open.

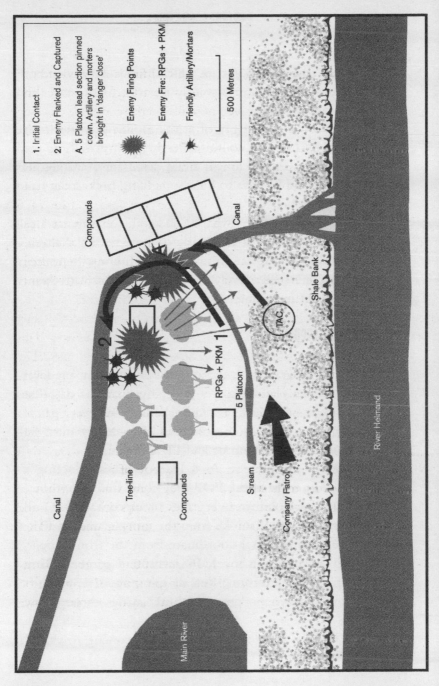

MONDAY 18 AUGUST

1. Initial Contact
2. Enemy Flanked and Captured

A. 5 Platoon lead section pinned down. Artillery and mortars brought in 'danger close'

Enemy Firing Points
Enemy Fire: RPGs + PKM
Friendly Artillery/Mortars

500 Metres

Compounds
Canal
Tree-line
Compounds
Stream
Company Patrol
Main River
River Helmand
Shale Bank
TAC
RPGs + PKM
5 Platoon
Canal

I never take afternoon naps which means that my energy comes and goes. I have a weekly report to write but this doesn't take long.

I am really enjoying myself at the moment. As our tour gets ever shorter it becomes easier to push myself, as the end is in sight. I'm no longer afraid that I am overdoing it, or that it would be wise to hold something back. I can rest when I get home.

I am really struck by what an incredible experience this all is. Professionally, I couldn't ask for more but I also realise that in the not-too-distant future I will be home with Andrea and Rufus. It is such a lovely thought, being back with them; it really keeps me going.

TUESDAY 19 AUGUST

The patrol programme is day on, day off for company-level patrols while a platoon patrol is deployed on the day that the company isn't out. It is quite relentless and every patrol is getting contacted at the moment. The enemy must be feeling the pressure from us and PB Emerald.

Today is no different. As 6 Platoon are conducting a patrol to the front of the FOB they come under machine-gun fire. They conduct a very slick break contact and pull back under cover of smoke from the mortars and an artillery fire mission that I coordinate from the front sangar. They all arrive back in covered in sweat and grime, sucking in air from the exertion, but all grinning. 'It's all shits and giggles when no one gets hurt' rattles through my mind.

I have been informed that the CO is coming to visit. I

am always slightly anxious when he is coming. The company is working so hard and enduring so much I just want him to see us in the best light. We aren't going to do any stage management, but I also want to make sure that we don't create the wrong impression. With my CSM – Thorpy – away on R&R, Mitch is standing in. He understands exactly where I am coming from and ensures that all the little things are seen to. I just want the CO to see exactly what B Company has been through and what we are achieving, considering the conditions.

I wander round and chat to any Toms that I bump into. The lads seem on good form and morale seems quite high. Most are quite chatty and are still keen to get out there and 'take it to the enemy'. All the Toms I speak to reinforce how relentless their workload is. They go on patrol, pull stag [sentry] duty in one of the sangars and then are invariably back on patrol again as we are so short on numbers, because of those off on R&R. Everyone needs a break from this though, so it is something we will just have to manage. I realise I need to keep an eye on the patrol programme and if it is getting too much I will have to throttle back.

WEDNESDAY 20 AUGUST

The CO, RSM and Padre Alan Steel arrive mid-morning by helicopter. It is great to see Alan as I haven't seen him in a long time and he has been desperately trying to come and visit. He is without shadow of a doubt the best army padre I have ever met. He has such a great touch with the lads and in turn they really like him and, importantly, talk to him. Likewise, the RSM is a superb guy and really good at his job.

The CO is relaxed and keen to talk. This suits me and we spend most of the day seeking cover, drinking coffee and talking about all sorts of stuff – the tour, the enemy, decisions, command, leadership, our respective R&Rs. It is good to have such a long talk with him.

We chat for a couple of hours and then he starts to wander round the FOB talking to the lads. This gives me a chance to catch up with Alan. We have known each other for years and I consider him a good friend. He has managed to visit all of the other companies, so it is useful for me to hear what everyone has been up to. It sounds like B, C and D Companies are having very different experiences in terms of terrain, enemy and challenges. Everyone is being put through the grinder, just in different ways. It's nice to be able to have a brew and a chat with a friend. It gives me an opportunity to air some of my feelings, especially those that I have kept bottled up after the loss of my three lads and Lance Corporal Rowe.

After lunch I head into the back office and plan tomorrow's patrol. I decide that we will go back to KA1, where Private Pope was injured. There is obviously a large enemy grouping there and they have demonstrated the ability to mass and coordinate quickly. There must be a local commander nearby. Plus, this grouping is north-west of the FOB and towards Sangin. If I can tie them down, I am achieving my mission.

I give orders mid-afternoon. The CO is happy with the plan and keen to get out on the ground and see the company in action. I don't think he will be disappointed.

After dinner I have another long chat with the CO. We talk about our post-tour plans. We will be getting quite a bit of leave and we both love Cornwall so most of our chat centres on that. It is good to see him so chatty. He is a good guy when he relaxes and the Toms are enjoying talking to him.

THURSDAY 21 AUGUST

We depart at 0330hrs with 6 Platoon leading, TAC, FSG, then 4 Platoon. I ask the CO where he would like to go, figuring he will probably stay with me. He decides to go with 6 Platoon in the lead section! The RSM goes with the CSM's group, commanded by Mitch.

Alan decides to come with the FSG and my group. The lads love this – they refer to it as 'religious top cover'. If the padre is with us, we must be safe. Alan doesn't even have a weapon, which the lads find baffling.

We make good progress weaving through the tracks and cornfields, through Jusulay and into KA1.

A compound which we suspect is an enemy sentry position, based on our experience last time, is secured by 6 Platoon, but it is found to be empty. I use the FSG to clear a compound I want to occupy and 4 Platoon secure a separate objective. This means that by first light we are all firm in compounds. We are in a position to provide mutual support to each other and, importantly, can see each other.

We have a break, remove our night vision and have a pause. The second wail from the mosques reverberates around the green zone, signifying the end of prayers. For us it signifies we will soon be spotted – and soon be in contact.

I like this secure position we are in and I like making the enemy expose himself by coming to us, but we aren't generating much intelligence.

This changes at 0600 and Brett comes on the radio to tell me that we have been spotted and that the enemy is in the process of pulling together a group to attack us.

Looking at the map, we are in a triangle formation with 6 Platoon at the apex, my group bottom left and 4 Platoon bottom right. I decide to swing 4 Platoon right, passing by 6 Platoon before going firm. My group will follow 4 Platoon and then the company will start to leapfrog forward with constant overwatch.

I move my group and the FSG to the rear of 4 Platoon and tell Dave – the platoon commander – to start his bound forward.

The canal is just to our rear, providing some semblance of cover but we will have to push out into the open to get to our next objective.

As soon as 4 Platoon leaves its compound the contact starts. RPGs, PKM and AK fire is poured down at 6 Platoon from multiple firing points. Due to the way we are orientated most of the fire is passing overhead of 6 Platoon and landing among us. This sends us all scrambling for cover but there isn't a huge amount. It is 'hug the ground' time.

We get opened up on from the right flank and quickly there are a number of enemy firing points shooting at us. This means we are now being fired at from the west, north and east. There are rounds flying everywhere and I am trying to get the mortars and artillery firing on to as many targets as possible.

Suddenly the dreaded shout of 'man down' goes up. This is only fifty metres from my position, so I crawl back down the track and look round the corner to see two Toms dragging someone back into a ditch. Mitch and the medics run forward and take charge.

I watch in amazement as Mitch casually stands there, under fire, supervising the casualty. He seems oblivious to the amount of fire that is flying around. His demeanour keeps those around him calm.

He runs up to me and tells me that the casualty is Lance Corporal Dipnall or 'Dippers' as he is known; he has been shot in the chest, causing a sucking chest wound. He was actually on the ground when he was hit. In the prone position a round passed just above the top of his body armour and down through his chest cavity. We need an immediate CASEVAC.

The FOB is to our rear – south – the only direction that we aren't being contacted from.

I increase the fire to our front to keep the enemy occupied while Mitch sorts out Lance Corporal Dipnall.

The QRF vehicles take huge risk again to rescue an injured comrade and race out to the track junction just on the other side of the canal. Within ten minutes Lance Corporal Dipnall is back in the FOB and away on a medical Chinook.

Once Dippers is away I increase the artillery barrage and get 4 Platoon to push forward.

As soon as we start to put the enemy under pressure with both fire and movement he backs off, allowing me to get some momentum going.

It all goes quiet, allowing 4 Platoon to secure its next objective – another compound and a track junction. I plan to bound from compound to compound, as the elevation from the buildings gives us an advantage. A Section of 4 Platoon and my group stay outside the compound next to the track as 6 Platoon starts its movement and we get a large contact rear. Obviously the enemy are trying to follow us. Yet again, the rounds are missing their intended target, passing overhead and landing among my group. Rounds slam into the trees that we are sheltering next to, causing us to scuttle for cover like beetles. I look up to see Alan grinning at me. He takes a picture of the tree I am sheltering behind and the strike marks one metre above my head where the rounds hit. It's amazing how people can always put a smile on for the camera.

The latest enemy firing point is identified by 4 Platoon. There is only one this time and I silence it with artillery.

We continue to push in a wide arc to the right, into KA2. During one of the halts a couple of Toms start to look around the edge of the compound that they are sheltering behind. They think they see a mortar round poking out of the ground so I get them to pull back and send in the 9 Squadron Engineer lads to have a look.

They have a poke around and discover a weapons cache. What looks like 30 Soviet 82mm mortar rounds. What a find. As luck would have it, we have another sergeant from the Royal Engineers with us and he is qualified to blow enemy ammunition.

They set to work and I ensure that they have security in place to allow them to work. Of course everything takes time and it is getting hotter and hotter.

After forty-five minutes they are ready and we all pull back. There is a large, satisfying explosion and one of the engineers reports that all of the rounds have gone.

I get the company moving again and we start to loop back towards the FOB, passing through KA5 and then straight back in. The enemy leaves us alone.

We get in at 1300; a nine-hour patrol.

I rush up to the ops room to find out about Lance Corporal Dipnall. Wes meets me on the way. Dippers is from 5 Platoon, the 3 PARA platoon, and was out with 4 Platoon today to make up numbers. He is very popular and a highly respected member of the company. Wes's pained expression makes me fear the worst.

Dippers 'crashed' on the helicopter. Effectively, he died. The medics managed to resuscitate him but gave him a category 9 chance of survival. Category 9 is almost zero chance; only one other casualty in the whole campaign at this point has survived this category.

Dippers, being the legendary fighter that he is, made it back to Bastion and is now stable. He went straight into surgery and they think he will lose half a lung, his spleen and a kidney. Amazingly, though, he is still alive.

I feel so sorry for him; he is such a good lad. I am just so grateful that he is still alive. So is Wes, although 5 Platoon are pretty shaken by the news.

I give the CO an update and he immediately phones HQ and tries to get some more information for us.

Later in the afternoon I have a chat with the CO and I realise that he has seen it all now – the ground, the enemy, CASEVAC, the decisions and the challenges we face here. He seems suitably impressed.

This leaves me very, very proud of my gang. They just suck all of this up and I am not sure that they are getting the recognition they deserve. I wanted the CO to see what we are up against and by going with the lead section there is no doubt that he has.

The CO is supposed to leave tonight but he seems to be enjoying himself and decides to stay an extra day.

FRIDAY 22 AUGUST

Changeover day today. A Company, 3 PARA have been recalled back to Bastion to begin their preparation for Op OT so D Company, 2 PARA will replace them at Emerald. This is good news as it means that Mike Shervington – 'Shervs' – will be just up the valley and we should get the chance to catch up again.

I deploy a platoon-level patrol into the local area and it passes without incident. This patrol is used as a diversion to allow the changeover at the PB. This all seems to work, as none of the Chinooks are contacted.

The CO spends all morning walking around talking to the lads. This gives him a really good feel for their workload and how hard they are pushing themselves. I am concerned that there will be pressure from HQ to mount even more patrols. As far as I am concerned, we are already working at full capacity.

I talk this through with the CO after lunch. The patrol yesterday and his chat to the lads leads him to agree with me. We can't really do any more.

I explain that I plan spikes of activity and then ramp things down to give people the chance to rest. He agrees with this plan and tells me to balance the patrol programme as I see fit and not to take unnecessary risk. I think the CO has really picked up on the fatigue that comes from our patrol programme and the overall grind that comes from our living conditions.

Late afternoon the Viking troop arrives from Sangin to take the CO back to his headquarters. He seemed to have had a good visit and drives off into the desert smiling and waving.

SATURDAY 23 AUGUST

I put in an 'equipment care' day. The lads really need a break as they have been grafting over the past week. There is so much pressure on the Toms but there really is no alternative. I wish there was more I could do but we are so short of manpower. The lads end up back-filling each platoon for the company-level patrols, so it is relentless for them. The only way I can give them a break is an EC day.

In the afternoon I get all of my commanders together and tell them how we will conduct the next couple of weeks. We have got to keep the activity up for Op OT and I understand the Toms' workload. We will surge patrols for a few days, as we have been doing, then put in EC days to give people a rest. It's hard, but we have got to keep pushing on. We can't afford to let the enemy gain any advantage.

SUNDAY 24 AUGUST

Star Wars village gets a patrol from 5 Platoon. This is a nice short one for them and we haven't been in there for a while.

Surprisingly, they discover a pressure plate improvised

explosive device (PPIED). It is a surprise, as we haven't seen much enemy activity in the village and this is a worrying development. I am amazed the elders have let the enemy put something so offensive and dangerous in their village.

I try to get the disposal team to come out but they are busy. I am told to mark the device and leave it! Absolute lunacy – as if it will still be there when we decide to come back!

I send for Corporal Berenger and we quickly craft a plan. He can set up an observation post on the roof of the 7 RHA sangar that can see the PPIED. The snipers will maintain 'eyes on' the device and if anyone goes near it they will fire flares and warning shots to keep people away until we can deploy a QRF. The snipers will observe at night and the sangar sentry will cover the day.

Once all of this is in place I tell Wes to head back in. I brief HQ on the plan and they are happy. They will keep trying to get me bomb disposal. I really don't want to leave the PPIED out there, there are far too many children in the village.

In the afternoon I get the FSG to mount a vehicle patrol to take me up to PB Emerald. Sergeant Lee Payne drives my Land Rover and two other vehicles accompany us. I haven't been in the vehicles much and I realise I am far happier on foot. The lads are really good on their drills – checking for mines and constantly providing overwatch – but I still can't shake the mental image of us hitting an anti-tank mine and getting blown to smithereens. As nice as it is driving in the desert, it is still pretty nerve-wracking.

We get to the PB and it is like a family reunion. All smiles and handshakes; we haven't seen any of our 2 PARA mates for months.

'Shervs' is there to greet me and so is Paddy, his sergeant major. Paddy makes his excuses and Mike and I get a brew on and have a good catch up. As ever, there is a lot of gossip to be exchanged and cross-referenced. It's just nice to see such a good friend and again reinforces the 'loneliness of command'. Shervs is a good friend and I know that I can say pretty much anything to him and he will be able to understand and empathise. I get on really well with people in my company, but there are certain aspects that are the company commander's alone. That is why it is so nice to talk to another one.

After a couple of hours of putting the world to rights I realise I need to head back. D Company is scheduled to be here for a couple of weeks so we should have plenty of opportunity to catch up and joint patrol in the future.

MONDAY 25 AUGUST

I am in the ops room having a brew when Corporal Berenger comes in. Our cunning PPIED plan has fallen apart. The snipers maintained 'eyes on' all through the night and handed the task on to a 7 RHA sentry in the morning. Unfortunately the sentries were not properly briefed and during a sentry changeover the PPIED 'disappeared'. I am both annoyed and relieved. I am annoyed that someone didn't come out and dispose of it and now it might be placed somewhere else for us to find, possibly with someone's foot. I am relieved that it is gone though, especially from the village. The moment the enemy knew that we had spotted it they would have been trying to get it back.

In the afternoon the CO passes through and says hello.

He is in the Vikings and off up to see D Company in the PB. He still seems on good form and doesn't stay long as he wants to get up and chat with Mike.

In the afternoon I give a set of orders for a company-level patrol tomorrow. I realise that I have got to keep driving the lads on. As the end of the tour gets closer and closer there is the possibility that people will start to become reluctant to go out. 'No one wants to get injured on the last patrol' is a common thought.

So, I throw everything I have got into my orders. I have come up with a good plan and I really add some passion and aggression to the delivery. A verbal set of orders is all that you have got to convince people that you passionately believe in your own plan.

The lads seem fired up and Mitch leans in afterwards and says 'good set of orders, that'.

I am flushed with pride and then Brett ruins it. He has just appeared from the ops room with bad news. D Company is now required for Op OT and are being extracted tomorrow. I will need to put one of my own platoons into the PB in order to continue maintaining the effect that we are focused on the 611 road.

No patrol tomorrow, despite my fire and brimstone speech and no Shervs just up the road. Double blow.

Brett, the platoon commanders and I go to the ops room and do some hasty planning. Wes volunteers 5 Platoon to go up to the PB first. I decide that the platoons will do week-long rotations up there.

Wes and his platoon will patrol up tonight and take over the PB, allowing D Company to extract first thing in the morning.

Just after last light I wave off Wes and his gang. This means I have even less manpower in the FOB.

TUESDAY 26 AUGUST

I am up early to go to the gym and I watch the Chinooks sweep into the desert just behind the PB to extract D Company. I think how rapidly the PB is shrinking. Matt established it with 160 people – it looked like every spare soldier from 3 PARA had jumped on that operation. Shervs took over with 70 people and now Wes is up there with his 30. At this rate there will be two Toms up there by the weekend.

As part of the Op OT deception plan the US Special Forces are working five kilometres north, up the 611. They work in smaller numbers and rely on air power to maintain their superiority. They seem to be having an interesting time and sucking the enemy in, as every twenty minutes or so a jet flashes over and drops a bomb on a target.

It is mid-morning when there is a large explosion to our north. The US SF has just dropped a 500lb bomb on an enemy patrol.

About twenty minutes later we get word that the US SF hit the enemy but, unknown to them, there were civilians sheltering in the same compound. Unfortunately there are civilian casualties. This is typical of the Taliban – complete disregard for the locals.

Twenty minutes later a taxi screeches to a halt at the front gate to the FOB and locals start dragging out severely injured men.

We have a new doctor – a TA captain – who seems a good guy and Thorpy is back from his R&R. They both head off to the front gate to start to create some order in the chaos that is ensuing. There are two casualties but at least 20 people shouting and gesticulating at the front gate.

The doc is superb, focused and not flapping; he starts to call for people to help. Thorpy quickly organises stretcher-bearers and the casualties are brought up to the medical centre.

I stick my head round the door and the doctor is quite happy to brief me. The scene is pretty unpleasant. There are two men, both of whom have lost their legs below the knees; one has also lost an arm. All of the medics are here working on the casualties.

We quickly organise an evacuation helicopter and within thirty minutes they are on their way to hospital. I am just congratulating the doc when the shout goes up that another taxi has arrived with two more men. These two aren't in such a bad way as the last two; they are pretty banged up, though. What strikes me is that they really look like Taliban: they are young, healthy-looking men with trimmed beards.

Once the next helicopter is on its way to remove these casualties I realise that I am hungry and that it is lunch time, so I head over to the cookhouse and grab some food. It then dawns on me that I am becoming pretty hardened to all this. The state of the four casualties hasn't affected my appetite at all.

In the afternoon it gets progressively worse. It looks like the Taliban get treated first, then civilians.

Late afternoon, two women and five children arrive, all injured. One of the children dies as soon as he gets here. For this number of casualties it is all hands to the pumps. Every patrol medic is sucked in. The doctor conducts triage, telling the medics what to do, before he moves on to the next casualty. He keeps working round and round the circle checking on each casualty's treatment and progress.

I am standing back watching the scene, helping Brett coordinate the CASEVAC and I have a huge sense of pride. Medics are with the casualties, there are Toms with all their gear on ready to do HLS security, and there are stretcher-bearers ready to go. All in all there are about 60 people involved in this and it looks to me like the British Army at its very best. It is impressive; we just fix problems.

After all the casualties are gone I sit in the briefing area with Thorpy and the doc, having a chat. I can see why people want to work in casualty, it is a real buzz. Like all adrenaline buzzes though, it wears off and you have to come down. We all start flagging and head off to bed. We are tired but pretty proud of our efforts helping people.

WEDNESDAY 27 AUGUST

In the morning I have a strange reminder of cultural differences towards death.

A middle-aged local man arrives with two more injured women. We treated his wife and children yesterday. He wants to find out how and where they are. I get news for him, then ask about the child who died. We still have his body in the medical store – there was no room on the CASEVAC last night. The man tells me that the child was his nephew and an orphan; he looked after him. I pass on my condolences through an interpreter and ask him if he would like to take the body.

His response stuns me. He tells me that he would rather not. If he takes the body, he will have to pay for the funeral.

I offer to pay for the funeral. He is happy with this so I get some dollars from my fund. The local's attitude changes once he has the dollars and he hefts the wrapped body on to his shoulders and heads off to get a taxi.

While I have been having this conversation the two women have been stabilised and a CASEVAC organised.

I head over for breakfast, which looks like it will be a real treat. With all the helicopters we have been receiving they have managed to send us some fresh food. For breakfast I have (real not tinned!) egg, sausage, bacon, baked beans and bread. It is magnificent. I make a mental note to ask Andrea to have plenty of fresh ingredients in the house when I return. When I get back I want to have really good sausage and bacon, plus eggs from my own chickens.

The day passes slowly. It is the day before D-Day. Op OT is due to start in the early hours of tomorrow morning so it is all quiet, right across the brigade. There are hardly any messages on the radio in the ops room. I imagine there are hundreds, if not thousands, of soldiers all 'waiting for the off', trying to push the inevitable anxiety to the back of their minds. Lots of soldiers sitting quietly reading a book or adjusting their kit.

This operation is big and very complex, with an incredible amount of moving parts. The brigade commander has moved forward to Kajaki with a small HQ to be in a better position to influence the battle; 3 PARA is running the bulk of the op, with everyone else in some form of supporting role. The deception plan appears to be working. The locals and the enemy are under the impression that the convoy will move up the 611. There is no intelligence to suggest otherwise. In our AO, the PB is achieving what we want it to. We have expanded our area of effect and it does look like we are trying to secure a valuable stretch of the 611. US SF are just beyond this, dropping as much ordnance as they can but still creating the effect that we are 'road' focused.

I am fascinated by how the op will go. I think that the deception effect will continue longer than people realise, but we will have to wait and see. I am also dubious whether the convoy will depart when it is supposed to; it is due to start just before first light.

The PB is limiting my available manpower so for the next few days we will concentrate on platoon-level patrolling. Tomorrow morning 6 Platoon will go out and picket the 611 – making it look like we are securing our stretch of road.

I volunteer to do the early watch-keeper shift in the ops room tomorrow morning, 0500–0800hrs. I want to listen to the op unfold on the radio.

THURSDAY 28 AUGUST

I get up at 0445 and am surprised at how chilly it is. I pull on my para smock, grab my mug and head round to the ops room. At this time in the morning it is great walking into its light, warm and welcoming atmosphere. I am replacing Sergeant Radcliffe who has been on since midnight. He greets me in his usual chirpy Scouse way and we put the kettle on.

I make everyone a brew. This always goes down well and it is a little thing that I have picked up on. The signallers will always make you a brew if you ask, but they all love having a brew made for them by a *major*. It is the least I can do, considering how well they look after me. My signals detachment is a great crew.

The op is on and it has started. Sergeant Radcliffe has been listening to it and all is going well. We listen to the radio traffic for an hour before 6 Platoon head out to the 611.

They move in front of the FOB and establish checkpoints, stopping drivers and letting them know that the convoy is on its way. Wes does the same with his platoon from the PB. It all seems to be working. It is not in the Taliban's interest to attack the convoy, anyway. Another turbine means more electricity, which means more tax for them.

After a couple of hours 6 Platoon heads back in; they have generated little intelligence. The enemy doesn't seem that interested.

FRIDAY 29 AUGUST

Today 4 Platoon conducts a low-level clearance patrol around the FOB and heads into Star Wars village for a chat with the locals.

Op OT is progressing well. The convoy has got itself deep into the desert and the route that the pathfinders found has been working.

It would appear that all of the activity is having an effect on the enemy. Intelligence has discovered that the enemy thinks that the desert convoy is a deception and therefore he will leave it alone. He is going to wait for the convoy up the 611. Brigade HQ must be delighted with their plan; it is working really well.

Just before last light the enemy fire an SP109 rocket at

the FOB from a compound 1500 metres to our north. The rocket sails overhead and lands in the centre of Star Wars village. I can't imagine that the locals will be happy with that. The firing point is quickly identified so we fire artillery back. It is all over quickly and is pretty much the most exciting thing that has happened today.

SATURDAY 30 AUGUST

I do the early watch-keeper shift again. I enjoyed it the other morning. I quite like getting up early and having a coffee and a chat with the signallers while it is all quiet.

It is pretty steady at the moment, which everyone seems happy with. We are concentrating on platoon-level activity. We are mounting a patrol each day but what is interesting is that for the first time in weeks the patrols aren't being engaged. There is intelligence that the enemy is still out there, but with the new PB and Op OT he has become more dislocated and is struggling to pull decent-size groupings together. This is good for us.

US SF are still operating up the valley and pummelling anything that comes near them. This tactic appears to be working. In Afghanistan they respect strength.

At the PB, 5 Platoon have been doing an excellent job. Wes has really been developing the intelligence picture and mapping out that part of the AO – discovering who lives where and what their views are on security. We have even had a local move back into his compound behind the PB. When questioned, he said that with us there he felt it would be safe to move back in. Although this is only one family, it is an indication that this can work; it is a matter of the numbers needed to achieve wider success.

SUNDAY 31 AUGUST

As Op OT is going so well, assets that were on standby to support are now being freed up, as they are not required. BGHQ has decided that a resupply will come to the FOB tonight to 'top us off' with rations and supplies.

I nominate 6 Platoon to do the task and have a chat with Tom, the platoon commander, as to what I want. He heads off reasonably happy.

I don't have much to do today so I spend most of my time wandering around chatting to the Toms. They are on good form but I start to pick up on an underlying thread. I get the impression that they feel we are pretty much at the end of this and that we should start to take less risk.

I understand their thinking, but it worries me. So much so that I have a good think about a presentation I would like to give and then schedule a briefing for all of 4 and 6 Platoons. I will chat to 5 Platoon when they get back from the PB.

SEPTEMBER

The company has momentum at the moment and I am confident we can keep this up until the end. We need to keep focused, though: it will take continual effort and a determined drive to move forward. I am mindful of how relentless this is for the Toms. Their workload is high. They end up on nearly every patrol as we are so short of numbers. They pull guard duty in the sangars that breaks up their sleep pattern and, invariably, there are other jobs that need doing around the FOB. It is solid graft for them and I am constantly impressed by their humour, resilience but most of all their driving focus. They want to get out there and take the fight to the enemy.

The challenges for the commanders are different. We have to create the conditions for the Toms to do what they do best – fight the enemy. There are constant challenges and frictions preventing us doing what we want to do but that is leadership. You have to be flexible. You have to understand what has to be done but also where you can be pragmatic. I am constantly reviewing the patrol programme with that in mind.

Inevitably, thoughts turn to home in the quieter moments and it seems strange that soon all of this will be someone else's challenge. What is also strange is that once we get back, B Company will immediately start to change face. The support company lads will head back to their own company. Lads will get posted to other jobs and new soldiers will join us. Very soon B Company will be a different group of people. Not a very pleasant thought, but for now I am determined to concentrate, in slightly megalomaniacal terms, on 'all of this being mine'.

MONDAY 1 SEPTEMBER

Finally, it is September. Quite a mental benchmark for us. As one of the Toms points out to me, at least we can now say 'We are going home next month'. Good point; well spotted, as ever.

I gather 4 and 6 Platoons in the briefing area and as much of the FSG as possible. I need to speak to them; they have to hear this from me. Speaking to the lads always brings out the best in me. I get really fired up and passionate.

I start with my favourite Apollo 13 quote, 'There is no such thing as a routine space flight'. I have picked up on the fact that people are starting to think that we are just going on 'another routine patrol'. There is no such thing as routine patrol when there is a real enemy out there.

I tell them that we have got to push on, right through to the finish, we are professionals and we have to maintain the traditions of the Parachute Regiment. If we hunker down in the FOB the enemy will close in and pick us apart with indirect fire. We would take more casualties than if we got out there and fought him in the green zone. Lastly, we have to honour those that won't be coming home with us. The enemy is still out there and we have unfinished business. We owe it to the fallen, we owe it to ourselves. Intelligence has now indicated that the enemy in our AO is increasing. I suspect Op OT and the US SF action is driving them down into our area. I think that we will now be dealing with disparate groupings of enemy and that gives us an opportunity. An opportunity to get out there and really pull him apart. I want us to hit the enemy with everything that we have got, so that he is left in no doubt as to whom he has been dealing with.

I think it is a good speech. The lads' shoulders are up, heads proud, making eye contact and nodding in agreement. I ask the Toms to leave and have a quick chat with the commanders. They all seem happy and understand where I am coming from. We have to keep getting out there and keep taking the fight to the enemy.

Just before heading off to bed we get some great news. We get an update about Lance Corporal Dipnall – 'Dippers'. He is back in the UK and making a fantastic recovery. Despite the extent of his wounds he is doing really well and should have far less damage than originally thought. This really cheers everyone up.

TUESDAY 2 SEPTEMBER

The resupply convoy passed without incident last night and 6 Platoon were in fairly early. All pretty quiet. The CSM is continuing with the low-level activity of preparing the FOB for handover. We want to try to get it into the best position possible, especially with winter approaching, so he takes small groups of spare Toms and sets them to work on various tasks – restacking, tidying, accounting etc. None of it is too arduous, so they don't seem to mind.

WEDNESDAY 3 SEPTEMBER

I am not sleeping very well at the moment and I have no idea why. I wake up at 0145hrs and by 0300 I am so bored with being awake I grab my head torch and read my book for an hour. It is a Tom Clancy novel that is proving engrossing.

I manage to drift off for a few hours but get up at 0645hrs and head to the ops room to make myself a coffee. I decide I won't train today. I have got into a good routine of doing a thirty-minute run followed by thirty minutes of weights most days. If I don't do this session I do a 'stretch' day, which is push-ups, handstand push-ups, dips and stretching. The stretching seems to help with all the weight we carry out on patrol. I decide to rest today as we have a company patrol tomorrow.

I deliver orders at 1000 for tomorrow's patrol. We are going to clear the western sector of the AO. I haven't been out for a while, so I have had the time to really study and plan this patrol.

We don't have a good picture of what the enemy are up to in this area so we need to go and have a look. This is the patrol that I planned for last week but it got cancelled due to us having to man the PB. The aim is to clear an area designated JB4 and the surrounding area. Op OT has 'muddied the waters', no one is sure if the enemy are still there, gone to Kajaki to fight, been blown up by US SF or … what? There is only one way to find out – 'saddle up' – get out there and have a look.

This should be a good patrol and we have the opportunity to use more firepower if necessary. The rules of engagement have been enhanced for Op OT, so it is much easier for us to pre-engage the enemy. I could do with 'Saddam' and a small pocket of enemy being out there so that I can wipe him off the face of the earth.

THURSDAY 4 SEPTEMBER

Fortunately I sleep well. I am woken at 0300hrs, I go through my usual routine and we depart at 0340.

First 5 Platoon patrol down to the FOB and then link up with the remainder of us at the rear gate. They leave a skeleton crew at the PB to guard it and I am content with their security as we won't be that far away. I am taking 4 Platoon and a strong FSG as well.

It is a low moon state, so our NVGs aren't that good. The going is hard in the darkness and the crops are still towering above us. We're led by 5 Platoon and Corporal Hawthorne, the lead section commander, does an excellent job at navigating us out. We are close to our objective by first light. After a short pause to remove our night sights and eat an energy bar we push on.

The atmospherics are strange. The locals are moving away from us at speed but we aren't getting much external intelligence. We haven't really seen this before.

We move into the target area and it is really close. The

corn is eight foot high and we can barely see each other. I am keen for us to clear as many compounds as possible to try to gather intelligence.

We hit quite a wide track that opens out the terrain and allows me to see a bit more of what is going on.

Suddenly a shout goes up and all hell breaks loose. The interpreter with 5 Platoon spots three enemy, one carrying an RPG, crossing over a track junction. They are completely unaware of our presence. At least they were, until the interpreter shouted.

The 5 Platoon section with the interpreter are awesome. They immediately spring in to a 'contact front' drill. The lead man starts firing and the remainder bring themselves on to line. As each man reaches the 'line', that is, he is looking in the right direction, he starts firing. They are so slick that within seconds all eight men of the section are firing at the enemy.

Due to the interpreter's shout, the enemy are alerted and have a slight lead as they dart into a cornfield. The section commander sensibly brings his GPMGs up and they hose the cornfield down at waist height, cutting down the three enemy.

While this is going on the next section from 5 Platoon bursts into the closest compound in order to clear it. Lance Corporal Smith, one of the snipers, cautiously moves across the inside edge of the compound to the far wall. There is a rickety old ladder there and he wants to use it to gain some height. He starts to quietly creep up it, rifle in right hand, using his left for stability. He gets to the top and pops his head over, to have a quick peek. He finds himself staring at three enemy, the lead one holding an AK, the remainder holding hand grenades.

Time stands still for all of them. 'Smithy' as he is known just stares into the eyes of the man with the AK.

Fortunately, at this precise stage the ladder begins to break. Smithy can feel it collapsing under him. Just as he starts to fall back he punches his SA-80 out with his right hand, flicks off the safety and fires one round right at the lead enemy. By the time he crashes to the ground grenades fly over the wall at him. He dives into a doorway for cover before throwing a grenade back. The remainder of the section push forward and start throwing grenades over as well.

I am calling a fire mission at this point and push up to the doorway to see what is going on. Smithy is there and quickly tells me what has happened. He looks gaunt and drained of colour.

'Sir,' he says, 'that was fucking bogging'.

I tell him he is a fully fledged gunfighter now that he has been in a duel. He is just relieved that he had an SA-80 and not his sniper rifle. I doubt he could have punched one of those forward, they are far too heavy.

I think he has just seen his life flash in front of his eyes, so I let him gather his thoughts and tell Mitch to quickly push the FSG round the compound and conduct a sweep.

The FSG soon find a discarded AK and an injured Taliban. He has been shot in the stomach. A further search discovers the other two.

The doctor comes forward from the CSM's group and starts treating the casualty. Smithy comes forward and confirms that it was the enemy he was staring at. We compliment him on a good one-handed shot.

Now that we have a casualty we need to head in. We are too deep in the green zone to call for a helicopter. Once the doctor is happy that the casualty is stable we load him on a stretcher and start to head back.

The journey back takes a long time. With a man on a stretcher it is hot, slow work and we are five kilometres from the FOB. We are putting ourselves under significant risk, bringing out one of their wounded. The CSM has to keep getting us to slow down and, fortunately, it stays quiet. I wonder if the enemy can see that we are treating one of theirs and deliberately leaves us alone?

It takes two hours to get in.

As soon as we get back the two uninjured detainees start spilling the beans. They are Taliban and they tell us that we have killed four today. They also tell us that the Taliban will kill them for being captured. They are only young, and obviously not that committed.

As the Chinook comes in to pick up the casualty the prisoners go nuts; screaming and kicking. They have to be dragged on to the helicopter with the casualty and firmly secured on board. They are clearly not happy about being captured.

In the afternoon Sergeant Radcliffe comes to see me. A local 'walk-in' has just been up to the rear gate for a chat. He confirms that we killed four enemy.

This is good news; a successful patrol, and the company is on a high. All except Smithy, who is still describing the whole thing as 'fucking bogging'.

FRIDAY 5 SEPTEMBER

After yesterday's patrol I decide that most of the lads will need a break. They are doing back-to-back patrols and yesterday's was quite taxing, especially with the long CASEVAC. I ask Mitch if he will take out a mobile patrol. The FSG have patrol Land Rovers and they can push out into the desert, past the PB and dominate the ground beyond the power station, just short of where the US SF is working.

Mitch, as ever, readily agrees. He is a professional and loves soldiering. His crew are soon ready and they head out the back gate, guns bristling on the cut-down Land Rovers. With 40mm grenade launchers and .50cal machine guns, Lord help any enemy they bump into. The lads look happy as well and they are all grinning as I wave them off.

This patrol maintains activity while allowing the remainder to get some rest.

They patrol for five hours, generating some intelligence and stopping at the PB on the way back for a chat with 5 Platoon. The patrol passes without incident and they are back in by 1500.

SATURDAY 6 SEPTEMBER

I get up at my usual time and everything is covered in sand. There has been a storm in the night and the conditions are still 'brown out' – although the wind has dropped, the sand and dust still linger like a low fog. It's like being in a cup of tea. Everything is brown and I can't even see the back wall of the FOB.

I head into the ops room and see if there is anything going on. We are due to deploy a platoon-level security patrol at 1000hrs. I am not convinced that this is a good idea, as in these conditions the helicopter pilots prefer not to fly. If there was a casualty they would come, but it seems an unnecessary risk. I will make a decision just before 4 Platoon deploy.

At 0945 the conditions haven't improved so I decide to cancel the patrol. I have just told the platoon commander to cancel when the message comes over the radio. 'Patrol minimise' is now in effect. This is right across the Brigade AO and means that all patrols are to be put on hold unless essential.

Just after lunch I deliver orders for a company-level patrol tomorrow. The conditions may lift overnight so I give a full set of orders and then let the lads carry out their battle procedure.

The sandstorm creates an odd atmosphere in the FOB. It feels really isolated, like a bubble floating in sand. We could be anywhere – cut off from the outside world by all means except radio and satellite phone. It creates a siege mentality in our minds. There is hardly anyone moving around; people just seek shelter and read books.

I wander around the FOB checking on the sentries in each one of the sangars. I am curious as to how far they can see. Not very far is the answer. They can see about 30 metres to their front. This makes the FOB feel even more eerie; enemy hiding in shadows? Of course this is just my imagination playing tricks but I have a chat with the CSM and we pass the message for everyone to stay vigilant.

SUNDAY 7 SEPTEMBER

I get up to more 'tea souper'. The conditions have improved slightly as we can now see 200 metres but the dust cloud is still lingering. 'Patrol minimise' is still in place, so I cancel the company patrol. This means I now have a whole day to fill. I don't really want to train as I will ingest so much sand and dust. So I follow the lead of everyone else and retreat to my camp cot. At least it is sheltered and I spend hours reading books. I think the tour has been great for my reading and study. I have had the time to read as much as I want. I try to have three books on the go at any one point: one factual/educational and then a couple of novels. That way I can bounce between them depending on my mood. I am reading Bill Bryson's *A Short History of Everything*, which is leading to some fascinating discussions in the ops room. I leave the book in there overnight and two of the signallers are reading it at the same time. This is creating some far deeper than expected debates. I walked in earlier and was asked 'Sir, what is the Large Hadron Collider?' Not the sort of question you expect every day from a Parachute Regiment Tom, but one that makes them such a wonderful soldier to command. Also, no pressure, as an officer and the company commander ... the lads expect us to be 'clever' and I don't want to disappoint. Fortunately, I recently read a magazine article on it so am able to answer the question. This leaves my – and the officer corps's – reputation intact. For now.

I am reading a book on NLP and creating some more drills to run myself through. Late afternoon I have an NLP session. I continue to mentally model excellence and also practise my state management using my anchoring routine. I find these sessions really help my concentration and focus. They are also quite calming. It leaves me feeling 'in control'. It is so important to try and perform at an 'optimum' level. I am constantly trying to find ways to ensure that, when needed, I can be on my 'A' game.

The NLP book belongs to one of the medics so I am

having physics debates in the ops room with the signallers and psychology debates with Lance Corporal Horton, the medic. It's great and really not what you would expect.

MONDAY 8 SEPTEMBER

I am up at 0630. The sandstorm has now lifted and when I check with the ops room 'Patrol minimise' is cancelled – patrols are back on. I go for a run round the perimeter, which feels quite hard work. I am only running for thirty-seven minutes but it seems to drag. I assume this comes from doing laps over and over again. Plus my stomach is unsettled. I feel all right; I am just conscious of it. I am eating quite a lot at the moment so I keep feeling bloated and uncomfortable. The run is good and after I have showered I have a decent breakfast and make myself a coffee in the ops room. Someone has brought a large tub of Tim Horton coffee from Kandahar which makes a pretty good brew.

I settle myself in to the 'command chair' at the back of the ops room and then sit for four hours having the odd chat, reading my books and watching the goings-on. The AO is pretty quiet after the dust storm – it seems to have quietened the enemy down as well.

Late morning I start to feel rough, like I have a migraine coming on. I have to go round to one of the back rooms and sit in the dark for an hour to get it to pass. It's horrible, but at least it does pass; I keep having bouts of 'roughness' after I eat. No idea what is going on; another indicator that we just need to get out of this place and get home where everything isn't covered in some form of germ or disease. It is such a dirty, stinking place. I love the way we are referred to by the locals as 'unclean' even though the green zone is covered in human faeces and the locals sleep with their animals. They must have cast-iron constitutions.

I am concerned that the lads might be growing bored so in the afternoon I have a wander round and talk to some of the more chatty [and honest!] Toms. They aren't bored and frankly they would happily sit this out until it is time to go home. Who wouldn't? So much is asked of the Toms and they consistently deliver. I check that my message has got through though – and it has. While they would like to sit it out, they know that we won't and we can't. Importantly, they understand the reasons why.

It is terrible to wish your life away but in all honesty this is such hard work. The conditions are challenging enough. When you then have to don 40 kilos of kit, wade out into a jungle and fight a very impressive opponent it is no wonder that we are getting ground down. The lads seem to have found 'war' to be as it has always been portrayed throughout history – a mixture of sheer boredom and sheer excitement (or perhaps terror? You decide). I can't claim to have been bored though; I have enough to keep me occupied.

Late afternoon I give a set of refresh orders. Tomorrow we are going out to do the company-level patrol I planned four days ago. I think it best to quickly go through things again, just to make sure that everyone is happy. It feels quite odd though, as I haven't been out for a while.

TUESDAY 9 SEPTEMBER

Up at 0300 and depart out of the rear gate – 4 Platoon, my group, 6 Platoon, CSM. This patrol is 'recce by force'.

I want to use it to confirm whether there are any enemy in a certain area, so we will go into it in force to see what we generate.

The insert is draining. There is no ambient light so walking in the green zone on NVGs is challenging. It is chilly and quite muddy and by first light most people are complaining that they feel drained. Maybe there is a bug going round the FOB?

We push deep into the eastern edges of the AO up into the 'KBs' (KB1,6,5,9). We haven't been here very often and we are quite a long way from home. The FOB is five kilometres away but PB Emerald is closer – only three, and 5 Platoon is on standby in the PB to come and assist if we need them.

It is a strange patrol though. Odd atmospherics, the people seem fairly indifferent to our presence and move off slowly, not the normal sprint.

We start to receive intelligence that the enemy is in the area but the messages are mixed, almost indifferent and half-hearted. I think the enemy are talking a good game to keep their commanders happy but they don't really want to attack us.

We continue on the planned route, receiving threatening intelligence that doesn't come to anything. Soon we have completed the top of the loop and are starting to head back.

Could this be it? Our first patrol in three months with no contact? It looks that way and fifty minutes later we are crossing the 611 back into the desert for our final leg back to the FOB.

Once in the FOB I stand there unloading my weapons, chatting to Lance Corporal Barker. Everyone is in semi-shock. A company patrol with no contact? In some ways it doesn't feel right. We have gone to all that effort, getting so many people on the ground, that it seems remiss on the enemy's part not to attack. 'All dressed up for the dance', so to speak.

By the time I get to the ops room Brett has looked through all of our patrol reports and checked. It is the first company patrol not to get contacted in three months.

WEDNESDAY 10 SEPTEMBER

We send out a platoon-level security patrol and once they are back in I have a chat with Sergeant Radcliffe to get his views on the lack of contact yesterday. I then go and sit on my own in the briefing area and think it through myself.

I think that there is a whole combination of factors going on at the moment. It is Ramadan, which is bound to slow activity down and makes the enemy 'weaker' during the day. Lack of food would do that to anyone. There is the blowback from Op OT and the effect that the patrol base has had on our AO. There is also the US SF activity, killing so many enemy and injuring civilians and there is our unfortunate incident injuring civilians as well. Out of all of these I suspect that the civilian casualties are the predominant driving factor. The dynamics in the AO started to change when I injured the civilians – the elder shouting at the 'fighting age male' springs to mind. The US SF have done this on a grand scale. I think this activity has forced the locals' hands – they have realised that it is easier and more realistic for them to tell the Taliban to go than it is to pretend that we are going to leave. Unfortunately, it has taken these events to show the locals the quality they respect the most – strength. Life is cheap round these parts, but it still has a price. The enemy have been capitalising on our rules of engagement and Western sensitivities – a good example is how they will use women and children as 'dickers' to monitor our patrols – knowing that we won't engage them. Unfortunately, by accident I think we have shown the locals what we are prepared to do to get at the enemy. It has made them think that we are 'serious', hence telling the enemy to leave is the easier option.

It is horrible though and it will sit in our minds for a long time. But potentially we have an opportunity. If we can combine the current situation with quick, tangible assistance programmes we have the chance to convince the locals that we are really here to help them.

THURSDAY 11 SEPTEMBER

I am up at 0630 and go for my usual run around the FOB. It gives me the opportunity to think.

It feels strange to be here, in Afghanistan on 11 September. The reason I am here is that seven years ago a group of religious fanatics boarded four planes and changed the course of history. I remember watching the plane strike the second building in the TV room at Warminster, where I was an instructor on the platoon commanders' battle course. I returned to the planning cell and told Toby Black – a fellow instructor – what I had just seen. I remember thinking at the time that I was witnessing something cataclysmic; that things would never be the same again. The USA had been directly attacked and someone would have to pay. I was actually impressed with how measured the American response was; I'd felt sure that nuclear weapons would be used.

The initial campaign in Afghanistan was impressive; it was an incredibly smart use of assets. The results were quick and tangible. But then, foolishly, flushed with over-confidence, they switched focus to the potential red-herring, Iraq. I wonder where we would be now in the Afghan campaign if the correct assets and focus had remained here, and not on Iraq. Who knows? I do think that we would be a lot further forward than we are now.

I suppose to some extent I should be grateful. As a professional soldier this is what I have spent my entire career training for – Northern Ireland, Kosovo and Iraq were, for me, not 'it'. If all of the effort had been invested in Afghanistan as opposed to Iraq there is a strong chance that this tour would be very different and more 'peacekeeping'. As far as I am concerned, this has been 'it'; war fighting. I can't see how we [B Company] would call it anything else. We have spent three months doing company advance to contacts and company attacks against a real enemy, so I am not sure what else you would call it. It has definitely been combat, though, and I am grateful to have taken part in it. The strange dichotomy of the soldier. He actually wants to go into combat even though for most people that would be completely counter-intuitive. For us, though, it would be like attending every training session and never playing a game. I think ultimately we want to see what it is like and also see how we will perform. We just want to *know*. 'Every soldier will think less of himself if he has not heard the guns fired in anger' is certainly true. I also feel so privileged to have led such incredible soldiers into battle. It is such an honour and one for which I will be eternally grateful.

FRIDAY 12 SEPTEMBER

The morning passes quietly as we aren't deploying a patrol until the afternoon. The CSM is in a flurry of activity continuing to prepare the FOB for handover. He has work parties out doing various pieces of manual labour and I have a wander round, chatting to some of the clusters of Toms. They seem in high spirits at the moment. The end is starting to come in sight and I think we all realise that we can manage this pace to the end.

In the afternoon Wes takes 5 Platoon out on a local area patrol. We quickly receive intelligence that the enemy are out there and they are planning on attacking both the patrol and the FOB. This information is passed to Wes, who gets his patrol into a formation that will allow him to fight back to the FOB if necessary. I grab my helmet and body armour and move round to the FSG sangar with Lance Corporal Barker. Mitch has got the sangar on full manning so all of the weapons and observation devices are being manned. At the same time, the CSM gets the message sent round the FOB that everyone is to move into cover.

Ten minutes later 5 Platoon comes under contact. They are now 500 metres directly in front of the FSG sangar, working their way along the belt of unoccupied compounds to our front. The enemy fires a long, inaccurate burst of machine-gun fire that passes over 5 Platoon's heads. I think the enemy are still having trouble accurately identifying patrols in the corn and they are probably using young inexperienced fighters.

The FSG sangar has seen the firing point so they start suppressing with the .50cal machine gun and the 40mm belt-fed grenade launcher while I start teeing up the artillery and mortars. At the same time, 5 Platoon starts conducting a break contact drill and begins to move back towards the FOB.

I am just telling Corporal Hickman what I want the mortars to fire on when an SPG-9 rocket sails over the FOB and lands in the Star Wars village. A second round lands in the FOB, splintering the toilets with shrapnel. Fortunately, as all the sangars are on full manning, the firing points are quickly identified. The sangars return fire and the mortars and artillery start to engage. Within seconds of the rounds impacting on the FOB the enemy firing points are being hit with heavy weapons, mortars and artillery.

The enemy then starts to make foolish mistakes and our weapons systems really come into their own. The FSG sangar identifies an enemy with an RPG near 5 Platoon. He is casually sauntering around with the weapon on his shoulder, probably thinking that he is out of our range.

The Javelin crew fire a rocket and it is just incredible to watch. It is a heat-seeking fire-and-forget missile – once it is locked on, you aren't getting away. The rocket deploys with an initial 'oomph' and then climbs directly up into the sky before slamming down on its target. The effect is pretty conclusive.

Private Andrew, a sniper, has the next best shot. He is very diligently covering his arcs from a covert position on top of the FSG sangar. Instead of being sucked into the action to the front he is observing our flank, towards the village. He sees two 'dickers' in a window that looks straight on to the artillery gun park. One of them has a walkie-talkie and it is obvious through Andrew's sniper scope that they are coordinating fire. He fires a warning shot and they both duck. Then the one with the radio pops back up and carries on talking into it. Intelligence confirms that enemy fire is being coordinated from that location. Last stupid decision he will ever make. Andrew shoots him with a .338 round.

Within twenty minutes Wes and his gang are back in, chests heaving with elation. It all goes quiet; I think the enemy have had enough for one day.

I make my way back to the ops room and the CSM bursts in to tell me about the toilets. The one the CSM had just been occupying was the one that got hit. The door has been peppered with shrapnel. We are all mock incredulous – how dare they hit our toilets! It is not as if we have many luxuries around here.

SATURDAY 13 SEPTEMBER

I seem to be getting up earlier and earlier. I wake up and lie there but in the end accept that I won't get back to sleep, so I get up and go for a run.

I like the weekends, as I can speak to Andrea. It is hard to catch her in the week so I tend to wait until the weekend when I know I will get her at home.

Once I have showered and changed I grab a satellite phone and have a lovely thirty-minute chat with her. It's hard not to get excited about going home, even though I know that the last patrol is going to be just as dangerous as the first. It doesn't stop us planning all the things we want to do when I get home and all the little luxuries I am after. It's mainly simple things, like fresh bread and decent wine. Plus, we are starting to plan a holiday in the USA.

After lunch we receive helicopters and another major

milestone on our tour is passed. The helicopters bring in soldiers from 59 Commando Engineers. The commandos are our replacements, so this marks the start of it. We still have over a month to go, but seeing these guys arrive is a real morale boost.

SUNDAY 14 SEPTEMBER

Some days just don't 'gel' and today seems like one of them. I think a lot of people are in bad moods and we all feed off each other. The day has a tense and 'wound-up' feel to it. All conversations are short and cursory. There is no escape when it is like this, nowhere to go. We are all locked in together – FOB fever. I just feel I need to get out of the FOB, which is handy as I will do so the day after tomorrow; on patrol. Sometimes the closeness of the FOB is overbearing and even being out in the green zone seems an interesting alternative. I assume this will get worse as the end gets closer.

We can't use the phones as two lads from the Viking troop have been injured in a mine strike. This always grates on people. We all understand that notification of next of kin must come first, but it always seems to happen just when a queue is forming for the phones.

It will be a busy night as we have a double resupply convoy coming to the FOB. The QM is building up all of the FOB's supplies as, once the changeover starts with the marines, helicopter space will be at a premium.

I sit in the ops room until the small hours listening to all of the radio traffic and the flurry of activity as the resupply vehicles arrive. Full shipping containers are dropped off and empty ones taken away. The CSM has his work cut out organising all of this in the dark and he is ably assisted by Sergeant Train.

We receive two new Jackal vehicles for which we have been waiting for months. They are very, very impressive; straight out of *Mad Max*. Two journalists are dropped off as well, one of them Bill Neely from ITN. They will be spending a few days with us.

MONDAY 15 SEPTEMBER

Despite a late and restless night I still wake up early. I get up at 0600hrs and have a very bracing cold shower. It is quite chilly in the mornings so a cold shower isn't as nice as it was when the day was already boiling by this point.

Once I have sorted myself out I head into the ops room for a chat. Private Gilbert is the duty signaller and he is a really pleasant, well-meaning guy. He loves a good natter so I make us both a brew and sit down and have a talk with him. It's general chatter but it is still nice. He is so positive he just cheers you up.

After breakfast I write my orders in the back office. I am planning a big one for tomorrow – back into the area north-west of the FOB where we have had some of our biggest contacts; and taken most of our casualties.

I deliver my orders at 1000hrs, with the ITN crew filming. No pressure, but they seem to go well. I grab the commanders and have a chat with them out of earshot of the journalists. I want to get a feeling of how morale is. The commanders are reassuring – the lads are really up for it at the moment. They just want to get out there and smash the enemy.

I am reassured and sense an opportunity. The enemy

appear weakened and they lack cohesion. If we can keep the pressure on at this stage we can deal him some serious blows. I wonder if this is what the Paras bring to the party? I think we have the ability to keep pushing right until the end. The fact that the lads are still keen to get out there is a huge credit to them, and to the commanders who keep driving them on. Or maybe it is just the 'FOB fever' – we all want to get out there and have a good old-fashioned fight!

We have a new secure laptop in the ops room so in the afternoon the CO and I are able to have a live 'email chat'. It works quite well and he seems upbeat. HQ is focused on a smooth transition with the Royal Marines to ensure that all of the good work being done in Sangin is carried on.

I then manage to get a phone and call Andrea. We have a lovely chat. I always find it surreal to be sat here in shorts and a T-shirt, propped on a sandbag, surrounded by all of the paraphernalia of war, staring off at snow-capped Afghan mountains, while Andrea is sitting in our lounge in Colchester.

I decide to have an early night before tomorrow's patrol, so I am in bed by 1900hrs and I read until 2000. I have four books on the go at the moment, so I have plenty to keep me occupied.

TUESDAY 16 SEPTEMBER

I am awake at 0130 and I spend the next hour rolling the plan around my mind before getting up. This gives me plenty of time for a nice gentle start to the day. I have a cup of tea and check that Bill and his cameraman are alright. They have a 'minder' allocated to them – Sergeant Hodgkiss – so I won't have to worry about what they are up to.

We leave at 0350, after a few radio dramas. All of the sets are so old and battered that it is a constant challenge for the signals detachment to keep them running.

The lead is taken by 6 Platoon and they pick a really good route; straight into the green zone and through KA1. My plan is to get to the target area undetected and then split into three groups, all able to support each other. My group will be 'overt' – that is, obvious – while the other two platoons will try to stay 'covert'. If all goes according to plan, the enemy will try to attack my group and will, effectively, walk into an ambush. It seems only right that my group is the 'tethered goat'. I couldn't ask anyone else to do it.

As the sun rises we are all in position. We are laid out in a 'V' with my group at the bottom and the other two platoons on the apexes about 100 metres away. We start to receive intelligence that the enemy knows that we are here but is having trouble locating us. In the end we have to generate some activity to give him a hand. Thorpy volunteers to take a small patrol out to our front, which would be obvious to any locals using the nearby track.

This works a treat. Thorpy stays on the edge of the track until a local walks by. He then heads back into the compound we are securing. Within minutes we receive intelligence that the enemy know where we are. Thank you, Mr Local and well done, Thorpy.

One enemy rifle shot cracks out and passes over our head. Minutes later a second one rings out. Very interesting; it is obvious he is trying to bait us into firing back and giving away our exact location. I give the order and no one returns fire. No point making life easy for him.

At 0810 an RPG flies straight over the compound my group is occupying and explodes just next to the entrance. Simultaneously, 6 Platoon open up with a huge weight of fire. It appears my plan has worked. The enemy that were trying to get to my location have bumped into 6 Platoon.

A serious firefight ensues for the next couple of minutes. The fire at 6 Platoon's location is heavy although there do appear to be fewer enemy firing points and RPGs than we have previously seen. I quickly call mortars and artillery on to the enemy firing points and their attack starts to tail off. The ITN guys are loving it.

I change my plan once the firing has died down. The original plan was to clear KA1 but 6 Platoon has been in a position to watch the enemy withdraw. I decide that we will keep the pressure on them and 'chase them down'. It dawns on me to follow our current doctrine – focus on the enemy, not the ground.

Bill Neely comes over and asks if he can do a quick interview. We have a few minutes so I give a quick explanation to the camera as to what has happened and what we are doing. We then head off.

I organise the patrol into two parallel columns 100 metres apart. I am hoping to trap the enemy in the gap between and it keeps us configured in a way that we can bring a lot of firepower to bear on a flank, if needs be. The left-hand column is 6 Platoon, 5 Platoon are the right-hand column, followed by my group.

As we head off the ground, as ever, starts to change. One minute we are in an open area of compounds, next minute we are in a cornfield, with corn towering three foot above us. It is a constant command and control challenge and I have to work hard to understand where everyone is. Then 6 Platoon come under contact again. It looks like the enemy have realised that we are following them and they have put in a quick ambush, so 6 Platoon have RPGs and PKM fired at them, but it isn't that accurate. Corporal Smith's section has been contacted and they respond with a well drilled 'contact left'. Within seconds the enemy has a ferocious amount of fire returned at him. I call in some artillery and it all goes quiet.

We continue on but it becomes obvious that the enemy has had enough for the day. We loop through KA5 and then head back to the FOB. Myself and Sergeant Train are interviewed again just outside the FOB. I really hope that B Company makes it on to the news. It would be great for all of our families and friends to see us.

Late afternoon Bill shows me what they have spliced together for ITN news. It is a four-minute piece and it looks brilliant. A few interviews, great 'action' footage and a really good voice-over that explains what is going on. We won't know until tomorrow morning if it makes it on to the news. Bill graciously keeps showing the clip back to back as everyone wants to see it; small groups of Toms cluster round his laptop.

WEDNESDAY 17 SEPTEMBER

We made it on to the news! By the time I get up Bill has already checked. The piece starts with 'Inkerman, the most dangerous place in the world for a British Army soldier'. We are all delighted.

I have put in an EC today. It is an important day for us:

17 September marks our most famous battle honour, Arnhem. It was during the battle of Arnhem that the Parachute Regiment's ethos and culture were formed – tenacity, courage and a determination to fight until the bitter end. I feel it right that we should mark this day in some way.

There is an inter-platoon volleyball competition organised by 7 RHA, who inevitably win. There will also be a themed meal tonight in the cookhouse. Not exactly 'Arnhem', I know, but it is the best we can do and it is right that the lads get to relax. I go and check on the chefs and they are working tirelessly to make it a special meal.

I spend quite a while chatting to Bill in the afternoon. He is a really nice guy and fascinating to talk to. I think that we are sometimes too cagey with journalists. He isn't really interested in the 'dirt'; he just wants to see what we are up to.

In the evening the chefs have done us proud – pizza and Italian night. The food is superb and even more impressive when the ingredients and conditions are considered.

After dinner and once the sun has set an 'open air cinema' – a white sheet on a wall, a projector and speakers – is set up. Two films are shown, *Theirs Is the Glory* and *A Bridge Too Far*, two classic Arnhem films. There must be a hundred people sitting on various improvised seats to watch them.

I watch a bit of *A Bridge Too Far* and Bill Neely walks over to me. I explain about Arnhem and our battle honour. He just can't stop grinning, he thinks it is brilliant.

He leans over to me and says, 'This is a really class act'. I have to agree. To be in a war zone watching the film version of one of your battle honours is very cool.

I take myself off and find a quiet spot. The film has made me think of heritage and regimental tradition. I feel very proud to be a part of 2 PARA during this tour; 2 PARA hasn't been through something like this since the Falklands. Unfortunately, the losses always make tours stand out. For us it is about the amount of close combat we have seen and the hardships we have endured. Months of it. So I think that we can all take pride in what we have done and realise that we have been a part of something great. We are an organisation that always pushes itself harder and further.

THURSDAY 18 SEPTEMBER

Bill Neely is stuck here as there are no flights and he is starting to get a bit restless. I talk to HQ and stress that it might be worth getting him out: he could use being stuck here to make a piece about the lack of helicopters. They agree and two hours later I am waving Bill off from the HLS. Amazing how quickly you can find a helicopter when you need one.

It was a pleasure having him here, and nice to talk to someone different.

FRIDAY 19 SEPTEMBER

A platoon-level patrol deploys in the morning and passes without incident. It appears that the enemy aren't interested. It may only be the company patrols that get any activity now as they tend to go deeper.

The CSM has been unpacking some of the shipping containers and loads of new gym kit has arrived. This has proved a sore point with the lads. They rightly feel that this should have been delivered far earlier. It has sat at Bastion for the whole of our tour and has arrived in time for our departure.

Never mind. It means that my early-morning gym session is more interesting. I am still doing my 13-lap run round camp each morning but it is becoming very tedious.

I have started watching my Ray Mears DVDs as well, which are great. I have admired Ray Mears for years. I like his calm, methodical approach and his depth of knowledge and understanding of bush craft is incredible. I have always enjoyed the woods and I have done some survival training in the past. It is another subject that I am interested in and also have a real passion for. Ray takes survival – which often looks like simple existence – and elevates it to living in the wilderness. His DVDs are full of environments that I would like to visit to practise these skills. The films are another form of escapism and it is nice to imagine myself practising fire-lighting or shelter-building on a desert island.

SATURDAY 20 SEPTEMBER

Another platoon-level patrol passes without incident. Could this be the end of the 'campaign season'? The winter tours have been traditionally quieter than the summer so maybe the fighters have had enough for this year and are heading back to their winter retreats. It is a strange thought, as we start to think about heading back to our families, that the enemy might be doing the same.

I sit in the ops room for most of the afternoon reading. It seems quiet across the whole area of operations. I am reading a book on the Special Operations Executive at the moment, which is good. It makes me think of my hero – Winston Churchill, the godfather of British airborne forces. It also reminds me that you have to keep 'buggering on', as Winston said.

SUNDAY 21 SEPTEMBER

More RiP (Relief in Place) activity. When we expect helicopters there is so much security involved – platoon deployed into the green zone, FSG securing the high ground above the HLS, command group in overwatch ready to call for artillery, artillery and mortars 'stood to' and all sangars fully manned – that it pretty much becomes our patrol activity for the day.

We receive two helicopters that deliver the rest of 59 Commando RE and my 9 Squadron Para Engineers have now gone. There were also two Royal Marines on board, the first ones to arrive. They seem to have sent the wrong guys, though. We suggested an intelligence specialist and someone from logistics. They have sent two section commanders.

MONDAY 22 SEPTEMBER

Quiet day. A good session in the gym trying out some of the new kit then plenty of book reading.

TUESDAY 23 SEPTEMBER

I get up and go for my usual run round camp, taking forty minutes. Although boring, it does set me up for the day. I am obviously pretty heat-tolerant as I find myself drinking only a litre of water a day. The rest is coffee; which is what real men drink anyway.

I spend most of the morning writing emails. I sometimes find myself 'in zone' and want to write emails and letters. Today is one of those days. Mike Newman has been sending me some great emails. It turns out that they supply Ray Mears with 5.11 clothing, so he is trying to get me his autograph.

Helicopters arrive with replacement artillery gunners and stacks of mail. I get copies of *The Spectator*, *The Field* and a few shooting magazines. Plus there were fresh rations on board, so breakfast should be good tomorrow.

I spend the afternoon sorting out platoon command rotation and our own mini-OMLT (Operational Mentor and Liaison Team).

I have a new platoon commander, Chris Collier. Plus there is now an ANA platoon here and they need mentors. David True – 4 Platoon commander – volunteers to mentor the Afghans, so that means Chris can command 4 Platoon. This will give him some experience before the tour ends. David has been working with the ANA for the last week now and is doing a good job. Plus two 2 PARA captains have arrived – Matt Neve and Adam Constant. They will come on patrol with us and then help David with the ANA. The plan is to get the ANA to take over manning the patrol base.

WEDNESDAY 24 SEPTEMBER

I have a good chat with David and Matt. They are taking the ANA up to the patrol base this morning. A couple of guys from 4 Platoon, which is currently there, will stay behind and act as 'close protection'. David seems to have bonded well with the ANA so I am hoping this works.

Once 4 Platoon are back in from the patrol base I issue orders for tomorrow's patrol. I am using 4 and 6 Platoons as 5 Platoon have been doing a lot and need a break.

Late afternoon the FOB gets shot at; individual rounds cracking over the FSG sangar. The snipers manage to identify the firing point and they can see one armed enemy on his own and another two 100 metres away. The snipers fire and kill the lone gunman, while the Javelin crew engage the other two. It is a slick and well coordinated piece of shooting.

THURSDAY 25 SEPTEMBER

Up at 0330. It is now quite chilly at this time in the morning. It is even nicer to have a cup of tea before you go out and the lower temperatures mean that dehydration is less of a concern. Private Crisp brings me a brew, which is good of him, and we head off at 0415. We are heading into KA5 and KA6 which are areas four kilometres to the north of the FOB, deep in the green zone. I have been staring at some maps and speaking to Sergeant Radcliffe and I am convinced that there are enemy up there. We are going to locate/clear/destroy – take your pick!

I get 6 Platoon to lead. It is Chris's first patrol in command of 4 Platoon, so I think it best to get 6 Platoon to lead.

The patrol is quite 'stop-start' and gets annoying quite quickly. We need to make the most of the darkness.

Just before first light Tom – 6 Platoon commander – leads the company into a 'secure location' that turns out to be completely unsuitable. The whole company is crammed into one small compound. Far too many of us in such a small area, so we head off quickly, continuing on the patrol route.

We get up to the top end of KA6. The country is particularly close here as it is predominantly cornfields. I decide to split the patrol into two columns with 6 Platoon northernmost and, therefore, closest to the threat. As always I am trying to trap the enemy between our two 'pincers'. I decide my group will follow 6 Platoon and the CSM will go with 4 Platoon.

We aren't receiving much intelligence and I am starting to wonder if there is anything here when 6 Platoon suddenly gets contacted. A heavy weight of rifle fire slams into them from the flank. They quickly return fire and get the firing point information to me. I hit it with artillery and mortars and it all goes quiet.

We push on and I wonder if that will be it for the day. It was quite half-hearted on the enemy's part. We are heading west and have just entered fairly open ground. It is the outskirts of the 'Austrian village', nice open areas with well-tended compounds and a river meandering through the centre.

The lead section from 6 Platoon suddenly gets into a huge contact. They have a massive weight of fire poured down on them. Due to the way we are orientated the enemy fire is passing over the heads of the lead section and is landing amongst the rear section and my group.

The fire is very, very close and it sends all of us sprawling for cover. There are bullets spraying up little clumps of dirt all around us. At times I have been a bit blasé about taking cover – it is important not to look like a flapping idiot in front of the blokes – but this time I am scurrying to get behind a tree. I get very flat on the ground and try to line my body up behind my helmet – as if that will help! RPGs start slamming in and suddenly we get contacted from the right. Seconds later 4 Platoon comes under contact from the left. It would appear my cunning pincer plan hasn't quite worked and the enemy now have a pincer on us. Not a problem though, as I have artillery and mortars.

I immediately start allocating assets on to enemy firing points, which decreases the enemy fire. He doesn't seem that determined and this looks more like 'shoot and scoot'. The situation is confusing and I can't even get my head up to have a look around. Quickly things start to swing in our favour and the platoons start to over-match the enemy's fire and get some manoeuvre going. As soon as we start to push forward the enemy starts to fold.

We keep 'working the problem' and after an hour it goes quiet. The snipers push to a flank and identify two enemy withdrawing. Due to the size of the contact I have requested whatever assets are available and an F-16 jet comes on station. The snipers maintain a watch on the two enemy and it looks like they have pulled back and set up to ambush us again. The F-16 picks them up as well.

The F-16 does an initial gun run with its cannon. The enemy pulls back another 50 metres and sets up again. All the while, we keep moving. Another gun run causes the same result. The gun runs aren't accurate and isn't scaring them off.

I request through HQ to use something bigger than the cannon and permission is granted. The F-16 wheels back round and puts a GBU-12 500lb bomb straight on top of them. This is the first time I have called in a 'bomb' from a jet and it is very, very conclusive. Those two enemies won't be annoying us any more.

We head back in without incident and sort ourselves out. Intelligence arrives saying that we have killed four enemy today, plus the two who had the bomb put on them. That combines with the three killed yesterday so I am hoping that this attrition is grinding the young fighters down. I have got to create space so that the RiP can happen as unmolested as possible.

FRIDAY 26 SEPTEMBER

It is 0700hrs and I am in the gym on an exercise bike. There are a few of us and I am reading a copy of *The Spectator* while cycling. Suddenly Sergeant Radcliffe arrives looking 'perturbed'. He tells me I am needed in the ops room. I ask if it can wait, as I want to finish my session. He says it can't.

As we walk back up to the ops room I ask him what is going on. He tells me there has been an incident at the patrol base and the information is confusing.

By the time I get to the ops room David is on the radio asking for a CASEVAC as he has two casualties. I ask him to tell me exactly what has happened.

At 0650 a junior sergeant from the ANA came off sentry duty, taking the PKM machine gun with him.

He calmly walked into the accommodation where the B Company OMLT lads were sleeping and fired two three-round bursts at the sleeping Toms. He hit Privates Clutton and Day in the legs and narrowly missed Private Wilson.

Wilson has holes through his mosquito net inches above his head.

The ANA sergeant then dropped the PKM, ran round to the side of the PB, jumped over the wall and ran off into the green zone.

In the ops room, we are stunned. What on earth is going on? We quickly organise for a CASEVAC and I send for Wes.

Wes arrives in the ops room and I tell him that I want to send his platoon up to the PB to replace the ANA as quickly as possible and, potentially, reinforce David.

David is assuring me that his team don't appear under threat but it is worrying that there are so few of them.

The CASEVAC comes in quickly and takes Clutton and Day away but it is such a challenge dealing with the aftermath. I want to disarm the ANA but I realise the impact that this could have on them. I don't want to offend them or belittle the ANA platoon commander.

David speaks to the ANA platoon commander. Fortunately, he is mortified and he offers to disarm his whole platoon. I tell David to disarm them and that Wes and 5 Platoon will be coming to take over from them.

The nightmare is that we have no idea how trustworthy the rest of the ANA platoon is.

Of course this is a very, very serious incident and BG HQ wants as much information as possible.

I spend the bulk of the day dealing with the aftermath. Mid-afternoon we get word that Clutton and Day are all right. One has been shot through the shin and one through the thigh. They are stable and will be flown back to the UK shortly. That is the good news. The bad news is that any trust we had in the ANA has evaporated.

Just after last light 5 Platoon head off and an hour later the ANA platoon arrives. They have been given their weapons back but their heads are hanging down with shame. The poor sentry who had replaced the disgruntled ANA sergeant has already been beaten by their platoon commander for not shooting the sergeant when he jumped over the wall.

I decide to leave them with their weapons. Afghan culture places a lot of emphasis on weapons and disarming them, I assume, would be highly humiliating. They are in their own compound and only we can let them into the FOB, so the threat is minimal. They are told quite clearly though that they are not to bring their weapons into the FOB and if they enter without permission they will be shot.

What a day! At times you think you just couldn't make it up. We receive intelligence that the Taliban are boasting about what has happened and the ANA sergeant has now joined their ranks.

By early evening things seem to have settled down, as much as they ever do round here. Matt and David have dealt with the whole situation really well and I tell them that we will sort the rest out tomorrow. For now we will leave the ANA alone, have a think and then start from scratch.

I need a quick, short-term solution. I realise that the only thing I care about is that no more of my guys get hurt. I am just desperate to get them all home, but the challenges just keep coming.

I feel weary by the time I go to bed; emotionally drained. It really is taking its toll now. I am starting to feel tired, mentally.

SATURDAY 27 SEPTEMBER

Unsurprisingly, senior ANA commanders want to visit and try to ascertain what has happened.

I am told to secure the Jusulay track junction so I send 6 Platoon out. An hour later the ANA brigade commander arrives with an entourage and a British OMLT team.

The brigade commander apologises to me, then heads down to the ANA compound to talk to his platoon; leaving me with the British Army major in charge of the OMLT.

He starts talking knowledgeably about the ANA and the problems that we all face out here. I ask him how long he has been in Afghanistan. Seven days is his response. I tell him that he might want to see a bit more before he starts offering advice.

At lunchtime the brigade commander heads off, leaving us to pick up the pieces.

In the afternoon I am in the ops room and one of the signallers draws my attention to one of the screens from our surveillance cameras.

Just down the road from the FOB is a power transformer and we have no idea whether there is power flowing from it.

We all watch round the screen as a local with a ladder, dragging a cable, approaches the transformer. He places the ladder, climbs up to the cable and holds up a set of jump leads.

'Is that live?' I ask.

'We'll find out in a minute,' Sergeant Radcliffe replies.

We stare transfixed at the latest applicant for the Darwin awards.

The local leans forward and places the clips on the cable.

There is a boom, a flash and the local is launched ten metres down the road.

It's terrible, but we all fall about laughing. A couple of other locals grab the injured man and run him round to the back of the FOB. We have already warned the doctor, so he is there to meet them.

The local is alive but he isn't in a good way. He has severe burns and is pretty shaken up so we call for a CASEVAC.

Once he is safely away I realise I should be grateful. I paid an influential local to get the transformer working. That poor local has just confirmed that Faisal did get it fixed.

SUNDAY 28 SEPTEMBER

You can feel the undercurrent of excitement in the FOB at the moment. It is nearly October, which is a huge mental benchmark for all of us. October is the month that we go home. We will be able to say 'we go home this month'. I am trying to keep everything as measured as possible. With a platoon at the PB and various other large activities on the patrol programme we have enough going on.

We receive some great news. Saddam, the local enemy commander and my arch-nemesis, has been seriously injured. It was during the contact on 25 September. At the time we received intelligence that one enemy had been killed and two injured. There was also a message requesting a car to collect Saddam. This sounded suspicious, but at the time we thought that he might just have been trying to flee quickly.

Sergeant Radcliffe held a security *shura* this morning with some of the local elders and one of them confirmed that

Saddam had been injured. This is good news; we finally got him. Shame he isn't dead, but this is better than nothing.

I wander into the ops room for a brew. Gilbert and Crisp are the duty signallers and we decide to start a 'mocha' club. We will take it in turns to see who can make the best mocha from what we have available – drinking chocolate, a variety of instant coffees and powdered milk. This is a serious business and the ratios are adjusted with scientific precision.

In the evening company HQ has a film night. The signallers set up the projector and borrow some speakers. It is a real 'blokes' night. For some reason it ends up with me and the signallers: Thorburn, Crisp, Gilbert and Greenfield. We watch *Days of Thunder*, which is a classic. We sit around chatting, smoking cigars and watching Nascar. What more could you want when you are a long way from home? We decide we will do another one next week and stick with the classics; next week will be a bit of Arnold Schwarzenegger action with *Commando*.

MONDAY 29 SEPTEMBER

Mid-morning we receive re-supply helicopters and the engineers change a few more people around. Plus another construction troop of Royal Engineers is arriving to do some major construction projects around the FOB. Time is dragging a bit. A very quiet day.

TUESDAY 30 SEPTEMBER

Today 4 Platoon conducts a local clearance patrol without incident and the day sort of drifts by. I do my normal training routine and I always have some paperwork to do. I am starting to get my thoughts in order for when the next company commander arrives. I have made a lot of notes and obviously have a lot of thoughts. What I need to do is get it into some form of structure. Another quiet day.

OCTOBER

We enter our final month in Afghanistan. The weather is getting colder and the contacts are tailing off so maybe the end of the 'fighting season' is approaching. As we prepare to head home maybe the enemy is doing the same? Back to his family to recharge his batteries. Who knows?

The tour, from a 16 Air Assault Brigade perspective, has gone well. The turbine was successfully delivered to the Kajaki dam. This was a huge operation with significant complexity and the brigade can take pride in pulling all this together.

From 2 PARA's perspective it has successfully focused on Sangin and really started to develop the local governance. It has pushed local reconstruction and development and is well positioned to hand over a coherent plan to the Royal Marines.

I think everyone has done all they can do with what they had available. There comes a point when you just can't develop things any further – you don't have the resources.

B Company has contributed significantly to all of this. Our part in the deception plan for the turbine delivery was successful. We have inserted a new patrol base which has definitely had *an effect on security within the area. Inkerman has served as the beacon, attracting the enemy to it and thus creating the conditions for development within Sangin. The FOB has been improved and is in good order to begin another winter.*

I think it has gone well. We have all faced a myriad of challenges and risen to the occasion. I continue to learn and every day there is something new and unexpected. I think in this environment leadership education is evolutionary; continuous small steps that add layer upon layer to your experience bank. I just hope I can capture it all and distil it into something useful.

WEDNESDAY 1 OCTOBER

It is just wonderful to wake up in October. We are now in the same month that we will go home. As much as I try not to think about it, it is there, all of the time. Home, I just can't wait to be back there, with Andrea and Rufus. I watch Ray Mears and Rick Stein DVDs every afternoon and it is making me desperate to be able to do more: light fires, cook, barbecue, go for a walk in the woods. I think it will be nice to leave the FOB as well. The general consensus is that six months in such an austere place, with such a high tempo of activity, is just too much. A move to a better-supported location would allow people to recharge and create variety. Walking over the same piece of real estate – realistically, the same five square kilometres – for six months is quite boring. Of course the flip side to the argument is that it takes a long time to learn your 'patch' and the people within it.

In the afternoon I have a chat with the CO on the radio

then send him an email. He seems on good form. HQ's departure is even more imminent than ours.

I check my emails and I have some really good ones. Mike Newman from Edgar Brothers has been in touch. I mentioned to him that I would like to get Ray Mears down for a barbecue. They have phoned him and his response was when and where? I want to follow this up. Having watched back-to-back episodes of Ray Mears for the last two months I would really like to meet him.

THURSDAY 2 OCTOBER

Most of the day is taken up with planning an air drop for tonight. As usual Sergeant Train takes over all of the planning and does a superb job. My only role is to ensure that he has got all that he needs. He is diligent, meticulous and thorough; a superb sergeant and one that I want to get promoted as soon as possible.

Just before last light the whole epic convoy heads off into the desert – 6 Platoon, heavy drop vehicles and a variety of other specialists. The air drops have been pretty pointless so far and there is no reason why tonight's will be any different.

Just before I go to bed I check my emails and have received one from Mum and Dad. Charlie, the family dog, has passed away. We have had him since I was commissioned from Sandhurst. He was old and had deteriorated so Mum and Dad made the inevitable decision. I find this news really upsetting and I realise that it is probably bringing out suppressed emotions. I find this quite hard to deal with. I am surrounded by so much death and destruction that it doesn't seem fair that Charlie is gone. I suddenly feel incredibly lonely, but I also want to be alone. I take myself off and sit on the roof of the old compound. I am struggling not to think about death, the lads that I have lost and Charlie. I suddenly wish I wasn't here. I wish I was anywhere but here right now, just for an hour, just for a break. It is only two weeks until I leave but, suddenly, that feels like a lifetime.

FRIDAY 3 OCTOBER

I am up early to welcome in the air drop crew. They pull back through the gate at 0600, covered in dust, grinning and laughing about the inevitable long night they have had. Yet again the pallets were dropped high so they scattered over a really large piece of desert. Sergeant Train, being the diligent guy that he is, refused to call off any search until all of the pallets were recovered; hence the long night.

SATURDAY 4 OCTOBER

I am awake at 0430 and I decide to get up. At 0500 I head into the ops room and make myself a coffee and then I go outside and sit on one of the benches. I decide to watch dawn come up and I am not disappointed. The red glow expands from behind the snow-capped mountains and it is truly stunning.

I then head back to my accommodation and grab my sniper rifle. I love shooting and I am a huge fan of the snipers. Corporal Berenger has signed one of the spare sniper rifles over to me. I decide that now would be a great time to have a shoot.

I head out the back gate and say hello to the sentry. I set myself up just in front of the rear gate on our improvised range and for the next hour I just lie there, taking my time, watching the sun continue to rise and shooting. I find the discipline and mastery of shooting very relaxing. It takes me a while to get the rifle zeroed but once I am there I shoot pretty well.

It's nice to start the day with a good shoot and I feel very content as I wander back up the FOB for breakfast.

Time keeps lurching at the moment. It speeds up and slows down; it is quite off-putting. In reality we are all just wishing the time away as we can't wait to go home. I try to put myself in denial; I try not to look at my watch and then I am suddenly surprised by the time and date. My routine helps. I get up, physically train, pop in the ops room for a brew, shower, ops room, lunch, ops room, DVD, evening commanders' brief, read, bed; start over again. I can feel the anticipation and excitement. The feeling that we are almost there and that we will soon be home. Some say that the tour has flown by. It doesn't feel that way to me at all. This has been a very long six months for me and I am looking forward to heading home. There is a relentless, constant pressure on the company commander.

I am so incredibly proud of my company. I am proud with how we have dealt with all of this. I am proud of how we have fought and I am proud of myself. Professionally, this has been incredible but I think we have all realised that enough is enough. Go when the going is good. Or, as Dirty Harry said, 'Know your limitations'.

SUNDAY 5 OCTOBER

It is Andrea's birthday today and I get into the ops room
to find that Op Minimise is in force and we aren't allowed
to use the phones. I am gutted; I really wanted to phone
her on the day. Minimise remains in force all day and, as is
so often the case, no one can find out who has been injured.

MONDAY 6 OCTOBER

Minimise has been lifted and I manage to get through to
Andrea. Fortunately she worked out that there must have been
a block on ringing and hadn't assumed that I had just forgotten!

We have a lovely chat. She had a quiet birthday as she
was duty officer at ATC Pirbright. Shame that she couldn't
have gone out for a meal. She has spoken to Mum and Dad,
who are still incredibly upset about Charlie being put down.
They are off to Cornwall for the week as a break. I really
hope that they are all right and they get another dog.

Mid-morning I deliver orders for the company-level patrol
tomorrow. I haven't been out for a while as it is so hard
generating enough manpower for a company-level patrol. I
am actually looking forward to getting out in the green
zone. There are a lot of new faces at the orders group.
Commando Engineers and Royal Marines stare at me blankly.
Their advance party has continued to grow and there will
be at least ten additional commanders out with us tomorrow.
It is already starting to feel like someone else's gang. The
orders go well and then I pick up my daily routine.

TUESDAY 7 OCTOBER

I am up at 0330hrs and it is really quite chilly at this time in the morning. I am grateful for the cup of tea that Gilbert brings me. He will be coming out on the patrol today as my signaller.

Today's patrol is broken into two phases. At 0400hrs 5 Platoon, FSG and my group head out. We are heading north-west into KA1 – the sight of some of our biggest contacts. We will establish an 'ambush', or in other words, get ourselves hidden in some compounds. At first light 4 Platoon will head out and conduct a 'routine' local security patrol. If all goes according to plan the enemy will try to get into a position to attack the security patrol and in the process bump into us. Failing that, we will attack them once they attack 4 Platoon. The KA1 area seems to be able to generate a lot of fighters quickly and I see no reason why today should be any different.

Phase one of the patrol goes successfully and we are up in KA1 before first light. As ever, 5 Platoon pick a cracking route which gets us into the target area in plenty of time.

The 5 Platoon lads occupy the first compound and the FSG and my group push on to the compound designated KA126. This is my traditional compound as I like it. It is the same one from where I watched Pope get injured in the RPG strike and Lance Corporal Dipnall was injured just up the track. I don't know why I like this one, it just feels right. We are not here that regularly and it is normally occupied, so we haven't set enough of a routine to make it worthwhile for the enemy to booby trap the place.

It is just before first light and we are all saying how cold we feel. We are sweating from the patrol out and wet from wading through an irrigation ditch. Fortunately the sun starts to come up and this takes the edge off the chill. Amusingly Adam, the FOO, checks his small temperature gauge. It is 20C! I can't believe it. Here we are, all complaining how cold we feel. Lord help us when we get back to the UK.

We quickly start to receive intelligence when 4 Platoon starts its patrol. A new enemy commander, 'Khaksar', is trying to coordinate activity. All the signs are here and it sounds like my plan is going to work. For the next hour the intelligence continues to build but nothing happens. There is talk that they have 'surrounded us' and they are about to start their attack, but nothing happens. In the end I get 5 Platoon to 'expose' themselves but even then it doesn't work. Today the enemy are all talk.

At 1030 we give up and start to head back in. As we patrol back I realise that this is potentially my penultimate patrol. What a strange feeling. The feeling that I will, probably, never see this piece of ground ever again, having spent six months learning it intimately. I am sure that I will be back in Afghanistan at some point but I am pretty sure I will never be here again. Very odd; I have ended up actually quite liking the green zone.

The patrol ends with no contact. Once we are back in I have a chat with Gilbert. That was his first time acting as OC's signaller, it is normally Lance Corporal Barker. He has done a really good job and I make sure I let him know.

WEDNESDAY 8 OCTOBER

More helicopter activity and the FOB is being flooded with Royal Engineers. The whole construction troop is now here and they start work tomorrow.

THURSDAY 9 OCTOBER

The FOB is a hive of activity. We are having an Equipment Care day, which is actually RiP preparation. Strange thought – we are preparing to hand over. Engineer plant vehicles are trolling around demolishing buildings. The Royal Engineers have spent half the tour building things and the other half knocking things down that haven't been built properly in the first place. I feel sorry for the 9 Squadron lads. They have worked like Trojans with the very limited resources they had, producing the best that could be expected. The construction troop rock up with all of the correct resources and knock everything down and build it properly. What a huge waste of time and effort.

After my afternoon dose of Ray Mears and Bush Tucker Man I find myself very reflective. I am getting more and more so each day. I think about how hard the tour has been and how hard it is just living here: drinking warm chlorinated water, washing your clothes in a bucket, solar showers, deep-trench latrines that make you retch when you are near them, rations, sleeping on camp cots and the myriad of other challenges. There are a lot of creature comforts missing but you can make yourself comfy. It is amazing how little you need.

The Ray Mears DVDs are really inspiring me and I make a list of projects and topics I want to pick up once I am home. I really want to study wild food. In my notebook I write out a 'things to do' list: build an outdoor oven, make hawthorn jelly, cook salmon native Indian style, bake bread outside, make a longbow, make charcoal, cook with hot rocks, go fishing, go foraging along the coast, do more shooting. The list goes on and it is interesting that these are all 'outdoor' activities. Sleeping outside for six months hasn't dented my enthusiasm for the wilderness. I realise I need to get out more and do more. I need to get out into the woods, take my time, see nature and see the wilderness more. I need to appreciate things more, especially woodland. I feel very comfortable out in the woods but I am sure I am missing half of it.

FRIDAY 10 OCTOBER

We are getting a lot of helicopters into the FOB at the moment as the unit change-around has started.

Early morning the CO, RSM and padre arrive. The CO wanted to come for a last visit before he heads back to the UK. His plan is to stay until tomorrow and then head back to Sangin prior to handing over to the CO of 45 Commando, Royal Marines.

The CO is also in a reflective mood and clearly wants to have a chat with me. I make us a decent coffee and we find a quiet spot. We end up talking for a couple of hours. Most of the talk revolves around how fantastic the lads have been. Their tenacity and endurance is unbelievable. We talk about the tour and how, roughly, it followed that path he thought it would. We talk about Afghanistan and the impact we have had and finally about where we both go next. He is due to be posted in December and I will leave next July. Neither of us are happy about this but it is the reality for officers. We come for two years and then have to go to staff jobs.

Just before lunch we are expecting some more helicopters and I have asked Brett to man the command sangar while I am chatting to the CO. I hear the two Chinooks arrive and they are on the ground for a long time, 'turning and burning'. During the handover, personnel arrive with all of their personal baggage and equipment so it takes quite a while for the helicopter to disgorge all of its contents. The poor pilots just have to sit there and wait for everyone to get off. We have a platoon on the ground and the sangars are 'covering their arcs', so we should be all right.

I hear the pitch of the helicopter engines increase and then they are away. More commandos in and more paras out.

Thirty minutes later Brett comes round and politely interrupts our chat.

'Russ, Rich Parvin is here,' he says.

I just stare at Brett, trying to comprehend what he has just said. Rich Parvin is the company commander of the Royal Marine Company that is replacing us. We are old friends, having spent two years as instructors on the platoon commanders' battle course together. I am not expecting him for another five days.

'What?' I ask.

'Rich is here. He managed to jump on an early flight. I told him you were chatting to the CO so he has gone to the cookhouse for a brew,' Brett replies.

I am still having trouble getting my head round this. Rich's arrival was the mental benchmark I have been working towards. Him being here means I am going home. I look at the CO, dumbfounded.

'Well, there you are, Russ. Once you are happy with the handover get yourself back to Bastion. Let's go and join him for a brew,' the CO says.

We walk over to the cookhouse and Rich is sitting there, cup in hand, beaming. I go over and we have an enthusiastic handshake and launch into a catch-up chat.

He was kicking his heels at Bastion; the opportunity arose to get here early so he took it. Better to be here than at Bastion. I still can't believe that he is here.

I spend the rest of the afternoon chatting to Rich and the CO. The CO is still keen to talk through a number of issues so I spend more time talking to him. Rich is just happy to be here so I leave him with Brett in the ops room.

We all have dinner together, which is good. CO, Rich, RSM, Padre Alan and I all sit around 'chewing the fat'.

SATURDAY 11 OCTOBER

I get up early and bump into Alan, the padre. Fortunately he is up early as well so it gives us a chance to catch up. With everything else going on I haven't really had a chance to talk to him.

He has had a challenging tour like the rest of us and is ready to head home. We have a decent coffee and chat for an hour before he has to get his kit ready.

The CO, RSM and padre leave early morning. I head down to the HLS to see them off. As I shake hands with the CO I realise that the next time I see him will be in Colchester. It's a very strange thought. I wave them off and then watch as more of my lads head off and more gunners from 29 Commando arrive.

Looking around I see that there are more and more commandos here. With Rich here as well I realise that the place is already starting to feel like someone else's. It's all a bit surreal; I am starting to feel like an observer. For six months this has been mine, all mine. Now as I look around I can feel it slipping from my grasp and before long it will be nothing to do with me. All the power that has been bestowed on me will soon be someone else's.

I head back up to the ops room and find Rich. His early arrival has caught me on the hop a bit but it does give us plenty of time to go through things slowly.

We spend the rest of the time in the briefing area chatting through the tour, the ground, the enemy and the challenges. I have organised for all of the specialist commanders (intelligence, snipers, mortars, fire support group) to do individual briefs to Rich to give him a feel for their point of view. This will start tomorrow.

SUNDAY 12 OCTOBER

I manage to get one of the satellite phones and ring Andrea in the morning. I am bursting to tell her that Rich is here. We have a lovely conversation but I know that I am now sick of using the phones. They are all in a poor state so they don't work very well and the phone is such a terrible way of communicating. Better than nothing, I suppose. It also dawns on me that if all goes according to plan we will be back in each other's arms in two weeks' time.

I go for my usual run round camp which leaves me feeling good and then I find Rich and we go for breakfast.

Rich gets bombarded with briefs for the rest of the day, leaving his head spinning. I spend the day sorting my kit out and moving out of my bed space so that Rich can move in.

After dinner I can feel stirrings in my stomach. Nothing too bad so I head off to bed and hope it will pass.

MONDAY 13 OCTOBER

I wake up early in the morning with my stomach tied in knots. I only just make it down to the toilets.

By the time I get back to my bed space my kidneys are on fire and I feel weak. I can't believe it; Inkerman's revenge! After six months here with nothing more than 'traveller's stomach' I am now struck down with the curse. I feel like someone has gone to work on my kidneys with a baseball bat. All I can do is lie on my camp cot.

Rich is very sympathetic and spends the day in the ops room. He is getting frustrated and can already see the challenges that you face at FOB Inkerman. The helicopters keep getting cancelled so while all of the commando artillery are here, none of his own blokes are. He starts calling people to ask if they can do something from the Bastion end.

Meanwhile I spend the day on my back, reading and watching DVDs. I can hardly move. I don't feel sick, just weak and battered in my lower back. My ever-loyal signals detachment is fantastic. They take it in turns to wander round, see how I am and ask if I want anything. I am hugely touched. I manage a cup of hot chocolate for lunch and a cup-a-soup for dinner.

As before, the sheer squalor of this place hits you when you are unwell. You can sense how unclean everything is, with the dust and sand swirling around, coating everything.

I manage to get up for our evening brief and just about stay on my feet for thirty minutes before collapsing back on to my camp cot. This is not fun at all.

TUESDAY 14 OCTOBER

I feel a bit better but I can't face getting up. My system just has no power. I have a chat with Rich and he is fine so I plan to do nothing except recuperate today. The fire in my kidneys is dying down but I still feel weak.

As I lie here thinking, I realise that this is the same as when I was going back on R&R. As soon as my system takes its 'foot off the gas', I practically grind to halt. I try to drive myself and those around me through personal energy and example and I think that I underestimate how much it is taking out of me. So the thought of a relaxing day is quite appealing. I probably should have done this more often!

I spend the day having the odd nap, watching DVDs and reading books. It is really relaxing and actually quite pleasant, if it wasn't for the pain in my lower back and the odd dash to the toilet.

The signallers continue to pop round and say hello, make the odd brew and generally have a chat. I am really appreciative.

WEDNESDAY 15 OCTOBER

I wake up and feel much better, back among the living. I have some cereal for breakfast and wait to see what happens. After an hour and no adverse side effects I realise that I am better, but I will still take it easy.

The last two days have actually worked well for Rich; they have allowed him to wander around and talk to people and form his own opinion on things. This has given him a good handle on how we do business and given him the chance to work out how he would like to do it. We can now spend some time together and he is keen to bounce his findings and ideas off me to see what I think. This is a good way to do it. My way is exactly that, my way – he will have his own ideas.

We spend the morning going through his findings and ideas. Rich is a very bright guy and he has already got some good ideas. The challenge he will have though is stark. His company is significantly smaller than mine; effectively, he has one less platoon. He is sold on the patrol base and all it is achieving but he will struggle to run it with his manpower. He is already having lengthy chats with his CO about this.

After a (light!) lunch helicopters arrive and Rich finally gets a load of his blokes in. I also send a platoon and a half of mine back. This is it now – the changeover is actually happening.

THURSDAY 16 OCTOBER

More helicopters arrive in the morning and Rich has the bulk of his force here. We now have enough to mount a joint company patrol. I plan a patrol for tomorrow that will allow Rich and all of his commanders to see as much of the ground as possible and, potentially, the enemy as well.

I have explained most of the 'hotspots' to Rich and I work out a route and a plan that takes in as many of these as possible.

I deliver orders after lunch. It feels very strange as I know that this is it; my last orders and my last patrol.

I also sense a slight feeling of trepidation amongst my lads. I know how they feel. No one wants to get injured on the last patrol. I grab all of my commanders and have a chat with them. We will keep moving on this patrol and not seek to get decisively engaged. The aim is to show the marines the ground rather than get in contact. If we keep moving it is that much harder for the enemy to mount anything too heavy. If they do attack us we will hit them with everything we have got and keep moving. We need to remain professional to the end and show the marines B Company at its very best. The guys get it and they assure me this will be communicated to the blokes.

FRIDAY 17 OCTOBER

I am up at 0500hrs and I sort my kit out, for the last time. I take my time strapping everything on, enjoying the moment. I am still a bit concerned about my health. I feel a bit weak from the illness and I am paranoid about the state of my stomach. I have not really eaten properly for five days. The thought of soiling myself is prevalent. The stakes are now that much higher. In front of my own lads would be bad enough; in front of Royal Marines would be a shame that I would never get over. I would be drummed out of the regiment.

Once Rich is sorted we head down to the rear gate. People are in good spirits. The marines are keen to get out on the ground and my lads are just keen to get it done.

We head out the gate and push north-east, up the desert before dropping down into the green zone. I take the time to really look around, to burn the images into my mind as I won't be coming back here. I am also struck by how cold it is. I am freezing and I wish I had brought my gloves. I think us summer veterans are quite happy to leave the winter to the marines. They like all that cold wet business.

We make good speed and, as directed, everyone keeps moving, making it very hard for the enemy to get it together. He is out there though. We quickly receive intelligence that the enemy is on to us and trying to put an attack together. Our constant movement is making it hard for him though.

I chat to Rich as we walk round and it is almost becoming a battlefield tour ... 'Here is the site of one of our biggest contacts ... this is where so and so was injured ...' We are covering a good chunk of ground though and Rich is seeing a lot of the area.

We hit the apex of our loop and the enemy picture is building. We all think it is going to happen. It is terrible, but I realise that I actually want a contact. I would like our last patrol to end in a final battle. I realise that if I pause the patrol here I can probably make it happen.

Reality sinks in though. It probably wouldn't be me in the initial contact; it would be one of my Toms. My job is to get them home, not gamble with their lives.

I order a rapid shift in direction and we start to head back towards the FOB. The enemy are confused and are losing sight of us. He obviously had an ambush set up.

The FSG sangar observe enemy movement behind us. They positively identify an enemy with a PKM machine gun, one kilometre behind us, so I give permission for them to engage. They use a Javelin. The rocket pops out of its launcher and then whooshes over our heads, slamming into its target behind us. A good strike; one less for the marines to deal with.

We continue to head in and by 0900 are back. All in, no one injured; a successful patrol. The lads are on a real high, all patting each other on the back and shaking hands. The marines are happy as well. They have seen the ground and had a Javelin fired overhead. There was something for everyone. I feel somewhat deflated, a feeling of anti-climax. I realise I probably won't do anything like this ever again.

I spend the afternoon going through the ground in detail with Rich in the briefing area. Now that he has been out there he can put it into some sort of context. He is happy with what he is getting, information-wise, which is the main thing.

Before the evening brief Rich and I head to the ops room and ask Brett and the marine 2IC to do the maths. Who has the most people here? It turns out that there are now more marines than paras, so I formerly request permission from BG HQ to hand over command of Inkerman to Rich as of midnight tonight. Permission is granted.

At the evening brief we go through all of the usual detail then I go last. I announce that as of midnight, Y Company, 45 Commando will be in charge of FOB Inkerman. I then take the time to wish them a very successful tour – and I mean it.

SATURDAY 18 OCTOBER

It feels odd to be here as an observer rather than commander. Odd but actually rather nice. Rich is all over this so I am trying to stay out of his way, to be there if he needs any advice, but very much at the back. As we know each other this is easy. He has graciously run some of his decisions by me just to see what I think, but this is very much over to him now.

Two helicopters come in mid-morning and we manage to get 4 and 6 Platoon out and back to Bastion. I am due to leave late afternoon.

I head back to my bed space and sort out the last of my packing. All of my possessions into one rucksack, one grip and a large postal sack. I leave most of my books behind as that seems only fair for those who have just arrived.

I have a light lunch as my stomach is still fairly fragile. I am completely run down and feel a bit pathetic. I have lost a lot of weight, my left eye is weeping and I have a mouth ulcer. It's like my system is piling in. I plan to take it easy and get myself energised for going home.

Just after lunch I am told that the helicopters are cancelled this afternoon as they are conducting a deliberate operation near FOB Gibraltar. This doesn't particularly bother me as I am happy enough here; it has been my home for the last six months so a few more days won't hurt. I do wonder why they are conducting a deliberate operation during the relief period though. Helicopter resources are stretched to breaking point during the changeover without adding further complexity.

I realise that I am better off here than at Bastion. I can do what I like here while there are a lot of rules and restrictions at Bastion. I would rather go from here straight to Kandahar, where there is more to do.

Late afternoon the enemy decide to welcome the marines to the FOB. There is a bang in the distance and an SPG-9 rocket flies over the FOB, just clearing the wall and crashing into the graveyard by the HLS. Everyone stands to and there is a huge commotion. I head round to the ops room and stay at the back, eating a bag of pretzels. Rich gives clear direction and then comes to the back to ask what I think. Everything he has done has been spot on, so I let him know. Plus Brett is still here and he is very slick on the procedural aspects of these incidents. The marines get some rounds down from the sangars so everyone is happy.

Once the incident is closed I drift back to my camp cot and start a new book, *The Afghan Campaign* by Steven Pressfield. The irony of reading this now is not lost on me. It is set during Alexander's conquest of Afghanistan and I get into it really quickly. It captures the difficulties of campaigning out here and I feel qualified to be able to say that now.

SUNDAY 19 OCTOBER

I get up early and go to the gym. Afterwards I have a good breakfast and then spend most of the morning reading a book and getting a bit of sun. I have spent the last six months trying to stay out of the sun and now I want a bit of colour to go home with. Theoretically, I will be leaving this afternoon.

It all feels like I am drifting with the current; I don't really have a purpose. There is nothing that can be done to speed things up so there is no point getting emotional. I am happy to get a good book and keep myself to myself.

After lunch I get all of my kit ready as the helicopters are expected at 1400hrs. I am just about to head down to the HLS when I am told that there is a delay of two hours. No problem, I get my book out and read for an hour.

At 1500 I get my kit down to the HLS as I have a feeling that this will be it. I spend the next hour wandering around the FOB. I then get told that the helicopters are on their way and are ten minutes out.

This all feels very strange. Finally, I am leaving.

I make my way to the memorial. I need to say goodbye to those that we are leaving behind.

I stand and stare at the four additional brass plaques from

our tour: Private Murray, Private Gamble, Private Cuthbertson, Lance Corporal Rowe. My lads. My lads that I won't be bringing home with me. I stare at the names and I can feel the emotion that I have suppressed start to bubble up. For six months I have seen the memorial only in my peripheral vision; my focus had to remain on the present and the future. Now I am staring at the past and I can feel myself going numb. I offer a prayer, a prayer to them. I tell them how sorry I am that they aren't coming with us, I tell them I am sorry that I am not bringing them home and I promise that they will live on in our hearts. To some extent we will all be leaving a small part of ourselves out here.

My reverie is broken by the distant sound of approaching helicopters. I give the fallen one last nod then jog down to the HLS.

Rich and his sergeant major are there to wave me off. I shake Rich's hand and wish him all the very best.

Before I know it the Chinooks are flaring and I am disappearing in the brown dust cloud.

I run up the back ramp and on to the helicopter, our kit is thrown on and, suddenly, we are off. From the melee of the dust and confusion to the relative calm of flight.

There are only ten of us on board, so we can spread out. I make sure I am in a position to see out of the open back ramp and watch my FOB shrink away in the distance. The helicopter gains height and soon we are thousands of feet up, looking down on the dusty, barren wilderness that is Afghanistan.

I sink back in my seat and say to myself, 'You've done it, you've done it, you are on your way home,' but it doesn't feel real yet.

Thirty minutes later we land gently at Bastion; no need for hasty landings here. The CQMS is there to meet us and we throw our kit into the back of an open truck. The CQMS offers me a seat in the cab but I opt to sit in the back, on top of the kit, with the lads. The sun is starting to set and the red sky is amazing. He drives us round to our de-kit area and we go through a rapid process that removes us of our ammunition, weapons, night sights and body armour and then takes us to our accommodation. Back where it all started six months ago. Flushing toilets, powerful showers and fresh food.

There are still a few from 2 PARA here but we are the last company to be heading home. Shervs and Simon are here but they depart late evening, with all of the captains, leaving B Company all alone, apart from 'Spock', a very pleasant Royal Scots Dragoon Guards major who has opted to stay back with us and assist with our journey home. He has been attached to BG HQ for the tour and thought that someone should be here to help us.

I feel shattered and drift off to bed.

MONDAY 20 OCTOBER

I am in the gym by 0630. I woke up early and, despite the air conditioning and the general pleasantness, I couldn't get back to sleep.

The gym is a real gym – almost the size of an aircraft hangar, and full of decent kit. I spend hours training, I am enjoying myself so much.

I then have quite an unpleasant day. I just feel very, very odd. Nervous, skittish, I can't hold a conversation and I don't want to speak to anyone. I keep making excuses and going off on my own; I just want to be on my own.

I skulk around for most of the day. I make sure that I go to meals with people but bar that I stay on my own, reading and thinking. I am also obsessed with washing. Our kit comes back from the laundry but I am not happy. Twice I strip off the kit I am wearing and hand-wash it in the sink. Even the locally employed civilian cleaners find it odd. They get their supervisor who speaks broken English and he politely tells me there is a laundry on camp. He is concerned that I didn't know. I thank him and explain I would rather do it by hand. He seems impressed, or so I think.

TUESDAY 21 OCTOBER

I get up early again and go to the gym. I am starting to feel a bit better today, less agitated.

After breakfast I round up my signals detachment and organise to meet at one of the coffee bars mid-afternoon. I have been promising I will buy them a brew for weeks now.

I spend the rest of the morning taking in the facilities at Bastion. It really is amazing. Great food, good gym, televisions in the accommodation, hot showers, flushing toilets, a big shop and even a Pizza Hut. How the other half live. I know that we need this facility to make it all run but the contrast is quite insulting to those from the FOBs.

As the day goes on I feel myself relaxing and mid-afternoon a crowd of us go to the coffee bar. I end up sitting there with Gilbert for hours just talking. It is great. We talk about the build-up training, the tour, different stories. It does me the world of good.

Early evening I am reading my Steven Pressfield book and am really struck by a passage in it,

'Does a lion hesitate? Does an eagle hold back? What is the call of a gallant heart, except to aspire to mighty deeds? Here is the standard of Alexander, held before us. By Zeus, men a thousand years unborn will curse bitter fate that they have not strode here at our sides. They will envy us, who have laboured in such a cause and wrought such feats as no corps-at-arms will ever achieve again.'

This pretty much sums things up for me. I feel such pride. Pride in my regiment, pride in my company, and pride in how we have taken all that has been thrown at us; pride in myself and proud to have finally been in combat.

WEDNESDAY 22 OCTOBER

I get up early and go to the gym again. I then spend the day reading and drifting around Bastion. We are supposed to fly to Kandahar today but, once again, flights are one minute on, the next, they are off.

After lunch I strip off my uniform and hand-wash it all in the sink. I am starting to find this therapeutic and I then sit outside in the sun, reading my book and waiting for my uniform to dry.

Early evening we move round to the 'departure lounge' – another tent with chairs and a TV. Our rucksacks and grips are taken from us and from this stage we are 'travelling light', living out of our daysacks right through Kandahar and until Cyprus.

We assume taking our bags away means that we are moving but the plane is delayed yet again. We sit and watch *Team America* on the big TV. Always good for a laugh.

Just after midnight the C-130 Hercules arrives and we are off on our next hop.

The Hercules flight is always interesting – very sharp take-off and landing, and although the flight to Kandahar is short, it is somewhat bumpy. But it's warm and dark in the back, so it is easy to get some sleep.

THURSDAY 23 OCTOBER

We are deposited at the transit accommodation at 0200hrs. This is a vast tent full of camp cots. I grab a bed and crash out. It is freezing here, definitely colder than Bastion. I end up sleeping fully clothed, wrapped in a lightweight silk blanket I carry.

I wake up at 0600 and realise that it is almost a year since this all began, right here. A year ago I was in this very tent, having just arrived for an eight-day reconnaissance trip. I felt so excited to be in Afghanistan. Now I feel so excited about going home. For some reason, though, I do love all of this: the travel, the feeling of adventure, moving around a war zone, living out of a daysack, washing where you can and sleeping where you are dumped. I think it is good for you, it recharges the soul.

I get up early and have an amazing shower. They are really powerful here. I then wander over to the Green Bean coffee bar and get a coffee and a muffin.

I have an obsession with coffee and coffee bars so this really does feel cool. Early morning, the huge sprawling camp is just coming to life. Fighter jets and helicopters are taking off in the background; a fresh day of war is just beginning. I just sit, taking it all in, thinking and writing my journal.

I spend a few hours reflecting. I find myself not wanting to talk about things though. I keep bumping into people that I know and they ask me how it was or how it has gone. I brush them off with simple answers like 'long' or 'hard work'.

I realise that I have had to make unpopular decisions. It is partly the nature of the job but I find myself returning to my mantra over and over again, 'The popular decision will be right some of the time; the right decision will be right all of the time'.

I stand by my decisions.

Late afternoon I bump into Gilbert, who has found a stash of wool blankets. They are locked in an adjacent storage tent but he has found a way of squeezing between some loose flaps. I sneak in and grab one. This will make a difference to tonight's sleep.

After a lovely evening meal of salad I head off for an early night. I wrap myself in silk blanket, then wool blanket, eye covers and ear plugs. I am completely cocooned and it feels wonderful, like I am drifting off in space.

FRIDAY 24 OCTOBER

I get up early and go to the superb gym. It is an even bigger set-up with even more top-end gym kit, so I have a great session. After a shower I bump into some of the lads and they pass on the predictable news – there is a delay. Inevitable really, as the RAF fleet is so stretched. It is a shame though as everyone is desperate to get home. I think we are all quite conscious that we are the last elements of 2 PARA still here.

I am quite relaxed about the delay though. There are worse places to get stuck. I actually quite like it here. I can be quite solitary and I am good at occupying myself, so this is no great hardship. The showers are great, the toilets are real – not a hole in the ground – the food is awesome, the gym is fully stocked and there are lots of coffee shops so I might as well just get on with it. If I can't be at home with Andrea then I might as well be here. Plus I am a bit of a military pest and there is a real buzz to places like this. I am just happy to be so comfortable.

I spend most of the day on the internet and in the coffee bars. I just drift around, thinking, which is actually quite pleasant.

At 2000hrs we have a brief from the RAF and we are told that we will be leaving for decompression tonight. Decompression is two days spent in Cyprus during your return journey where you get to relax on a beach, have a few beers and 'blow off steam' if necessary. It keeps everyone together in a very relaxed environment to allow them to start to share and process their experiences. It also helps with the transition back to normal life. We have been in a very abnormal and very violent environment and there are bound to be implications from that.

The lads are quite mutinous at this stage. They want to skip the two days and go straight home. I have to say I agree with them. I find the highest-ranking officer I can and ask if there is any way of going straight home but the answer is a flat no. You can't beat a bit of compulsory fun.

SATURDAY 25 OCTOBER

If the mood of the lads was bad last night it is ten times worse this morning. The whole company is standing on a beach in Cyprus, tired, cold and very, very pissed off.

We left Kandahar last night at 2230. We flew for two hours to Muscat, refuelled for two hours and then flew for three hours to Cyprus. We were basically woken every hour for something.

We arrived in Cyprus at 0400. The previous group hadn't left yet so we had to wait in temporary accommodation – an old aircraft hangar full of bunk beds. We were told to strip off our uniforms and then these were bagged and sent off to the laundry. With a sergeant major shouting at us, it was comical. We are told that we can now sleep until 0615 when we will then be taken for breakfast. I grab a bunk bed and Private Ayers grabs the top bunk.

'It's like being a prisoner of war,' he says to me and I burst out laughing. He is spot on.

At 0615 we are herded to breakfast and then driven to the beach. The sun is only just starting to come up, so it is still chilly.

We are told that we have to do a swim test. We have to swim out fifty metres, swim round a buoy and then swim back. We can then use any kit that we want – canoes, wind-surfers and so on. There is a lot of stuff here but the lads are not happy.

I hear a voice behind me.

'Fuck them,' someone says.

I realise that this is a moment for good old-fashioned leadership so I strip down to my shorts.

I look over at Lance Corporal McEvoy. His dad is an army physical training instructor.

'Your dad would never forgive you if you didn't do a swim test,' I say to him, 'Go on, come with me.'

'All right,' he says and strips off as well.

We both wade in and I can't believe how warm the water is. It is lovely. We start swimming and I look back. No one else has joined us. There are 50-odd people still on the beach watching us.

I realise that I'm not going to force them, this is supposed to be fun.

As we round the buoy I can see that the whole company is in the water following us. It looks great. I am so pleased.

Lance Corporal McEvoy and I finish the test and head straight out to a floating platform. The sun is now heating up and I suddenly realise that we are in paradise. Lovely beach, warm sun: it is perfect.

The atmosphere has completely lifted. The lads are now laughing and smiling. There is an inflatable climbing tower on the platform so the inevitable climbing, fighting and throwing people off the top has broken out. I am just happy that the lads are happy.

The rest of the day is spent having fun on the beach. Some of our casualties have been flown out to join us and it is great to see them. Corporal Hickman's shoulder is on the mend and Corporal Philip's shin is much better. There are lads that I haven't seen for months and I am so happy to see them.

Alan, the padre, is here and we manage to find a quiet spot and have an ice-cream and a really good catch up. We talk for hours. It is so nice to see him and start to link up some of the threads of the tour.

Major Dave Lee, the quartermaster, is also there and we end up having a long talk late in the afternoon. Dave is a Falklands veteran and a wise old sage. He is probably the only one in the battalion who has seen and done all of this before.

He asks me if I think it was worth it. I realise that, despite all of my thinking, this is the question I have avoided. To some extent I still am. I give him a non-committal answer but I know I will have to face this at some point. One thing I know is that the army can't keep doing this each summer.

In the evening they lay on a party. There are six free cans of beer each, entertainment, satellite phones to call home, internet and even a cinema. I don't need much beer to get drunk. I am shattered quite quickly and end up going to bed quite early. There is nice fresh bedding and a clean towel, which feel like luxury.

The lads are on top form and the decompression serves its purpose. There is the odd scuffle as old scores are settled, but nothing serious.

SUNDAY 26 OCTOBER

We are all woken early and some people are a lot worse for wear than others. I head to the toilet block to shave and I can hear someone being sick. The banter is all good though and it seems everyone enjoyed their evening.

There is also a sense of anticipation. It feels like Christmas morning. We are going home today.

After a nice breakfast we are driven back to the airport and there is a Monarch Airlines plane waiting for us. Before long we have boarded and we are on our way.

I can feel myself and the whole aircraft getting more excited as the flight goes on.

As we start to come in to land I look out of the window and realise how green everything is. The English countryside looks incredible.

We land at Stansted airport, which is great for getting to Colchester. We climb on to coaches and start the 45-minute journey. The countryside this close looks even more spectacular.

As we pull up to the front gate of our barracks my heart is in my mouth. I am so excited to be home and I can't wait to see Andrea.

Jo, the media officer for 2 PARA, climbs on the bus and lets me know that there are media here to capture our arrival.

'Which ones?' I ask, thinking he must be talking about the local papers.

'All of them,' he replies, referring to all the national newspapers and television.

'Blimey,' I think to myself.

As the coach sweeps into the car park I can see a sea of cheering families. All smiling, waving and clapping. It is just wonderful.

I climb from the bus and the CSM is there to meet me – he was on a previous flight to get things ready for our arrival.

It is great to see him and we shake hands and say hello to each other.

'You better go and see your wife,' he says laughing.

Andrea is there and we grab each other and have a huge hug. We get two seconds together before the press are on me and the questions start.

Andrea just smiles at me and motions for me to carry on.

I spend the next hour answering questions. The press are great and ask really good questions. They seem to be swept up in the moment as well and everyone is happy.

An hour later, as the remaining journalists drift off, I realise we are pretty much the last people here. Thorpy has stayed behind to make sure I am all right. He briefs me up that we have four days off and then he heads off himself, leaving Andrea and I alone in the car park.

We grab my bags and head to the car for the last piece of the puzzle. I open the boot and Rufus leaps out, squeaking and wagging his tail.

Our house is only five minutes from the barracks. Suddenly I am doing what I have dreamt of for so long. I walk through my front door, breathe deeply, kiss Andrea and stroke Rufus. B Company is home. The odyssey is over.

EPILOGUE

In the Ray Mears DVDs he continually asks the question 'What have I learnt?' It is a good question and a very good discipline and, towards the end of the tour, I found a quiet spot in the FOB and contemplated this question for a few hours before making notes in my journal. What have I learnt?

I have learnt that I don't panic in a crisis situation. I have learnt what it is like to be in combat. I have learnt that you have got to keep calm because panicking really doesn't help. I have learnt that six months is too long somewhere like this, with the conditions and the tempo the way they are. I have learnt that you have got to temper your expectations. I have learnt that people will surprise you in both a good and a bad way. I have learnt that combat is a great leveller; people's true self comes out, you just can't hide it. I have learnt that command is very lonely and that you have to make unpopular decisions. I have learnt what leadership really is.

As I reflect, I think that leadership hinges around the following five tenets:

- *Make the decisions, both big and small. That is what you are there for.*
- *Shape events and the situation. You have to exert your influence all of the time and try to drive things in the direction you want them to go. There may be many twists and turns on the way, but you have to know where you want things to go and what you want them to look like.*
- *Energise. Your personal energy and passion is infectious, so use it. Inspire, be courageous and, if in doubt, get to the front and say 'follow me'.*
- *Think a lot. Take time to reflect, take time to 'meditate', as Napoleon said, and take time to visualise. The leader often has to spend more time thinking than doing but that is the only way to identify all of the friction points within the plan. As is often said 'a plan is just a series of things that haven't gone wrong yet'. It is the leader's job to try to identify as many of them as possible.*
- *Finally, identify the difference between what you want to do and what you need to do. This cropped up all the way through the tour and is probably my key takeaway. A decision based on what you need to do will stand the test of time. A decision based on what you want to do may not.*

I realise there will be so much more for me to learn and it will take time and reflection to formulate this experience. It has been incredible. This has been war fighting and I have commanded a Parachute Regiment rifle company. I have fulfilled my tactical ambitions, far beyond my expectations. I have been in the crucible. We are now in the group of warriors who have actually done it. I have studied the theory and now I understand the practical.

It is an amazing feeling.

At the tactical level the company has fought a superb fight. Badly resourced, with little intelligence, we have continually gone out there and taken the fight to the enemy. I don't think the full extent of all of this will sink in until it is over. I think we can walk away with our heads held high. Bloodied, but in no way bowed.

Each tour in Afghanistan is different and unfortunately they are all marked by death and casualties. There feels to be a timeless aspect to Afghanistan, that it has existed for hundreds of years in the way that it exists today, and that it is very unlikely to change. We look so out of place with all of our technology. In Helmand, theirs is really an ancient existence. It will take a long time and a lot of investment to change this.

THURSDAY 25 JUNE

I am standing in the beer garden of the Maypole pub in Colchester. Eight months have passed since we returned home and the day I have been dreading has arrived. This is my leaving party with the company. From tomorrow I will no longer be the company commander of B Company, 2 PARA.

It has been strange since we returned. Settling back into normality and life in barracks has been a challenge for all of us. We have taken the time to remember our fallen and deal with our casualties. We have got back into a routine. People have left and people have joined the company.

I am standing here now, looking at my company with such mixed emotions. I am so proud of B Company and I am so sad to be leaving it.

Chris Collier makes a nice speech and then I am presented with a gift. It is the Parachute Regiment flag that flew over the FOB. It has been framed and it looks brilliant. It leaves me speechless; it is such a wonderful present.

I need to say something though.

I decide to tell them about my journey. I tell them about reading *2 PARA Falklands* by John Frost when I was eleven and how I thought at the time what incredible soldiers these must have been to go and face such hardship and prevail. I talk about wanting to join the army from a very early age and how I don't recall having a long-term plan; I just wanted to be a part of the army and the Parachute Regiment.

I let them know that if I could chose, now or then, what I wanted, it would be to lead paratroopers into battle. And how I have done just that.

I decide to wrap up with a recollection. A recollection of the bravest man I have ever met. The lone Tom I observed through my NVGs down at the back gate of FOB Inkerman. Watching him struggle to his feet under the load, shrug his kit into place and then head off into the dark. Confidently, determined, without a backward glance. Knowing that within hours he would be fighting for his life, but still showing no hesitation.

As I look round the sea of faces listening to me I know what an incredible honour it has been to command men such as these. They really are amazing.

I finish with a toast and everyone raises their glass.

'B Company,' I say.

'B Company,' they echo back.

AN APPEAL

Every day service personnel and their family's lives are changed for ever by the nature of current conflict. If you have been inspired or touched by the stories from this book then please consider donating to one of the following charities:

1. The Afghan Trust (www.afghanistantrust.org). Founded in 2007, it primarily supports the relief of all Parachute Regiment soldiers injured in Afghanistan, and the families of those wounded or killed, with welfare services, support and financial assistance, and sustains the memory of loss of life and the sacrifices made there by soldiers of the regiment.
2. The Parachute Regiment Charity (www.paracharity.org). A new charity carrying on our best traditions in the relief of hardship, need and distress amongst members of the regiment and airborne forces and their dependents.
3. Combat Stress (www.combatstress.org). Thousands of ex-service men and women are not able to leave the

horrors of war on the battlefield. They bring the combat home and re-experience it in their minds each and every day. This wonderful charity, founded in 1919, treats veterans experiencing psychological difficulties.

4. Help for Heroes (www.helpforheroes.org). Since its inception, Help for Heroes has done an incredible job raising money for those that need it. They are as important today as they have ever been.

5. The Royal Hospital Chelsea (www.chelsea-pensioners. co.uk). An amazing institution that has to self-generate an incredible amount of funding to keep doing the wonderful job that they do. They are there for when today's soldiers retire.

Please give generously. The horrors of modern combat touch us all in different ways. These five charities do an incredible job looking after those that need it most, but they can't exist without all of our help.

GLOSSARY

ACOG	Advanced Combat Optical Gunsight
ANA	Afghan National Army
AO	area of operations
ATO	Ammunition Technical Officer
BG	battle group
BGHQ	battle group headquarters
C-130	Hercules aircraft
CASEVAC	casualty evacuation
CH-47	Chinook helicopter
CO	commanding officer
COIN	counter-insurgency
CPR	cardiopulmonary resuscitation
CQMS	company quartermaster sergeant
CSM	company sergeant major
EHT	environmental health team
F-16	fighter jet
FAC	forward air controller
FOB	forward operating base
FOO	forward observation officer

FSG	fire support group
GMG	grenade machine gun; 40mm belt-fed grenade launcher
GMLRS	GPS multi-launch rocket system
GPMG	general purpose machine gun; 7.62mm belt-fed machine gun
H-hour	time that assault troops cross the line of departure
HLS	helicopter landing site
HMG	heavy machine gun; .50cal belt-fed machine gun
IED	improvised explosive device
MERT	medical emergency response team; specialist medics on a CH-47
MFC	mortar fire controller
NCO	non-commissioned officer
NLP	neurolinguisitic programming
NVG	night vision goggles
OC	officer commanding
OMLT	operational mentoring and liaison team
Op	operation
OP	observation post
OPTAG	operational training advisory group
PB	patrol base
PKM	Kalashnikov's Machine-gun Modernised; Soviet belt-fed machine gun
PPIED	pressure plate improvised explosive device
QM	quartermaster
QRF	quick reaction force
RiP	relief in place
RMP	Royal Military Police
RPG	rocket-propelled grenade

R&R	rest and recuperation
SA80	assault rifle
SIB	RMP Special Investigations Branch
Sitrep	situation report
SPG-9	Soviet recoilless anti-tank gun
TAC	company commander's tactical headquarters
Tom	Parachute Regiment private soldier
UAV	unmanned aerial vehicle
107mm	Soviet rocket
611	road connecting Sangin to Kajaki
7 RHA	7th Parachute Regiment Royal Horse Artillery

ACKNOWLEDGEMENTS

As a serving soldier, writing this book has been a surreal experience and would not have been possible if it wasn't for a number of people whom I need to thank.

I want to thank the Mikes – Newman and Malsz – for looking after me when I was away and continuing to be such good friends.

Thank you to Jumbo and D-P for coaxing me into considering writing a book in the first place. Ed at Virgin has been great, politely listening to my 'pitch' and then confirming that it could actually be a book. He linked me up with Humfrey Hunter who has been a superb agent and, I would like to think, has become a good friend. Without Humfrey's expert advice and guidance I would have struggled to find a way to portray all of this information. He has always been there to guide me through this alien process.

Fi Peebles was incredibly helpful, proofreading the initial proposal.

It is easy to forget how much we put our parents through when we go to far-off places and do dangerous things, so I am grateful to my Mum and Dad for being so supportive and I am sorry for the stress I have put them through. My sister, Vanessa, has always been there for me and now that she has a doctorate in psychology she been able to help me process some of the more challenging aspects of the tour; she has a gift for helping people.

Last is my wonderful wife, Andrea, who never stops believing in me and has been my rock throughout.